Phan Châu Trinh and His Political Writings

Cornell University

Phan Châu Trinh
translated and edited by Vinh Sinh

Phan Châu Trinh and His Political Writings

SOUTHEAST ASIA PROGRAM PUBLICATIONS
Southeast Asia Program
Cornell University
Ithaca, New York
2009

Cornell Southeast Asia Program Publications
640 Stewart Avenue, Ithaca, NY 14850-3857

Studies on Southeast Asia No. 49

Printed in the United States of America

ISBN: hc   978-0-87727-779-8
ISBN: pb   978-0-87727-749-1

Cover Design: Maureen Viele

TABLE OF CONTENTS

ACKNOWLEDGMENTS

My interest in Phan Châu Trinh and his writings dates back two decades to earlier work I completed on Phan Bội Châu. Phan Châu Trinh's vision appeared to be so different from that of Phan Bội Châu and his contemporaries, and I felt it required further study. Since that time, two occasions and a number of friends and colleagues have contributed to my understanding of Phan Châu Trinh and his world. The first occasion was in 1990, when an international conference was held in Vietnam for the first time since Đổi mới (Renovation). At that conference, I met the late Mr. Nguyễn Văn Xuân for the first time. Nguyễn Văn Xuân was a specialist in Quảng Nam học (studies about Quảng Nam province). Among his many monographs, the most well-known is Phong trào Duy Tân, a brilliant and enlightening analysis of the modernization movement. Nguyễn Văn Xuân believed that this movement began in Quảng Nam, Phan Châu Trinh's home province, and not in Hanoi, as some people think. Throughout the years, Nguyễn Văn Xuân and I became very good friends. He helped me a great deal in finding research materials, particularly those in literary Chinese by Phan Châu Trinh. Thanks to Nguyễn Văn Xuân, I have confidence in my understanding of the culture and history of the Quảng Nam area, and I would like to take this opportunity thank him.

Another occasion was in July 1991, when I had the privilege to attend a symposium on Vietnamese history at Cornell University. The symposium was small in size, but the ideas and collegiality were truly inspiring. It was a wonderful learning experience. I would like to take this opportunity to thank Professor Keith W. Taylor for inviting me to this stimulating symposium.

In the process of revising this work, I am indebted to the anonymous reviewers for Southeast Asia Program Publications (SEAP), Cornell University, who offered pertinent comments and suggestions. In particular, I would like to thank the anonymous reviewer who offered such insightful and detailed suggestions to add to the discussions and to clarify the argument and prose. The changes suggested strengthened my argument and made this work more accessible. As well, it was my good fortune to have SEAP's Deborah Homsher as editor. Her efficiency in overseeing the publication is much appreciated. Financial support from Canada's Social Sciences and Humanities Research enabled me to travel to Vietnam and France, and to continue my research. I would like to thank Nicholas Wickenden, who read a section of the manuscript and gave me his valuable help. I am very grateful to Carol Janigo, whose highly capable and conscientious help is beyond what one can look for in a student assistant. I thank Kyôko, Tan, and Grace for their assistance and support.

NAMES AND ABBREVIATIONS

In this monograph, Vietnamese and other East Asian names are given in customary order, with the family name first and the personal name last. In the case of Vietnamese names, the form of name used is that by which the person would have called himself or herself as an adult, thus retaining the person's local pronunciation. For this reason, we use Phan Châu Trinh and not Phan Chu Trinh, because Phan himself and his friends, particularly those in Quảng Nam, used it in that way. In Sino-Vietnamese, the names *Chu* (cycle, circumference, vicinity) and *Châu* are written using the same Chinese character. The recently published three-volume *Phan Châu Trinh toàn tập* (The Complete Works of Phan Châu Trinh), edited by Chương Thâu, Dương Trung Quốc, and Lê Thị Kinh (Phan Thị Minh) (Đà Nẵng: Nxb Đà Nẵng, 2005), and the two-volume *Phan Châu Trinh qua những tài liệu mới phát hiện* (Phan Châu Trinh through Newly Discovered Materials), edited by Lê Thị Kinh (Phan Thị Minh) (Đà Nẵng: Nxb Đà Nẵng, 2003) correctly used the same spelling for Phan's name. For the same reason, Huỳnh Thúc Kháng is preferred to Hoàng Thúc Kháng. In present-day Vietnam, the use of one's personal name has become very popular, even when referring to a person with a formal title (e.g., "President Thiệu" for South Vietnam's former president, Nguyễn Văn Thiệu). By contrast, in the Vietnam of Phan Châu Trinh's time, it was customary for literati like Phan to use a person's family name, full name, or pseudonyms (or pseudonyms with family or full names) in addressing each other formally. For this reason, no one would have used his personal name (*Trinh*) to refer to Phan Châu Trinh. The same restriction was still observed by those a generation or more younger, such as Nguyễn Ái Quốc or Hồ Chí Minh (thus one might refer to Mr. Nguyễn Ái Quốc or Mr. Nguyễn, or to President Hồ, but never to Mr. Quốc or to President Minh). Indeed, if one were to use the name "President Minh," the person being referred to might be Dương Văn Minh, president of South Vietnam immediately before 1975, as he belonged to the post-Second World War generation, a different generation.

Translation abbreviations. Throughout the monograph, Sino-Vietnamese and Vietnamese words and terms are indicated by the abbreviation "Viet.," Chinese as "C." in *pinyin*, and Japanese as "J." in the Hepburn system. Also note that the terms "literary Chinese" and "classical Chinese" are used interchangeably.

Phan Châu Trinh

Phan Bội Châu

Huỳnh Thúc Kháng

Portion of text from "A New Vietnam Following the Franco-Vietnamese Alliance"

BIOGRAPHICAL CHRONOLOGY

1872   Phan Châu Trinh was born in Tây Lộc village, Tam Kỳ prefectural city, in the province of Quảng Nam.

1887   Phan's father, Phan Văn Bình, died. He was probably murdered by members of the "patriotic" Nghĩa Hội Cần Vương (Righteous Loyalist Society), who unjustly suspected him of working against them.

1892   Phan became Huỳnh Thúc Kháng's close friend.

Sino-Japanese War, 1894–95

1898   Phan became Trần Quý Cáp's close friend.

1900   Received the degree of *Cử nhân* ("Recommended Men") in the imperial city of Huế.

Boxer Rebellion in China

1901   Received the *Phó bảng* ("On the Supplementary List of 'Presented Scholars'") degree.

1903   Hired to work as *Thừa biện* (secretary) in the Ministry of Rites.

1904   Exposed to Liang Qichao's reformist writings, i.e., the *tân thư* ("new books") and *tân văn* ("new journals").

Met with Phan Bội Châu.

Together with Trần Quý Cáp and Huỳnh Thúc Kháng, he retired from officialdom.

Russo-Japanese War, 1904–05

1905   Made a landmark trip to the South with Trần Quý Cáp and Huỳnh Thúc Kháng.

China abolished the Mandarinate Examination System

- At the Bình Định provincial examination, Phan, Trần Quý Cáp, and Huỳnh Thúc Kháng disguised themselves as candidates.

- Phan wrote the poem *"Chí thành thông thánh"* (Utmost Sincerity Would Be Understood by the Sages), and Trần Quý Cáp and Huỳnh Thúc Kháng wrote the *phú "Lương ngọc danh sơn"* (Precious Stone in a Famed Mountain).

- At Khánh Hòa, Phan and his friends disguised themselves as merchants selling foodstuffs to go on board and examine a Russian ship (part of the Russian Baltic Fleet at anchor in Cam Ranh Bay).

- In Bình Thuận, the group discussed practical modernization projects with prominent figures, including the establishment of the Liên Thành fish-sauce company and the Dục Thanh School. Phan became ill, and the trip to the South was terminated.

Arrived in Hanoi in December. After exchanging ideas on modernization with prominent figures, including Lương Văn Can and Đào Nguyên Phổ, Phan went to Nghệ-Tĩnh to meet Ngô Đức Kế. Phan then went North, straight to the Yên Thế resistance base to see Đề Thám. Privately, Phan thought of Đề Thám as "nothing more than a military commander," and strongly believed "if one only sits tight in a corner, how can one survive?"

1906   From Yên Thế, Phan proceeded to Hải Phòng, disguising himself as a laborer to cross the border into China. Arrived in Hong Kong in late February.

- In Shahe (Guangdong), Phan met Phan Bội Châu and Marquis Cường Để, and visited the former military commander Tán Thuật (Nguyễn Thiện Thuật), who was staying at the home of Liu Yongfu (Viet. Lưu Vĩnh Phúc.)

- In April, went to Japan with Phan Bội Châu. Inspected schools and met with prominent figures, who probably included Phan Bội Châu's Japanese acquaintances, such as the statesman Inukai Tsuyoshi, Kashiwabara Buntarô of the Tôa Dômeikai, and the famed Chinese scholar and publicist Liang Qichao. The two may also have visited Fukuzawa Yukichi's Keiô Gijuku University, located in Mita, Tokyo. When returning to Vietnam, Phan Bội Châu accompanied Phan to Hong Kong.

1907   Following his return to Vietnam, Phan wrote a letter to Governor General Paul Beau, *"Đầu Pháp chính phủ thư"* (Letter Addressed to the French Government), denouncing the social evils of the situation in Indochina and demanding improvements in colonial policy.

He appealed to the Vietnamese to unite in building schools and creating academic institutions.

In July, he gave the first "speeches" (*diễn thuyết*) at the newly founded Đông Kinh Nghĩa Thục, Hanoi. Urged the youth to cut their hair short, to wear

Western clothes, and to support domestic products. The term "Tây Hồ style" (*mốt Tây Hồ*), i.e., "Phan Châu Trinh's style," was in vogue.

1908   ***Tax revolts erupted in Quảng Nam and other cities in central Vietnam***

Phan was accused of initiating the movement for popular rights (*dân quyền*) and of maintaining surreptitious contacts with Phan Bội Châu to instigate the public to join in revolt. He was sentenced to life imprisonment on Poulo Condore Island.

Huỳnh Thúc Kháng and many of Phan's friends were also sent to prison on Poulo Condore Island. Trần Quý Cáp was murdered in Nha Trang; this tragedy greatly shocked Phan.

1910   Phan was released in June through the efforts of Ernest Babut and other French admirers, who protested his imprisonment. The colonial authorities tried to hold Phan under house arrest in Mỹ Tho city, Mekong delta, but when he protested vehemently, the authorities gave in and agreed to allow him and his son, Phan Châu Dật, to depart for France.

Before leaving Vietnam, he wrote the draft, in classical Chinese, for "Pháp Việt liên hợp hậu chi Tân Việt Nam" (A New Vietnam Following the Franco-Vietnamese Alliance),* to expose the differences between the divergent political stances adopted by him and Phan Bội Châu.

1911   Arrived in France in April. Raised his voice to urge the French government to liberalize its colonial policy in Indochina. Writing in classical Chinese, he composed the drafts for *Đông Dương chính trị luận* (On Indochinese Politics) and *Trung Kỳ dân biến thỉ mạt ký* (History of the Insurrection in Central Vietnam).

1912   Retranslated into Vietnamese the novel *Giai nhân kỳ ngộ diễn ca*, Liang Qichao's Chinese translation of *Kajin no kigû* (Chance Encounters with Elegant Females), probably during 1912–14. *Kajin no kigû* is a political serialized novel that explored popular rights and revolution, first published in Japan from 1885 to 1897 by the Japanese ex-*samurai* Tôkai Sanshi.

First World War, 1914–18

When Germany attacked France, Phan refused to be conscripted for French military service. Was arrested and thrown into Santé prison for nearly ten months (September 1914 until July 1915) on suspicion of asking for help from Germany to fight against France.

1915   ***Japan's Twenty-one Demands issued to China***

1919   At the international conference at Versailles, Phan, with Phan Văn Trường and Nguyễn Ái Quốc, presented a list of demands, including that the French grant a complete amnesty to all Indochinese political prisoners, reform the justice system in Indochina, and provide the Indochinese with laws similar to those of the Europeans.

May Fourth Movement (China)

1921   Huỳnh Thúc Kháng was released from the prison on Poulo Condore Island after thirteen years.

1922   Emperor Khải Định arrived in France to attend the International Exposition, in Marseilles. Phan drafted in classical Chinese a letter accusing the emperor of seven offences. The letter, commonly known at the time as "Thư thất điều" (literally, "The Letter of Seven Clauses"),* stunned French and Vietnamese intellectuals.

1925   In June, Phan finally returned to Vietnam. A campaign began to demand the release of Phan Bội Châu, who at the time was confined in Hỏa Lò prison, Hanoi. Phan Bội Châu was released from Hỏa Lò prison 1925 and lived in Huế under house arrest until his death in 1940.

Phan gave his two last lectures, entitled "Đạo đức và luân lý Đông Tây" (Morality and Ethics in the Orient and the Occident)* and "Quân trị chủ nghĩa và Dân trị chủ nghĩa" (Monarchy and Democracy).*

His health deteriorated due to tuberculosis and dysentery, and he had to set aside plans of going to Hanoi to give lectures and to meet Phan Bội Châu in Huế.

1926   Huỳnh Thúc Kháng arrived in the last minutes before Phan died. This final reunion took place some sixteen years after Phan had left Poulo Condore Island in 1910.

Phan died at the age of 56, on the evening of March 24.

* Included in this collection.

INTRODUCTION: PHAN CHÂU TRINH AND HIS POLITICAL WRITINGS

Phan Châu Trinh (1872–1926) was the earliest and most eloquent proponent of democracy (Viet. *dân chủ*) and popular rights (Viet. *dân quyền*) in Vietnam. Throughout his life, he consistently favored a moderate approach and pleaded for making gradual progress within the French colonial system. As a result of his exposure to Chinese reformist literature through *tân thư* (new books) and *tân văn* (new journals), Phan assigned top priority to the promotion of democracy and popular rights and to the improvement of the Vietnamese people's standard of living (Viet. *dân sinh*).

Phan Châu Trinh's stance was sharply different from that of the other most prominent Vietnamese patriot of Phan's time, Phan Bội Châu (1867–1940). In contrast to Phan Bội Châu and many other political activists who believed that military resistance was the only means by which Vietnam's national independence could be restored and that foreign help was indispensable, Phan Châu Trinh emphatically maintained throughout his life that "to depend on foreign help is foolish and to resort to violence is self-destructive" (Viet. *vọng ngoại tắc ngu, bạo động tắc tử*). Indeed, he argued that this route to independence would only perpetuate the colonial cycle. In the context of early twentieth-century colonial Vietnam, Phan Châu Trinh believed that true independence could only be achieved by changes within Vietnamese political culture. Thus he articulated penetrating criticism of the corruption and superficiality of Vietnam's official class. His emphasis on changing the fundamental values governing the ruling class's behavior, rather than simply focusing on removing French colonial rule, sets Phan Châu Trinh apart from his contemporaries and marks him as a true revolutionary. These views were shaped by Phan Châu Trinh's life experience and his understanding of Confucianism, with its emphasis on Mencius's thought regarding the position and well-being of the people.

The formation of Phan Châu Trinh's ideas and his intellectual development were intrinsically bound up with the period in which he reached young adulthood. When one considers the quest for modernization in Asia, 1904 is a crucial turning point that challenged Vietnamese intellectuals to ponder seriously their own country's position and future. In China, the two-thousand-year-old civil-service examination was to be abolished in 1905. One should remember that it was from China that, in 1075, Vietnam adopted the examination system to recruit officials for the government. Moreover, Kang Youwei (1858–1927; Viet. Khang Hữu Vi) and Liang Qichao (1873–1929; Viet. Lương Khải Siêu), two well-known Chinese reformist intellectuals, had escaped to Japan after the failure of the 1898 coup. Liang continued to write and edit his journal in Yokohama, near Tokyo, and these journals reached Huế, the imperial capital of Vietnam, where all the candidates were gathering for the metropolitan examinations in 1904. The year of 1904 also marked the outbreak of the Russo–Japanese War, and the world watched with great interest as Japan, a newly emerged East Asian power, fought against Russia, a world-class empire. As he learned more about modernization and the realities of the modern world during this period, Phan Châu Trinh became convinced that domestic reform, rather than violence, was indispensable to Vietnam's future success. Throughout his life, Phan continued to refine his ideas, but he never deviated from these principles. On the altar of modern Vietnam's "heroes," Phan Châu Trinh thus stands in a class of his own, and his enlightened thought, as expressed in his writings, requires a further look.

Part I
Background—Vietnam in the Face of Western Expansion

For us to understand the development the Phan Châu Trinh's thought, it must be placed within the context of the development of French colonialism in Vietnam. In the second half of the nineteenth century, French colonialism expanded to Southeast Asia. Caught off guard by European expansionism and unable to see beyond its own anachronistic outlook, Vietnam paid a high price as the French moved quickly to take control and dominated most of the country by 1883. By the turn of the twentieth century, the reality of French colonialism had shaped a generation of young Vietnamese intellectuals, including Phan Châu Trinh, who completed his education and formative years against this backdrop and would spend his political and writing career addressing the issues of the time. Indeed, an understanding of this period and the crucial changes that occurred between 1900 and the 1920s is essential to a deeper understanding of Phan Châu Trinh's writings and the urgency with which he expressed his ideas. Besides the loss of sovereignty and the political implications of French colonialism, these crucial changes ranged from the abolishment of the examination system to unprecedented change in the writing system of the country, that is, from classical Chinese to Romanized characters—*quốc ngữ*.[1] Phan Châu Trinh's written work reflects this upheaval and his intimate understanding of the implications of the time, not only in his ideas, but also in the forms of writing he used: he studied and took the examinations in classical Chinese, but by the end of his life, in the 1920s, he wrote two of his most important works in *quốc ngữ*—"Morality and Ethics in the Orient and the Occident" [*Đạo đức và luân lý Đông Tây*] and "Monarchy and Democracy" [*Quân trị chủ nghĩa và Dân trị chủ nghĩa*]—which are included in this monograph.[2]

---

[1] *Quốc ngữ*, or "national language," is the Romanized form of the written language, attributed to Alexandre de Rhodes, who published the first Vietnamese-Latin-Portuguese dictionary in 1651. After the Chinese-style examinations were abolished in 1919, *quốc ngữ* was adopted and became the official script of Vietnam. Though very well-versed in literary Chinese, Phan Châu Trinh was an enthusiastic promoter of *quốc ngữ*. He once said: "Without the overthrow of Chinese characters, we cannot save Vietnam." See David G. Marr, *Vietnamese Anticolonialism* (Berkeley, CA: University of California Press, 1971), p. 169.

[2] In the present volume, these two articles in *quốc ngữ* are respectively collected from these works: 1) Thế Nguyên, *Phan Chu Trinh* (1872–1926)[Phan Châu Trinh (1872–1926)] (Saigon: Tủ sách Những "Mảnh Gương" Tân Việt, 1956); and 2) Thái Bạch, ed., *Thi văn quốc cấm thời thuộc Pháp* [Poems and Prose Prohibited During the French Colonial Era] (Saigon: Nhà sách Khai Trí, 1968).

THE MAKING OF COLONIAL VIETNAM

France invaded Vietnam in July 1857 and began what was a rather late start for a European power in the imperialist race in Southeast Asia.[3] Although the history of relations between France and Vietnam dated back to the seventeenth century,[4] France's interest in expansion in this area during the second half of the mid-nineteenth century was motivated by imperial aspirations and competition with other European powers, particularly the British. Since there were few non-colonized areas left, and with vigorous encouragement from the French Roman Catholic church, which advocated military intervention to prevent the persecution of missionaries,[5] the French directed their efforts to Vietnam, and neighboring Cambodia and Laos. Intervention in Vietnam had the added incentive of providing a route to China's vast and rich markets through the backdoor from northern Vietnam to southwestern China.

The first French invasion of Vietnam, carried out with the Spanish in 1857, occurred in Vũng Thùng Bay, which is presently Đà Nẵng, Quảng Nam, the province where Phan Châu Trinh was born. Remembrance of this event was recorded in the following popular folk poem:

> *Tai nghe súng nổ cái đùng,*
> *Tàu Tây đã đến Vũng Thùng nghe anh!*

"Boom!" Suddenly I heard a tremendous sound,
Alas! French ships have arrived in Vũng Thùng Bay, brother!

After attacking Đà Nẵng, the French moved south to Saigon. Following France's initial military success in taking Saigon and its adjacent provinces in 1861, Emperor Tự Đức (1847–83) signed a treaty in 1862, which provided the French with direct control of the three provinces around Saigon and increased access for French trading ships to Vietnamese ports. Over the next decade, additional territories in the south were placed under French direct rule, and the entire colony was named Cochinchina (i.e., Nam Kỳ).

---

[3] By 1857, the British were in India, Burma (now Myanmar), Penang, Singapore, Malacca, and Hong Kong; the Dutch were in Indonesia; the Spanish were in the Philippines; and the Portuguese were in Macao and Timor.

[4] Most well-known among the French in the seventeenth century was the Jesuit missionary Alexandre de Rhodes, who completed a transcription of the Vietnamese language into Roman script, which was later adopted by modern Vietnamese in the early twentieth century as their official writing system, *quốc ngữ* (see footnote 1).

[5] The second emperor of the Nguyễn dynasty, Emperor Minh Mạng, though very capable of handling daily matters, proved to be out-of-date in dealing with Western affairs and Christianity. Deeply embedded in the East Asian traditional way of thinking, Emperor Minh Mạng saw the West as "barbarian," and thus from his perspective the most effective response was to exclude the West and repress Christianity. (See Marr, *Vietnamese Anticolonialism*, p. 44.) During Emperor Minh Mạng's reign, all French advisers were dismissed, while seven French missionaries and an unknown number of Vietnamese Christians were executed.

The hope of finding a route to China through Vietnam continued to motivate the French. In 1868, naval officer and explorer Francis Garnier's[6] expedition from Saigon up the Mekong River via Cambodia and Laos demonstrated that the Mekong River could not serve as an accessible trade route into southwestern China. The French then turned their attention to developing the Red River (Viet. *Sông Hồng*) delta to transport goods to the rich markets of China. In August 1883, the French successfully concluded a treaty with the Vietnamese court that turned northern and central Vietnam (Tongkin, i.e., Bắc Kỳ; and Annam, i.e., Trung Kỳ) into French protectorates, a step that contributed to expanding direct rule by the French throughout Vietnam. Within the French colonial system, Vietnam became part of a larger entity, the Indochinese Union, after Laos was annexed (1893). The Indochinese Union was governed by a French governor-general, who resided in Hanoi but also maintained a stately palace in Saigon, capital city of Cochinchina. A resident superior administered each protectorate in Tongkin and Annam, and a lieutenant-governor served in Cochinchina. The union consisted of the colony of Cochinchina and the four protectorates of Annam, Tongkin, Cambodia, and Laos.

Although at the beginning it appears that Vietnamese court officials may have had some leeway, in reality it was too late for them to maneuver.[7] To make matters worse, after Emperor Tự Đức passed away in 1883, key court mandarins were ignorant of the implications of the dire situation facing Vietnam, and their policies and actions tended to be destructive.[8] The French were able to take advantage of this lack of court mandarin leadership to increase their political and economic control in the area.

The arrival of Governor-General Paul Doumer[9] in 1897 was a turning point in the development of colonial Vietnam. A former Parisian budget analyst and minister of finance, Doumer (1897–1902) was an uncommonly shrewd and active administrator, who became the architect of French empire-building in Southeast Asia—balancing the budget of Indochina and extending the administrative and

---

[6] The French pioneering explorer Francis Garnier can be compared to Gordon and Kitchener, the English soldier-administrators in Egypt; Dr. Karl Peters, the German explorer in East Africa; or Savoignan de Brazza, founder of the French Congo—all were soldiers, diplomats, explorers, traders, or missionaries in the imperialist competition. Francis Garnier was later killed in a battle during China's Taiping Rebellion while fighting with remnants of Liu Yongfu's (Viet. Lưu Vĩnh Phúc) forces near Hanoi (see footnote 54 under "Liu Yongfu"). For a survey of nineteenth-century expansionism, see Louis L. Snyder, ed., *The Imperialist Reader: Documents and Readings on Modern Expansionism* (Princeton, NJ: D. Van Nostrand, 1962).

[7] For a discussion of Vietnam during the French occupation and the consequences of French colonialism for the Vietnamese people, see, for example, William J. Duiker, *The Rise of Nationalism in Vietnam, 1900–1941* (Ithaca, NY: Cornell University Press, 1976), pp. 31–100; and Neil L. Jamieson, *Understanding Vietnam* (Berkeley, CA: University of California Press, 1993), pp. 42–99.

[8] After Emperor Tự Đức passed away, because the new emperor was young, the government's affairs were left in the hands of three regents (Viet. *Phụ chánh Đại thần*): Nguyễn Văn Tường, Tôn Thất Thuyết, and Trần Tiễn Thành. The court mandarins, especially the first two regents, were responsible for the death of three emperors in a row. They were Emperors Dục Đức, Hiệp Hoà, and Kiến Phúc. Emperor Kiến Phúc was enthroned in December 1883, but he died in July the following year, presumably through the machinations of regents Nguyễn Văn Tường and Tôn Thất Thuyết.

[9] Paul Doumer was president of France from 1931 to 1932. He was shot in Paris by a mentally unstable Russian émigré and died of the wound.

economic infrastructures required for efficient exploitation.[10] Doumer began his term by swiftly imposing a significant degree of direct rule on every level of administration. He initiated a series of major fiscal reforms: the colonial bureaucracy was streamlined, unnecessary expenses were cut, and the five autonomous colonial budgets in Indochina were consolidated under a centralized treasury. Doumer gathered the natural resources of Indochina, as well as government monopolies on the production of highly profitable products like salt, opium, and alcohol, under the governor-general's control. These changes in France's approach were long-lasting and continued throughout the colonial period, even during the tenures of more liberal administrators during Phan Châu Trinh's lifetime, such as Paul Beau's (1902–07) and Albert Sarraut's (1911–14 and 1917–19). So complete was Doumer's authority and pursuit of colonial achievement on behalf of France that, toward the end of his mandate, in 1901, he could proudly report to Paris that not a single French soldier had died on the battlefield in Indochina.[11]

Doumer engineered the division of Vietnam into three parts: Cochinchina, Annam, and Tongkin. In Tongkin, according to the treaty signed in 1884, imperial authority was designated to an imperial viceroy (Viet. *kinh lược sứ*). Doumer abolished this position and transferred its prerogatives to the French resident superior in Hanoi, effectively detaching Tongkin from the Vietnamese emperor.[12] Also in 1897, the Privy Council (Viet. *Cơ mật viện*) in Annam was replaced with a Council of Ministers, which was responsible to the French resident superior in Annam. It is significant to note that Doumer removed the imperial government from financial independence. In the same year, the colonial government began to collect the taxes the people of Annam owed to the imperial court. The resident superior then transferred those funds to the imperial treasurer annually, "putting the imperial government on an allowance."[13] Thus the emperor lost any real authority and became "in effect a puppet of the French, on the throne at the whim of the local resident superior, with French advisers at all upper levels of the bureaucracy."[14] It is no surprise that Phan Châu Trinh had so little respect for monarchism and that in 1922, when Emperor Khải Định went to France, Phan wrote a terse letter, included in this volume, denouncing the emperor's display of illusory power.[15] This system essentially continued until 1945, and regardless of

---

[10] Truong Buu Lam, *Colonialism Experienced: Vietnamese Writings on Colonialism, 1900–1931* (Ann Arbor, MI: The University of Michigan Press, 2000), p. 8.

[11] Ibid., p. 1.

[12] See Truong Buu Lam, *Colonialism Experienced*, p. 16; and Duiker, *The Rise of Nationalism*, p. 106. ("Imperial viceroy" in Duiker's book had *kinh lược* as the Sino-Vietnamese equivalent, but it should be *kinh lược sứ*.)

[13] Truong Buu Lam, *Colonialism Experienced*, p. 17.

[14] Duiker, *The Rise of Nationalism*, pp. 106–07. The French sent Emperor Thành Thái into exile in 1907, first to Vũng Tàu and then, in 1916, to Reunion Island, on the Indian Ocean, where his son, Emperor Duy Tân, was also sent into exile in 1916.

[15] During his trip to Japan in 1906, Phan Châu Trinh met Marquis Cường Để, a pretender to the throne who was supported by Phan Bội Châu and his associates. Phan Châu Trinh was not impressed with the emperors on the throne and did not hide his "antipathy" toward Cường Để. For Phan's attitude toward Marquis Cường Để, see Vũ Đức Bằng, "The Viet Nam Independent Education Movement" (PhD dissertation, University of California, Los Angeles, 1971), p. 68 (viewed via University of Michigan microfilm, Ann Arbor, MI). For an account of a first meeting between Marquis Cường and Phan Châu Trinh and Phan Bội

various minor reforms, the country was still administered along the lines laid down by Doumer, that is, French officials dominated the bureaucracy and Vietnamese were employed only in minor positions and at very low salaries.

During Doumer's tenure, the French also began to build the infrastructure necessary to solidify their political control and allow them to dominate the economy. This infrastructure facilitated the exploitation of Vietnam's resources for export. Other than a few domestic industries, little industrial development was encouraged. Instead, the French concentrated on extracting natural products such as coal and minerals, and harvesting tea, rubber, tobacco, and other crops. The result of this economic policy was that the economy remained largely in the hands of the French, and the Vietnamese saw little benefit. French colonialism prohibited the development of an entrepreneurial middle class, offered few meaningful options for the educated elite, and left the peasantry in an increasingly impoverished state.

Perhaps most significant in the long run was the French establishment of an opium franchise in Indochina. In 1899, Doumer restructured the opium business, expanding sales and sharply reducing expenses. He consolidated the five autonomous opium agencies into a single opium monopoly. Doumer constructed a modern, efficient opium refinery in Saigon to process raw resin from India and China's Yunnan province into prepared smokers' opium, then sold it at official outlets in Vietnam at a profit of 400 to 500 percent. More dens and shops were opened to meet expanded consumer demand, and business boomed.[16]

By the 1920s, France began to consider Indochina to be the "jewel" of Greater France (*la plus grande France*). The entrenched economic interests and French national pride in its "civilizing mission" (*mission civilisatrice*) were unquestionably related to what Doumer had proclaimed in 1905: "Truly it is time that France put on this land her stamp, which is civilization."[17] It was this sentiment that contributed to France's attempts to hold on to Indochina until its military defeat at Điện Biên Phủ, in 1954.

TWENTIETH-CENTURY VIETNAMESE NATIONALISM

From the time that France began its intervention in Vietnam, resistance sprang up throughout the country. Many local officials and members of the scholar-gentry, such as Trương Định, Nguyễn Trung Trực, and Nguyễn Đình Chiểu,[18]

Châu in Canton, see Phan Bội Châu, *Overturned Chariot: The Autobiography of Phan-Bội-Châu*, trans. Vinh Sinh and Nicholas Wickenden (Honolulu, HI: University of Hawai'i Press, 1999), pp. 104–05. (See footnote 50 under "Marquis Cường Để").

[16] Joseph Buttinger, *The Smaller Dragon: A Political History of Vietnam* (New York, NY: Praeger, 1961), pp. 464–65.

[17] Paul Doumer, *L'Indo-Chine française*, Ouvrage couronné par l'Académie française et la Société de Géographie, second editon (Paris: Vuiberg & Nony, 1905), p. 215; cited in Vũ Đức Bằng, *The Viet Nam Independent Education Movement*, p. 20.

[18] Trương Định (1820–64) was an overseeer (Viet. *quản cơ*) in southern Vietnam under Emperor Tự Đức. After Vietnam had concluded the Treaty of Saigon, in 1862, Trương Định refused to recognize the treaty, which ceded three southern provinces. He fought on until he committed suicide to avoid capture. Nguyễn Trung Trực (1837–68) carried out resistance in Tân An (presently Long An) and Rạch Giá (presently Kiên Giang). He staged an attack on the French warship *L'espérance*. The French tried to capture him, but they were not successful. Finally, they arrested his mother, so he gave himself up and was executed in

refused to collaborate with the French. The largest resistance movement was led by Phan Đình Phùng, once the chief censor (Viet. *ngự sử*) of the Nguyễn court in Huế. In response to the Cần Vương (Loyalist)[19] edict by Emperor Hàm Nghi in 1885 calling for all-out resistance, Phan Đình Phùng organized a guerrilla army in Nghệ An, Hà Tĩnh, and Quảng Bình provinces, which kept the colonial forces at bay until 1896, when Phan Đình Phùng died of dysentery.

Frustrated by the failure of previous anticolonial ventures, the scholar-gentry began to look for new alternatives. Phan Bội Châu was the major figure within this group of literati.[20] A founder of the Vietnam Modernization Association (*Việt Nam Duy Tân Hội*, 1904), Phan Bội Châu went to Japan in 1905, primarily to ask for military aid. Through discussions with Liang Qichao, a famed Chinese reformer who lived in Japan as an exile at the time, as well as a number of prominent Japanese politicians, Phan Bội Châu came to recognize the necessity of providing Vietnamese youth with a modern education following the example of the Meiji Restoration. It should be added that Phan Bội Châu's commitment to education must not be overemphasized, as even during his years in Japan—when he appeared most optimistic about the potential of education—he was never fully committed to it. Thus it is not difficult to understand why Phan Bội Châu advocated "extreme violent action" (Viet. *bạo động kịch liệt*) in 1912, and saw it as the most effective route to restoring Vietnam's independence, seeking "a life in ten thousand deaths."[21] Nevertheless, as the key figure behind the Đông Du Movement, Phan Bội Châu helped to bring some two hundred Vietnamese youth to Japan to study between 1905 and 1909. It was hoped that these youth would acquire the knowledge and experience necessary to contribute to the modernization of Vietnam.

In 1907, however, Japan and France concluded a treaty by which they pledged to respect their mutual spheres of interest in East Asia. Consequently, between 1908 and 1909, the Japanese authorities ordered the Vietnam Modernization Association to disband, and Phan Bội Châu himself was expelled from the country. Phan Bội Châu and his associates went to Siam (Thailand). When a revolution broke out against the Ching (Manchu) dynasty in China, he moved to Canton in 1910 and formed the Vietnam Restoration League (*Việt Nam Quang Phục Hội*), a

---

1868. Nguyễn Đình Chiểu (1822–88) was a famed poet, also known for his opposition to the French colonization of southern Vietnam when the 1862 Treaty of Saigon was concluded. He was born in Gia Định (later called Saigon) and passed the regional examination for *tú tài* (the first degree) in 1843 in Gia Định. When he went to the imperial city of Huế to take the metropolitan examination, he heard that his mother had died, so he decided to return home. During the journey south he contracted an eye infection and became completely blind. When the French took Saigon in 1862, he moved to Bến Tre province. Despite his blindness, Nguyễn Đình Chiểu opened his private school and authored famous works such as the story, written in verse, of *Lục Vân Tiên*, which is a masterpiece of Vietnamese literature; *Văn tế nghĩa sĩ Cần Giuộc* (Eulogy for the Righteous People of Cần Giuộc), praising the heroic action of villagers in Cần Giuộc against an attack of the invaders; and *Ngư tiều y thuật vấn đáp* (Fisherman and Woodsman's Discourses on Medical Art), which conveyed his feelings of the situation of Vietnam under French colonialism.

[19] See footnote 29 later for more information.

[20] For Phan Bội Châu's works in English, see Vinh Sinh and Nicholas Wickenden, trans., *Overturned Chariot: The Autobiography of Phan-Bội-Châu.*

[21] Phan Bội Châu, *Tự phán* [Self-judgment] (Huế: Nxb Anh Minh, 1956), p. 150.

government in exile. After the French arranged Phan Bội Châu's arrest and imprisonment in south China (1914–17), the Restoration League began to decline.

In 1924, Phan Bội Châu dissolved the Restoration League and renamed the organization the Vietnamese Nationalist Party (*Việt Nam Quốc Dân Đảng*). In the following year, Phan Bội Châu was seized by French agents in Shanghai and transported back to Hanoi for trial. He lived in Huế under house arrest from the end of 1925 until his death in 1940. Although Phan Bội Châu's attempt to create a strong and independent Vietnam was both conceptually subjective and short-lived, it spurred generations of Vietnamese thereafter to work for national causes. Consequently, Phan Bội Châu is placed as the foremost national hero in modern Vietnam.

Phan Châu Trinh and Phan Bội Châu were contemporaries, but had divergent perspectives on crucial points. In contrast to Phan Bội Châu's, Phan Châu Trinh's approach was nonviolent and envisaged a gradual path to national independence through anti-feudal/anti-monarchical reforms and modernization undertaken within the French colonial system. The first essay in this volume, "A New Vietnam," is Phan Châu Trinh's account of his relationship with Phan Bội Châu, and it supplies several previously unknown crucial details related to Phan Bội Châu and his role within the Vietnamese independence movement.

PHAN CHÂU TRINH AND THE HISTORIOGRAPHY ON MODERN NATIONALISM

After the Second World War, many of the monographs, edited works, and journal articles on the early revolutionary movement that were published in Vietnamese focused on Phan Bội Châu as a national hero. While highlighting his militant resistance, they are often ideologically biased in their interpretation.[22] Furthermore, the information provided in these works generally lacks detail and is occasionally erroneous. Within this scholarship, with the exception of Huỳnh Lý and Nguyễn Q. Thắng's works,[23] Phan Châu Trinh and his ideas were sidelined, and for the most part he was seen as sincere and devoted to his people, but misguided.[24] Despite this interpretation and the crucial differences between Phan Châu Trinh's ideas and those of Phan Bội Châu's, Phan Châu Trinh remained popular among the Vietnamese people and was "customarily ranked immediately after Phan Bội Châu in the pantheon of modern Vietnamese heroes." Based on his

---

[22] See, for example, Tôn Quang Phiệt, *Phan Bội Châu và Phan Châu Trinh* [Phan Bội Châu and Phan Châu Trinh] (Hà Nội: Nxb Văn Sử Địa, 1956); Tôn Quang Phiệt, *Phan Bội Châu và một giai đoạn lịch sử chống Pháp của nhân dân Việt Nam* [Phan Bội Châu and a Stage in the History of the Anti-French Resistance of the Vietnamese People] (Hà Nội: Nxb Văn Hoá, 1956); and Trần Huy Liệu, "Nhớ lại Ông già Bến Ngự" [Reminiscing on "The Old Man of the Imperial Quay" (Phan Bội Châu)], *Nghiên cứu lịch sử* [Journal of Historial Studies] 47 (February 1963).

[23] Huỳnh Lý, originally a Southerner but living in North Vietnam before 1975, was the first person in the North to publish a book about Phan Châu Trinh: Huỳnh Lý, *Thơ văn Phan Châu Trinh* [Poems and Prose by Phan Châu Trinh] (Nxb Văn Học, 1983; second edition, 1993). Nguyễn Q. Thắng has been living in the South before and after 1975; he is the first person in the South to publish a book on Phan Châu Trinh: Nguyễn Q. Thắng, *Phan Châu Trinh: Cuộc đời và tác phẩm* [Phan Châu Trinh: Life and Works] (Hà Nội: Nxb Thành phố Hồ Chí Minh, 1987).

[24] See William J. Duiker, "Hanoi Scrutinizes the Past: The Marxist Evaluation of Phan Boi Chau and Phan Chu Trinh," *Southeast Asia: An International Quarterly* 1,3 (Summer 1971): 242–54.

lifelong struggle for democracy and against oppression, Phan Châu Trinh's position demonstrated his "enduring popularity."[25] Since 1992, scholarly interest in Phan Châu Trinh has substantially increased. For the most part, this new interest has resulted in a number of Vietnamese collections of Phan Châu Trinh's writings.[26] For scholars working in Vietnamese, these works provide an excellent introduction to the breadth of Phan Châu Trinh's studies.

There are a number of excellent scholars writing in English who have discussed Phan Châu Trinh within their works on wider topics concerning modern Vietnam and thus have made several important contributions.[27] Within these broader perspectives, attention has focused on Phan Châu Trinh's contributions to the modernization movement, and his ideas about democracy. Until now, however, no single monograph focusing solely on Phan Châu Trinh and his enlightened thought has been published in English.

With Phan Châu Trinh's enduring popularity in mind, one must ask why and how his memory elicited such a warm response through both non-Communist and Communist regimes. There are several reasons for Phan Châu Trinh's distinctive place within the history and historiography of Vietnam. In contrast to Phan Bội Châu, who was a popular man of action, Phan Châu Trinh was an enlightened thinker (J. *keimô-ka*), who prescribed deep and enduring changes to society. He made invaluable contributions to the modernization movement: for example, his suggestion to young men to cut their hair short and wear Vietnamese-made, Western-style clothing; his innovative efforts to introduce speech-making to Vietnam; and his ideas about democracy and other significant political concepts. While scholars have mentioned these contributions when discussing the Đông Kinh Nghĩa Thục (Đông Kinh Free School), more attention should be paid to the development of a Vietnamese enlightenment movement patterned after the Japanese *keimô* (enlightenment). This movement emerged almost immediately after Phan Châu Trinh returned from Japan in 1906. In Japan, the Meiji enlightenment in the late 1860s and early 1870s was inspired by Fukuzawa Yukichi, who presented the first *enzetsu* ("speech," a term coined by Fukuzawa himself), and included reforms such as the *danpatsurei* (short-hair-cut law) in 1862, and *minshūshugi* (democracy), a term also invented by the Japanese during this period. Although

[25] Duiker, *The Rise of Nationalism*, p. 90.

[26] Major works include the following: Phan Châu Trinh, *Phan Châu Trinh toàn tập* [The Complete Works of Phan Châu Trinh], ed. Chương Thâu, Dương Trung Quốc, and Lê Thị Kinh (Phan Thị Minh) (Đà Nẵng: Nxb Đà Nẵng, 2005), three volumes; Phan Châu Trinh, *Phan Châu Trinh qua những tài liệu mới phát hiện* [Phan Châu Trinh through Newly Discovered Materials], ed. Lê Thị Kinh (Phan Thị Minh) (Đà Nẵng: Nxb Đà Nẵng, 2003), two volumes; Nguyễn Văn Xuân, *Tuyển tập Nguyễn Văn Xuân* [Selected Works of Nguyễn Văn Xuân] (Đà Nẵng: Nxb Đà Nẵng, 2005); Huỳnh Lý, *Phan Châu Trinh: Thân thế và sự nghiệp* [Phan Châu Trinh: Life and Works] (Đà Nẵng: Nxb Đà Nẵng, 1992) and *Tuyển tập Huỳnh Lý* [Selected Works of Huỳnh Lý] (Đà Nẵng: Nxb Đà Nẵng, 2005); Nguyễn Q. Thắng, *Phan Châu Trinh: Cuộc đời và tác phẩm* [Phan Châu Trinh: Life and Works]; and Phan Châu Trinh, *Tuyển tập Phan Châu Trinh* [Selected Works of Phan Châu Trinh], ed. Nguyễn Văn Dương (Đà Nẵng: Nxb Đà Nẵng, 1995). Note that Lê Thị Kinh (Phan Thị Minh) is one of Phan Châu Trinh's granddaughters, and Nguyễn Văn Xuân and Huỳnh Lý are two specialists on Phan Châu Trinh.

[27] For example, William J. Duiker, David G. Marr, and Neil L. Jamieson are worth noting. See Duiker, *The Rise of Nationalism*; Marr, *Vietnamese Anticolonialism*; and Jamieson, *Understanding Vietnam*.

many have mentioned what Phan Châu Trinh accomplished when he was at Đông Kinh Nghĩa Thục or in his home province of Quảng Nam, until now no one has clearly identified Phan Châu Trinh as an enlightener.

An important omission in this literature is the lack of an examination of Phan Châu Trinh as the founder of the Vietnamese political-discourse style (Viet. *văn chính luận*). Part of the problem in understanding Phan's contribution lies in the fact that he wrote in both literary Chinese and *quốc ngữ*. Few contemporaries schooled in literary Chinese were able to master the new *quốc ngữ*, let alone do so with excellence and clarity. For example, although Phan Bội Châu was known as the most prolific writer in modern Vietnam and lived until 1940, he never learned to write using *quốc ngữ*. Phan Châu Trinh's use of both languages, and his encouragement to others to learn *quốc ngữ*, reflect his own efforts to address the changing times and to promote modernization. One should remember that he was trained as a scholar in the old tradition and had to struggle to learn *quốc ngữ*. As noted above, two essays in this monograph, "Morality and Ethics in the Orient and the Occident" and "Monarchy and Democracy," were written in *quốc ngữ*, and should be read with that in mind. The works selected to be translated and included in this monograph reflect the issues most important to Phan Châu Trinh and the effort he spent to enlighten his people.

Part II
A Unique Path to Adulthood

Phan Châu Trinh (pen name Tây Hồ)[28] was born in 1872 in Tây Lộc village, Tam Kỳ prefectural city, the province of Quảng Nam—a region that over time produced many individuals involved in Vietnam's national and foreign affairs. Phan's father was Phan Văn Bình, originally a military official in charge of regional defense in the mountainous area, who answered the call of the Cần Vương (Loyalist) Movement[29] and worked for it as a transportation officer. His father's

---

[28] Phan Châu Trinh used his Tây Hồ pen name quite often. Tây Hồ means literally "West Lake," the name of a large lotus pond in his home village. This name reflected his desire to invoke his birthplace, and it had classical Sino-Vietnamese literary connotations. Phan also adopted Hy Mã as his pseudonym. Hy Mã implies "wishing to become someone like the Italian revolutionary Giuseppe Mazzini [1805–72; Viet. *Mã Chí Nê*]." Phan must have come to know of Mazzini's career through the works by the Chinese reformer Liang Qichao (1873–1929), living in exile Japan in 1899 since the failure of China's Reform Movement. Apparently Phan read Liang's works when he was staying in Huế in 1903–04. Phan also used Tử Cán as his courtesy name, though his use of this name was comparatively rare.

[29] "Cần Vương" was a term first used in *Zuo zhuan* (Viet. *Tả truyện* [*Xuân Thu Tả Thị truyện*]; A Commentary on the Spring and Autumn Annals), meaning "doing one's best for the emperor." See *Kadokawa Daijiten* [Kadokawa Great Dictionary of Etymology], ed. Ozaki Yujirô et al. (Tokyo: Kadokawa Shoten, 1992), p. 224. The term is thus equivalent to "loyalism/imperialism," with a Confucian connotation. In the context of Vietnam under French expansion, the term "Cần Vương" began to be used noticeably when the young Emperor Hàm Nghi fled from the imperial palace in Huế to resist the French expansion with Tôn Thất Thuyết in Tân Sở, Quảng Bình province, in July 1885. Although Emperor Hàm Nghi was captured in 1888, any attempts to resist the French in Vietnam—most notably that of Phan Đình Phùng's resistance at Vũ Quang, Hà Tĩnh province in the 1896, and the resistance by Đề Thám from 1887 to 1913—were still called "Cần Vương." In fact, resistance movements until as late as 1917, including the Đông Du movement from 1905 to 1909 and the abortive uprising by Emperor Duy Tân in 1916, can be referred to collectively as the Cần Vương movement. From May 1916, however, as the throne had been transferred to Emperor

death in 1887 was tragic: he was murdered, probably a victim of unjust suspicion, by members of the patriotic Nghĩa Hội Cần Vương (Righteous Loyalist Society). As a typical Confucian *literatus*, Phan refrained from discussing private and family matters in his writings, nor did he ever say anything about his father's tragic death. Looking back at Phan's life, however, one may surmise that his father's unjust fate left a lasting, meaningful impression on his outlook and contributed to the moderate and nonviolent approach that he consistently adopted throughout his life.

Phan Châu Trinh's early training concentrated on martial arts, i.e., "the sword" rather than "the pen." This background also set him apart from other Vietnamese intellectuals. Unlike most Vietnamese boys at this time, Phan received his early education from his mother, Lê Thị Trung, an educated woman who came from a celebrated family in Phú Lâm village of the same prefecture. After his mother died, at the age of fourteen Phan "left his school to follow his father, often going out hunting in the mountains or practicing shooting arrows and riding horseback."[30] At this age, most literate young men in Vietnam focused on studying books, so Phan's more active education, focusing on martial arts training, fostered his self-confidence, independence, determination, and practicality—qualities that one may readily observe in him in his later years. His mastery of martial arts (Viet. *võ/vũ*) as well as the literary arts (Viet. *văn*) set him apart from the many effete intellectuals (Viet. *văn nhược*) at the time, and reminds one of the Japanese *shishi* (men of high purpose), imbued with *bushidô* (Viet. *võ/vũ sĩ đạo*), who dedicated their life to the movement that would eventually lead to the Meiji Restoration. Indeed, Phan Châu Trinh's unique background and education account for his independent thought.

Phan Châu Trinh's early experiences were coupled with an extraordinary intellect. Following his father's death, Phan's eldest brother brought him home and hired a private tutor to teach him. After more than four years of studying at home, Phan was sent to take lessons with the most renowned Confucian scholars in the province. Notwithstanding his rather late introduction to formal schooling, thanks to his intelligent disposition, Phan "was quick to understand, and was able to read books perceptively"—according to Huỳnh Thúc Kháng (1876–1947),[31] Phan's

---

Khải Định, who was not interested in resisting against, but rather preferred to collaborate with, the colonial rule, the Cần Vương movement came to an end. Because this transition was clearly significant, Phan Châu Trinh's letter to Emperor Khải Định is available in this volume. For the Cần Vương Edict (1885) of Emperor Hàm Nghi in English, see David G. Marr, *Vietnamese Anticolonialism*, pp. 49–51; or Nguyên Thê Anh, "The Vietnamese Confucian Literati and the Problem of Nation-building in the Early Twentieth Century," in *Religion, Ethnicity, and Modernity in Southeast Asia*, ed. Oh Myung-Seok and Kim Hyung-Jun (Seoul: Seoul National University Press, 1998), pp. 231–50.

[30] Mính-Viên Huỳnh Thúc Kháng, *Phan Tây-Hồ tiên sinh lịch sử* [A Biography of Phan Châu Trinh (Tây Hồ)] (Huế: Nxb Anh Minh, 1959), p. 11.

[31] Huỳnh Thúc Kháng (1846–1947) was an anticolonialist and a close associate of Phan Châu Trinh, Trần Quý Cáp, and Phan Bội Châu. His pseudonym was Mính Viên. He passed the *tiến sĩ* ("presented scholars") degree with distinction (Viet. *Hoàng giáp*) in 1904, but did not pursue a bureaucratic position. As he was a leader of the modernization movement, following the Trung Kỳ uprising in 1908 he was arrested and sent to Poulo Condore Island for thirteen years, until 1921. In prison, he mastered the basics of the French language, and until his death he had an impeccable memory (because his first manuscript was lost, he had to rewrite the *Thi tù tùng thoại* twice from memory). In 1926, he was elected to be the chairman of the Trung Kỳ House of Representatives (*Viện Dân biểu Trung Kỳ*) for three years, until 1929. He was editor-in-chief of the *Tiếng dân* (People's Voices) newspaper from

lifelong close friend. As a writer, Phan developed "his own style, and would not simply use flowery and superfluous words like ordinary mediocre writers."[32] Among the Chinese classics, Phan's favorites were the *Analects* (Viet. *Luận ngữ*), *Mencius* (Viet. *Mạnh Tử*), and *The Historical Records* (Viet. *Sử ký*). He also browsed through *The Book of Poetry* (Viet. *Kinh thi*), *The Book of Documents* (Viet. *Kinh thư*), and the *Spring and Autumn Annals* (Viet. *Xuân Thu*), but "would not set his eyes upon the other classics."[33] Phan's preference for reading material is significant. Instead of simply studying a set of texts prescribed for the examination, he had a strong sense of purpose, which included a focus on the well-being of the people. Considering Phan's natural intellect, the lasting influence of Chinese-style studies, and his independent attitude, the following comments by Huỳnh Thúc Kháng are noteworthy because he was only four years younger than Phan and thus experienced the same educational system:

> In our country the examination system developed an atmosphere in which fathers gave instructions to children, teachers taught students, and friends gave advice to one another; apart from that, there was no other thing worthwhile in this life. For this reason, the country has become so weak and the people are exhausted and isolated, yet the learned have remained intoxicated in that abyss and cannot wake up...

> Living in such an atmosphere, one could not help but be more or less influenced by it, so Phan pursued this examination system. Nevertheless, he was naturally intelligent, his aims were high. Though Phan was older when he began his studies, he did not have to read a lot to know things profoundly. When reading books, Phan had a special eye, and when writing he used a new approach—different from those who picked up small words and sentences from others to show off, like nonsense writers.[34]

Phan Châu Trinh was particularly fond of Mencius. This passion for Mencius, interestingly enough, was shared by Liang Qichao, whose books Phan would devour, and Nakae Chômin (1847–1901), the celebrated spokesperson for people's rights in Japan, whose ideas were surprisingly similar to Phan's. In response to the government's drastic efforts to modernize Japan during the early years of the Meiji period, 1868–75, when Japan was introduced to Western civilization, Chômin asserted that "traditional Confucian morality was of great significance" as "it constituted a spiritual support for the people." The key ideas of Chômin were

---

1927 to 1943. After 1945, he was Minister of Home Affairs of the Democratic Republic of Vietnam; when Hồ Chí Minh was attending the Fontainebleau conference (France) in 1946, Huỳnh Thúc Kháng was entrusted with looking after the government in Vietnam. When the peace talks broke down and the resistance war began, he was dispatched to the area around his hometown, where he died in 1947. Huỳnh Thúc Kháng authored several books, including *Thi tù tùng thoại* (Stories Related to Prison Poems), *Phan Tây Hồ tiên sinh lịch sử* (A Biography of Phan Châu Trinh [Tây Hồ]), and *Huỳnh Thúc Kháng niên phổ* (Huỳnh Thúc Kháng's Chronological Records).

[32] Huỳnh Thúc Kháng, *Phan Tây-Hồ tiên sinh lịch sử*, p. 12.

[33] Ibid., p. 12.

[34] Ibid.

"truth" or "principle and justice" (Viet. *lý nghĩa*) as in "the principle [Viet. *lý*] of equality" and "the justice [Viet. *nghĩa*] of freedom." The word *lý nghĩa,* in fact, was taken from the work of Mencius, where it had the meaning "what all persons in common perceive to be good."[35]

THE WINDS OF CHANGE

In 1903, Phan Châu Trinh went to Huế to assume a junior position as "secretary" (Viet. *thừa biện*) in the Ministry of Rites. Important developments in his thought and activities occurred at this point in his life. According to Huỳnh Thúc Kháng, at this time "new books" and "new journals" from China "overflowed into our country; among them the most influential were the writings of Liang Qichao and Kang Youwei. These books discussed popular rights and freedom, and revealed a great many facts about Western civilization."[36] After the humiliating loss in the Sino-Japanese War (1894–95), the Chinese emperor had acted on the advice of Liang and Kang to implement the "Hundred Days of Reforms" in 1898. The intent of these reforms was to promote modernization and to revitalize the civil service examination system and bureaucracy, but they were interrupted as a result of the Empress Dowager's interference, and Liang and Kang were forced to flee to Japan. From Yokohama, the new "headquarters" for the reformist Chinese literati after the failure of the 1898 coup, Liang's iconoclastic writings spread and eventually crossed back to the mainland, where they influenced a whole generation of young Chinese.

Vietnamese intellectuals remained even more isolated than their Chinese counterparts from the ideas about modernization that were transforming Japanese society. It was not until the Chinese reformist literature reached Vietnam that Phan Châu Trinh and his associates began to explore these new ideas. It is important to note that Liang's works were written in Chinese but published in Yokohama, Japan, and thus made their way into Vietnam through the Chinese merchant boats, which meant they were rare and valuable manuscripts, even among Vietnamese official scholars. As his friend recalled, Phan's reading of these manuscripts had a significant affect on the development of his thought: Phan "often went to see Thân Trọng Huề and Đào Nguyên Phổ," two prominent scholars,

> ... to borrow [these manuscripts] to read, and he was so fascinated by them that he would even neglect eating and sleeping, and from that point on his ideas were completely renewed, and not only was his knowledge broadened but his patriotic fervor was also further heightened.[37]

Previously, Phan had thought that there were "things in this world that cannot be done [Viet. *thời sự bất khả vi*], but now, as he had a clear vision in his mind's eye, he

---

[35] See Sannosuke Matsumoto, "Nakae Chômin and Confucianism," in *Confucianism and Tokugawa Culture,* ed. Peter Nosco (Honolulu, HI: University of Hawai'i Press, 1984), pp. 255–56.

[36] Huỳnh Thúc Kháng, *Phan Tây-Hồ tiên sinh lịch sử,* p. 12.

[37] Ibid., pp. 14–16.

could find out how to set to work in his own way."[38] Phan Châu Trinh had begun to engage in the work of saving his country through modernization.

Around 1904, the imperial city of Huế was a place where Vietnam's intellectuals would meet one another to discuss national affairs, but also where pedants and self-serving, greedy, "white-robe" mandarins found it possible to ignore the humiliating loss of their nation's independence. It was around this time that the Russo-Japanese War (1904–05) broke out, and news of the initial victories by Japan—a small East Asian country that had begun to modernize itself less than forty years previously—reached Vietnam, convincing Phan and his colleagues that modernization was an urgent necessity. Finding it impossible to remain indifferent to the situation,[39] Phan Châu Trinh and his close friends retired from their official positions in late 1904 and agreed to travel toward the south on a "fact finding" mission.

THE CRITICAL TURNING POINT

At this time, important changes occurred within the Vietnamese examination system. Although it was not officially dismantled until 1919, few talented young men remained in the system after 1905, when it became known that the examinations had been abolished in China. The end of the era was dramatically signified by Phan Châu Trinh, Trần Quý Cáp, and Huỳnh Thúc Kháng's landmark trip to the southern provinces in 1905. It is worth noting that all three men had previously received the highest degrees—Phan had received a *phó bảng* (lit. "on the supplementary list of 'presented scholars'") degree in 1901, and Trần and Huỳnh had just passed the 1904 metropolitan examinations to obtain the *tiến sĩ* ("presented scholars") degree.[40] When they passed through Bình Định province, a provincial examination was being held. The examination assignments included writing a poem on "Chí thành thông thánh" (Utmost Sincerity Would Be Understood by the Sages) and a *phú*[41] on "Lương ngọc danh sơn" (Precious Stone in a Famed Mountain). The three scholars disguised themselves as candidates, adopted "Đào Mộng Giác" as their common name, and collaborated in writing the examinations—Phan wrote the poem, and Huỳnh Thúc Kháng and Trần Quý Cáp wrote the *phú*. Their submission, however, was a denunciation of traditional studies and the whole outdated mandarinate examination system. Phan's poem on "Chí thành thông thánh" became notorious as it was energetic and full of spirit, and it expressed the futility of maintaining the outdated examination system at a time when Vietnam was suffering under the yoke of French colonialism:

> *Thế sự hồi đầu dĩ nhất không,*
> *Giang sơn vô lệ khấp anh hùng.*

---

[38] Ibid.

[39] Ibid., p. 16.

[40] *Phó bảng*, literally "a substitute or an alternate" degree, was a second-level *tiến sĩ* degree. Clearly, it was a higher degree than *cử nhân*. It signified that the candidate was too qualified to fail the metropolitan examination, but that the examiners were not as satisfied as they were with those earning a full *tiến sĩ*. Depending on the examiners, the granting of degrees could be tinged by subjective judgment. Nevertheless, the earning of a *phó bảng* would have been seen as a great success.

[41] Irregular, metrical, and rhythmical composition.

Vạn dân nô lệ cường quyền hạ,
Bát cổ văn chương túy mộng trung.
Trường thử bách niên cam thóa mạ,
Bất tri hà nhật xuất lao lung.
Chư quân vị tất vô tâm huyết,
Bằng hướng tư văn khán nhất thông.

The affairs of the world at the beginning were naught,
The country has no tears to cry for heroes,
Thousands of people are slaves, underneath the stronger,
Eight-legged literature[42] is just a dream.
You have been spoken ill of, for hundreds of years,
And do not know the day you may be set free from the
    prison-like cage.
If you are to do your utmost,
Read this writing from the beginning to the end and you'll understand.[43]

Later, the two pieces were circulated among the public and made a strong impact, like "a thunderbolt shaking the entire country."[44] As Huỳnh Thúc Kháng observed, "this was the first time literary works were written to make a heavy attack on the examination system and promote modern studies."[45]

While in Khánh Hòa in April 1905, the three friends heard that the Russian Baltic Fleet, on its way to reinforce the Russian naval force in the Japan Sea, was then anchored in Cam Ranh Bay to secure fuel and provisions. They disguised themselves as merchants selling foodstuffs in order to board a Russian ship and observe it to "their heart's content." Later on, Huỳnh Thúc Kháng simply explained that this bold endeavor was prompted by their "curiosity."[46] The act, nevertheless, reveals the bold temperament and inquisitive spirit that would later prompt Phan Châu Trinh to journey to Japan so that he could see for himself a country that had been modernized only recently but was able to defeat the Tsar's "invincible" navy; the same spirit informed his travel to and sojourn in France, where he spoke out for the interests of his compatriots and observed firsthand the

---

[42] A classical Chinese style that was required for the candidate examination. "Eight-legged" literature was used to discuss the *Four Books* (i.e., *The Great Learning, The Doctrine of the Mean, Analects,* and *Mencius*) and followed a strict couplet style. This rhythmic format was composed of four sections, each containing two couplets. Thus, it came to be called eight-legged literature (*bát cổ văn*). It was introduced as an essential component of the candidate examination during the Ming dynasty (1368–1644) and lasted in China until 1905, when the examination system was abolished during the last years of the Qing dynasty (1644–1911). Vietnam had adopted the candidate examination system from China, but continued to use it until 1919. Phan viewed eight-legged literature as typifying the antiquated nature of the Vietnamese examination system, probably owing to his reading of the "New Books" by Liang Qichao in Huế in 1903–04. There are several translations of the *Four Books*; among the most popular is *Han-Ying Sishu* [The Four Books in Chinese and in English], trans. James Legge, annot. Luo Zhiye (Hunan: Hunan Chubanshe, 1992).

[43] Huỳnh Lý, *Thơ văn Phan Châu Trinh*, p. 68.

[44] Huỳnh Thúc Kháng, *Phan Tây-Hồ tiên sinh lịch sử*, p. 18.

[45] Huỳnh Thúc Kháng, *Huỳnh Thúc Kháng niên phổ* [Huỳnh Thúc Kháng's Chronological Records] (Thph Hồ Chí Minh: Nxb Văn Hóa Thông Tin, 2000), p. 36.

[46] Ibid., pp. 36–37.

motherland of the colonial power with which the Vietnamese had to reckon.[47] Phan once said: "You cannot just sit in a corner and talk about things in the outside world, especially in the present state of affairs, when the winds of change are blowing in all directions; you have to go and look to see what is happening."[48]

In Bình Thuận, the group stayed in the city for some time to meet and discuss practical modernization projects—including the establishment of the Liên Thành fish-sauce company and the Dục Thanh School—with prominent figures. Phan Châu Trinh's original plan was that from Bình Thuận the group would head to Cochinchina, but he fell ill and was forced to part with his friends for treatment. Despite his illness, Phan continued to be active: when the Phú Tài Society was created in Bình Thuận to disseminate democratic and self-strengthening ideas through the study of Liang Qichao's and Kang Youwei's writings, Phan was the main speaker of the lecture series.

JAPAN AS SEEN BY PHAN CHÂU TRINH

Meanwhile, Phan Châu Trinh heard that Phan Bội Châu had gone to Japan. He returned to Quảng Nam to consult with his colleagues about the prospect of traveling to Japan himself. The two Phans had previously met each other for the first time in Huế in early 1904. Phan Châu Trinh was impressed by Phan Bội Châu's ardent patriotism, but his ideas, he thought, "did not escape from the traditional straitjacket."[49] Upon reading the materials sent by Phan Bội Châu from Japan, Phan Châu Trinh supported the idea of dispatching students to Japan for study, but did not agree with Phan Bội Châu's monarchical inclination to designate Marquis Cường Để[50] as leader of the Vietnam Modernization Association, his

---

[47] I have discussed the visit of Phan Châu Trinh and his two friends to Cam Ranh, where they dared to board a ship of the Baltic Fleet, in "Chuyện một trăm năm trước—Tháng 4, 1905 ở vịnh Cam Ranh" [The Story That Happened One Hundred Years Ago: April 1905 in Cam Ranh Bay], *Diễn Đàn* [Forum] (April, 2005), pp. 20–22.

[48] Huỳnh Thúc Kháng, *Phan Tây Hồ Tiên sinh lịch sử*, p. 18.

[49] Ibid., p. 17.

[50] Marquis Cường Để (1862–1951) was a descendant in the fourth generation of Emperor Gia Long. Gia Long's eldest son, Crown Prince Cảnh, died before he was enthroned, and thus the throne was passed on to the second son, Emperor Minh Mạng, in 1820. From that time, the imperial line of the Nguyễn dynasty followed Minh Mạng's descendants and never returned to Prince Cảnh's descendants. Those who are familiar with Japanese history would tend to suspect that this situation would have created conflicts between the senior and junior lines, as it did in Japan during the fourteenth century, but in Vietnam Emperor Minh Mạng's line was seen as the only legitimate imperial line. Thus, although he was a descendant of Prince Cảnh, by the time Marquis Cường Để was solicited by Phan Bội Châu in 1905 to join the political movement, he was a virtually unknown figure. Marquis Cường Để's title was "Kỳ Ngoại Hầu," which literally meant "outside-of-the-capital marquis." He was made titular head of the Vietnam Modernization Association (*Việt Nam Duy Tân Hội*) when it was founded. Early in 1906, he went to Japan and studied first at the Shimbu Gakkô and then at Waseda University. After his forced departure from Japan in 1909, he traveled successively to Hong Kong, Siam (currently Thailand), and China, returning to Nam Kỳ via Singapore in 1913 to make contacts and raise funds. He then returned to Hong Kong, was arrested, and was able to escape to Europe. He came back to Japan in 1915; according to his own account, the famed Japanese politician Inukai Tsuyoshi (see footnote 56 for Inukai) promised him that if France were defeated in Europe, Japan would help Vietnam to gain independence. Inukai further advised the Marquis not to accept any assistance from the Germans and also not to venture too far away from Japan in case the right time arrived for

endorsement of violent actions, or his reliance on foreign help, which Phan Châu Trinh considered to be "rushing forward when one cannot see ahead" (Viet. *dục tốc kiến tiểu*). For this reason, Phan Châu Trinh wanted to meet Phan Bội Châu again for further discussion, and also to observe modernized Japan firsthand.

Phan Châu Trinh arrived in Hanoi in December 1905. After exchanging ideas on modernization with prominent figures, such as Lương Văn Can, Đào Nguyên Phổ, and Võ Hoành,[51] Phan went to Nghệ-Tĩnh to meet Ngô Đức Kế, another life-long friend. From there he traveled north, straight to the Yên Thế resistance base, to see Đề Thám, a renowned resistance leader, and exchange views on national affairs. After their discussion, Đề Thám asked Phan Châu Trinh to stay on to work with him, but he declined. Privately, he sized up this resistance leader as "nothing more than a military commander,"[52] and under the current circumstances, Phan strongly believed "if one only sits tight in a corner, how can one survive?"[53] He believed that military tactics were not sufficient for the tasks ahead and that he would need a greater understanding of the wider world.

From Yên Thế, Phan Châu Trinh proceeded to Hải Phòng, disguised himself as a laborer to cross the border to China, and arrived in Hong Kong in late February 1906. Probably things had been arranged in advance, so that when Phan Châu Trinh arrived in Shahe (Guangdong) to visit the former military commander Tán Thuật (Nguyễn Thiện Thuật), who was staying at the home of the legendary Liu Yongfu (Viet. Lưu Vĩnh Phúc),[54] Phan Bội Châu and Marquis Cường Để were also there. Phan Bội Châu showed Phan Châu Trinh "An Appeal to My Fellow Countrymen to Study Abroad" (Viet. *Khuyến quốc dân du học văn*), and Phan Châu Trinh commended it highly, but when he saw the program of the Vietnam Modernization Association drafted by Phan Bội Châu and his colleagues in Japan, which designated Cường Để as monarch, Phan Châu Trinh remained silent, and then said that he wished to go to see Japan just once. According to Phan Bội Châu's autobiography, whenever the two were engaged in discussions on national affairs, Phan Châu Trinh bitterly denounced monarchism, "as much as to say that if the system of monarchical autocracy were not abolished, simply restoring the country's independence would bring no happiness."[55]

Japan to come to his aid. After the Japanese coup in Vietnam in March 1945, the Marquis expected to replace Emperor Bảo Đại, but his hopes were never fulfilled, as Bảo Đại was retained by the Japanese. The Marquis died a disappointed man in Tokyo on April 5, 1951.

[51] See Nguyễn Hiến Lê, *Đông Kinh Nghĩa Thục* [Đông Kinh Private School] (Saigon: Lá Bối, 1974), p. 40.

[52] Đào Văn Hội, *Ba nhà chí sĩ họ Phan* [The Three Phans—Men of High Purpose] (Saigon: Nhà in Maurice, 1951), p. 60.

[53] Huỳnh Thúc Kháng, *Phan Tây-Hồ tiên sinh lịch sử*, p. 19.

[54] Exiled from China, Liu Yongfu (?—1917) came to northern Vietnam in 1863 and became leader of the "Black Flags" (Cờ đen), who assisted the Vietnamese in their efforts to resist the French. Before returning to his base in Guangdong, China, in 1895 he went to Formosa to combat the Japanese.

[55] In Phan Bội Châu's autobiography, he comments that "it seems at that time, deep in his heart, he [Phan Châu Trinh] already had a different aspiration ... Every day, when we talked about the affairs of our country, he singled out bitterly the wicked conduct of the monarchs, the enemies of the people. He ground his teeth when talking about the ruler of the day, who was bringing calamity to the country and disaster to the people, as much as to say that if the system of monarchical autocracy were not abolished, simply restoring the country's independence would not bring happiness ... The Marquis [Cường Để], who was

The Japan that Phan Châu Trinh visited in April 1906 was a dynamic one, connecting what he had read in Huế with the real world. In Tokyo, Phan Bội Châu took Phan Châu Trinh to inspect schools and to meet with prominent persons. Though neither Phan Châu Trinh nor Phan Bội Châu recorded the places they visited and people they met, we can assume that, apart from the Vietnamese staying in Japan at the time, they met Phan Bội Châu's Japanese acquaintances, such as the statesman Inukai Tsuyoshi[56] and Kashiwabara Buntarô of the Tôa Dômeikai. They probably also met with the famed Chinese reformer Liang Qichao (although there is no direct evidence of this) because Phan Châu Trinh greatly admired Liang Qichao; they shared the same view in relation to education, and Phan Châu Trinh would spend at least two and a half years in Paris retranslating *Tôkai Sanshi*, a work that Liang had translated from Japanese to Chinese.[57] The two may also have visited Fukuzawa Yukichi's Keiô Gijuku University, located in Mita, Tokyo.

After observing Japan's social conditions, Phan Châu Trinh commented to Phan Bội Châu, "The level of their people is so high, and the level of our people is so low! How could we not become slaves? That some students now can enter Japanese schools has been your great achievement ..." Phan Châu Trinh then suggested to Phan Bội Châu,

> Please stay on in Tokyo to take a quiet rest and devote yourself to writing, not to making appeals for combat against the French. You should only call for "popular rights and popular enlightenment." Once popular rights have been achieved, then we can think about other things.[58]

When Phan Châu Trinh left to return to Vietnam, Phan Bội Châu accompanied him as far as Hong Kong.

For Phan Châu Trinh, his visit to Japan confirmed his conviction that modernization was necessary before one could even contemplate independence—an independent Vietnam without modernization would be vulnerable to the greater powers in the area, which would compromise any hard-won independence it achieved. It is unfortunate that, apart from the above sporadic information, nothing was written concerning Phan Châu Trinh's sojourn in Japan, but this trip seems to have been very important in crystallizing his ideas and shaping his future course of action. Much later, in 1925, after some fourteen years in France, before returning to Vietnam, Phan Châu Trinh wrote a letter to a Vietnamese student that sheds light upon his understanding of Japanese modernization and the response of Vietnam and other Asian countries:

---

sitting nearby, became very excited. Thereupon he wrote out a letter of admonition for himself; at the end of the letter he signed himself 'Enemy of the People,' then 'Cường Để.'" See Phan Bội Châu, *Overturned Chariot: The Autobiography of Phan-Bội-Châu*, p. 105.

[56] Inukai Tsuyoshi (1855–1932) was born in Okayama prefecture and used the pseudonym Bokudô. In 1882, with Ôkuma Shigenobu and others, he founded the Rikken kaishin-tô (Constitutional Reform Party). In 1910, he formed the Rikken kokumin-tô (Constitutional People's Party) and became its leader. He was elected prime minister in 1931, but was assassinated by a radical rightist in the same year. Inukai was interested in Asian affairs.

[57] For *Tôkai Sanshi*, see detailed explanation below, in the section "Fourteen-Year Sojourn in France."

[58] Phan Bội Châu, *Overturned Chariot: The Autobiography of Phan-Bội-Châu*, p. 108.

I wonder why you and your friends do not open your eyes and look at the examples of East Asia. Very clever, when facing European civilization. With one slash Japan cut its old customs and began to follow the new way. The Japanese became arrogant to the Chinese, they became arrogant to the Koreans. The two countries, China and Korea, could not decide what to do with the old habits, refusing to follow the new way. When the Japanese achieved modernization, they scorned their fellow Asians. China and Korea began to wake up, but they were still confused about what to do at that time. With regard to ourselves, we have also been scorned, but we decided to close our eyes. We have continued in our self-destructive habits. Now we open our eyes, but still look for a dream without facing the truth and finding a way to go. What can we expect of our country? What is the nation? Shall we wait for our grandchildren, or our great-grandchildren?[59]

Phan Châu Trinh's public return to Vietnam was cause for speculation. Some people were surprised by the fact that he did not conceal his return from Japan; they took it for granted that Phan Châu Trinh was in agreement with Phan Bội Châu and Marquis Cường Để, who opposed the French vehemently, thus they expected Phan Châu Trinh to return as surreptitiously as he had departed. Some suspected that Japanese troops would follow his return to Vietnam. Others rumored that Phan Châu Trinh carried with him a very important message from Japan. One group sent a letter directly to Phan Bội Châu, saying that because Phan Châu Trinh was in favor of democracy and against Marquis Cường Để, his return to Vietnam would compromise the revolutionary movement. [60]

In the midst of all this speculation, Phan Châu Trinh thought the best way forward was to engage directly with the French; he hoped that among them he would find sympathetic, knowledgeable people who would advise the Vietnamese concerning the best route to modernization, as well as the potential drawbacks and disadvantages. With help from the French there might be a chance to save Vietnam.[61] As a result of his visit to Japan, Phan Châu Trinh had a concrete vision of how a "modernized" country should look; his experience in Japan had confirmed his belief that a modern education was the key to progress and that his country's move toward independence should be gradual. At the same time, he showed an awareness of the potential danger of Japanese expansionist tendencies, though he only talked about this aspect of Japan as a secondary concern and mainly focused on the positive advances he had seen, the results of modernization. The significance of Phan's trip to Japan was revealed in his open approach toward French authorities after he returned to Vietnam.

Soon after his return, Phan Châu Trinh took a calculated risk in writing a letter to Governor-General Paul Beau; this was the first letter that had ever been written by a Vietnamese directly to the highest French authority in the colony. This letter,

---

[59] Phan Châu Trinh, "Bức thư trả lời cho một người học trò tên là Đông" [Letter to a Student Named "Đông"], Paris, January 24, 1925, in *Tân Dân—Tuần báo Văn hoá, Chính trị, và Xã hội* [The New Citizen—Weekly on Politics, Culture, and Society], no. 3, March 24, 1949.

[60] The letter is included in *Tự phán*.

[61] Huỳnh Thúc Kháng, *Phan Tây-Hồ tiên sinh lịch sử*, p. 21.

usually known as "Đầu Pháp chính phủ thư" (Letter Addressed to the French Government; 1907),[62] denounced the social evils of the situation in Indochina and demanded improvements in colonial policy. It was widely circulated. It infuriated the officials at the Huế court because they thought that they were the main targets of his criticism; Phan became a *persona non grata*[63] in their eyes. Although the Governor General's response is not known, Phan's letter was well received by the progressive French living in Vietnam, and their support would eventually prove crucial to Phan. French support was important, yet Phan Châu Trinh knew that only the Vietnamese themselves could change their fate.

MODERNIZATION EFFORTS AND THE ĐÔNG KINH NGHĨA THỤC SCHOOL

Almost immediately after his return to Vietnam from Japan, Phan Châu Trinh started working on a plan of modernization, though he did not mention it in his writings. He seemed to absorb the positivist message of Enlightenment quickly. From what he saw and had discussed during his trip to Japan, Phan Châu Trinh had developed a good understanding of the modernizing elements that had made Japan strong, and he tried to duplicate this modernizing experience in Vietnam.

Phan Châu Trinh began by appealing directly to the Vietnamese to join hands to build schools and create academic institutions (Viet. *học hội*), commercial societies (Viet. *thương hội*), and agricultural societies (Viet. *nông hội*). Adopting "Using commerce to unite people together" (Viet. *dĩ thương hợp quần*)[64] as a slogan in Trung Kỳ, he encouraged people to focus on the particular strength of their region, for instance by planting cinnamon trees (Viet. *quế*), tea (Viet. *trà*) and sugar cane (Viet. *mía*), and producing a variety of sugar products (Viet. *đường*) and textiles (Viet. *dệt*) in Quảng Nam. Phan Châu Trinh founded a commercial company of his own and owned a cinnamon tree plantation. Hoàng Tăng Bí, one of Phan Châu Trinh's acquaintances, had learned the new weaving and dyeing techniques and began producing textiles on a larger scale, whereas other people established businesses producing handicrafts, hats, clothes, feather fans, wooden shoes, and Oriental medicines.[65] Phan Châu Trinh was determined to "invigorate the people's spirit, broaden the people's mind, and enrich the people's well-being" (Viet. *chấn dân trí, khai dân khí, hậu dân sinh*).[66] To Phan, "invigorating the people's spirit" was all-important because their patriotism and their enthusiastic spirit had been buried by colonialism and therefore needed to be revived. Furthermore, he wanted the people to realize the futility of Chinese-style civil service examinations. "Broadening the people's minds" by opening schools to teach the new curriculum with an emphasis on modern technology was required to nourish the people's intellect and the nation's talents. Finally, it was necessary to enrich

---

[62] For an English translation of this letter, see Truong Buu Lam, *Colonialism Experienced*, "Document 2, Phan Chau Trinh (1872–1926), Letter to Governor-General Beau (1907)," pp. 125–40.

[63] Ibid., p. 22; and Đào Văn Hội, *Ba nhà chí sĩ họ Phan*, p. 62.

[64] Nguyễn Văn Xuân, *Phong trào Duy Tân* [The Modernization Movement] (Đà Nẵng: Nxb Đà Nẵng, 1995), p. 223.

[65] Vũ Đắc Bằng, *The Viet Nam Independent Education Movement*, pp. 103–04.

[66] Huỳnh Lý, *Phan Châu Trinh: Thân thế và sự nghiệp* [Phan Châu Trinh: Life and Works], pp. 36–37.

living conditions by improving the standard of living though the development of domestic products and industries. Arguing from this point of view, Phan Châu Trinh was truly an enlightened thinker.

As early as the latter part of 1906, we are told, Phan Châu Trinh began to promote short haircuts; for a man to have his hair cut short became a powerful, symbolic act that represented courage, modernization, and eventually even rebellion. Phan Khôi,[67] later a celebrated personality but at that time an eager, promising nineteen-year-old, related the following story about Phan Châu Trinh. In the winter of 1906, Phan Châu Trinh, having just returned from Japan, arrived in Quảng Nam with another friend. The way Phan Châu Trinh spoke to people was like "giving a speech." He then suggested three persons in the group, including Phan Khôi, be the first to cut their hair short. "The hair cutting was clumsy," Phan Khôi thought, "but Phan Châu Trinh kept praising: 'Nice cut indeed! Nice look indeed!'" Afterward, about fifty or sixty people followed their example and had their hair cut. By early 1907, the haircutting business was flourishing throughout Quảng Nam. Wherever there was a school, then there was haircutting. That year, the superintendent (Viet. *kiểm khán*) of the Diên Phong School was working as a barber in his spare time. Phan Khôi wrote this popular song (Viet. *ca dao*) for the superintendent to sing while he cut hair.

> *Tay trái cầm lược,*
> *Tay mặt cầm kéo,*
> *Cúp hè! Cúp hè!*
> *Thẳng thẳng cho khéo!*
> *Bỏ cái hèn mầy,*
> *Bỏ cái dại mầy,*

---

[67] Phan Khôi (1887–1960) was from a renowned family; he was the son of Phan Trân, a *phó bảng* graduate and former prefect (Viet. *tri phủ*) during the Nguyễn dynasty, and his mother was the daughter of governor Hoàng Diệu, a man who committed suicide when the French attacked Hanoi in 1882. Phan Khôi was born in Bảo An, prefecture of Điện Bàn, Quảng Nam province. The pseudonym he used most often was Chương Dân (Brightened Citizen). Phan Khôi was brilliant in many fields: as a writer, a philologist, a critic, a journalist, and a poet. He took part in the Duy Tân movement at the Đông Kinh Nghĩa Thục school. In the 1908 Trung Kỳ uprising, he was arrested in Hanoi, transported back to Quảng Nam province, and imprisoned until 1911. After that, he participated in the literary world and became one of the most famous literary figures in Vietnam, owing to his penetrating observations, marked by a distinctive style. In 1932, he wrote the poem *Tình già* (Aging Love), which marked the beginning of "New Poetry" (*Thơ mới*) in Vietnam. When the resistance war against the French erupted in 1946, Phan Khôi was invited by Hồ Chí Minh to join. He participated in the struggle and traveled from the South to the Communist guerrilla zone in Việt Bắc. In 1956–58, he was involved as leader of the *Nhân văn* (Humanities) group, demanding political freedom and democracy. The two newspapers this group published, *Nhân văn* and *Giai phẩm* (Beautiful Issues), were eventually suppressed by the authorities. Phan Khôi died in 1960. He published many works. The major ones are: *Việt ngữ nghiên cứu* (Study on Vietnamese Language; 1955), *Chương Dân thi thoại* (Poems and Stories by Phan Khôi; 1936), *Tình già* (Aging Love; 1932), *Học thuyết và đạo đức Khổng Phu Tử* (Theories and Morality of Confucianism; 1924), and *Giáo dục nghiên cứu* (Study on Education; 1919). Phan Khôi's article, "Lịch sử tóc ngắn" (History of the Short Haircut), appeared in the magazine *Ngày nay* (Hanoi), no. 149, on February 15, 1939. Until now, several scholars have cited this article from anthologies and, for some reason, indicated that the author of the above popular song (*ca dao*) was "anonymous." Previous translations of the poem have not been very precise, either.

Cho khôn, cho mạnh,
Ở với ông Tây!

The left hand holds comb,
The right scissors,
Clip! Clip!
Straight, straight, be careful!
No more with cowardliness,
No more with foolishness,
Get wise, get strong,
You are living with the French!

Phan Khôi went on to relate:

> During the 1908 Trung Kỳ [Annam] uprising, I was not there at the time, but I heard that if one followed the demonstrations, one had to have his hair cut. When one passed by a market and a leader was giving a speech, men in the market had to have their hair cut before they could participate. After the incident [the demonstrations that took place prior to the uprising], the price for haircutting increased quite a bit.

During the Trung Kỳ uprising, protesters caught with short hair could be imprisoned for eighteen months; thus the riot was called the "Revolt of the Hairs Cut Short" (*Révolte des cheveux tondus*). Observing from the French point of view, one can see why the Vietnamese haircut was perceived as a serious act during this time. Writing in 1939, Phan Khôi noted that, thanks to the Trung Kỳ haircutting movement in 1908, the short hairstyle had spread throughout Annam, whereas in Tongkin and Cochinchina more than thirty years later many still wore their hair long with top knots. Also in 1908, Western dress began to appear sporadically in Hanoi.

Phan Châu Trinh strongly believed education was the most important element in modernization. Đông Kinh Nghĩa Thục, a new school established mainly by Phan Châu Trinh, was opened in March 1907. "Đông Kinh" could mean either Hanoi or Tokyo. "Nghĩa Thục" is the Vietnamese equivalent of the Japanese *Gijuku* of Keiô Gijuku in Tokyo, which was a private "community school," somewhat reminiscent of an English "public" school. The name thus reveals the admiration felt by Phan Châu Trinh and his associates for Fukuzawa's educational institution, dedicated to the teaching of modern subjects, which was the inspiration for theirs.[68] The principal (Viet. *thục trưởng*) of Đông Kinh Nghĩa Thục was Lương Văn Can, and the director of academic affairs (Viet. *giám học*) was Nguyễn Quyền, both of whom were Phan Châu Trinh's good friends. It may be added parenthetically that once after Nguyễn Quyền and Phan Châu Trinh had gone to get their hair cut together in Hanoi, Nguyễn Quyền wrote his now famous poem:

---

[68] This university had been founded in 1873 by Fukuzawa Yukichi. Đông Kinh is not only the old name of Hanoi but also the Vietnamese equivalent of the name of Tokyo. See Phan Bội Châu, *Overturned Chariot: The Autobiography of Phan-Bội-Châu*, pp. 12–13.

Phen này cắt tóc đi tu,
Tụng kinh Độc Lập ở chùa Duy Tân.

This time I had my hair cut and became a monk,
I will chant the "Independence" sutra, and I will live
in the "Modernization" temple.[69]

There were about six hundred students enrolled in Đông Kinh Nghĩa Thục. The "curriculum was based on New Learning, relying on the Chinese and Japanese reformed education systems. The school taught physical education, natural sciences [Viet. *cách trí*], arithmetic [Viet. *toán pháp*], geography, history, literature, and civics (Viet. *công dân giáo dục*)."[70] The Đông Kinh Nghĩa Thục especially encouraged students to learn *quốc ngữ* by translating texts discussing new Western ideas. Phan Châu Trinh was convinced that writing in an alphabetical script was essential to modernization, and he argued, "Vietnam cannot be saved without getting rid of Chinese characters."[71]

During 1907, Phan Châu Trinh spent most of his time in Quảng Nam, but made several trips to Hanoi to deliver speeches and check on progress made at the Đông Kinh Nghĩa Thục. As noted above, the Vietnamese concept of "speech" (Viet. *diễn thuyết*) itself was unquestionably modeled after the speeches of Fukuzawa Yukichi, the founder of the Keiô Gijuku University, who gave the first public speech in Japan in 1873.[72] In delivering his own speeches, Phan Châu Trinh was introducing a new and exciting form of public discourse; prior to this point, public speeches were unknown in Vietnam. His topics focused on modernization. For example, the subject of one was "Vietnam cannot be saved without abolishing Chinese characters" (Viet. *Bất phế Hán tự, bất túc dĩ cứu Nam quốc*).[73] Phan Châu Trinh's speeches were extremely popular and attracted substantial audiences.[74] The following poem describes one such occasion:

Buổi diễn thuyết người đông như hội,
Kỳ bình văn khách đến như mưa.[75]

Those who went to hear the speeches were crowded as if at a festival,
Then came the time of composition expositions, guests came like rains.

Phan Châu Trinh urged the youth to cut their hair short, to wear Western-style clothes, and to support domestic producers by purchasing their products. These

---

[69] Đặng Thai Mai, *Văn thơ Cách mạng Việt Nam Đầu Thế kỷ XX, 1900–1925* [Revolutionary Prose and Poems in Vietnam at the Beginning of the Twentieth Century, 1900–1925] (Hanoi: Nxb Văn học, 1964), p. 66.

[70] Ibid., p. 57.

[71] Marr, *Vietnamese Anticolonialism*, p. 169.

[72] Fukuzawa Yukichi gave his first speech in Japanese at the Mita Hall. The Japanese term for "speech"—*enzetsu* (Viet. *diễn thuyết*)—was also coined by him. It was later adopted by the Chinese, Koreans, and the Vietnamese.

[73] Marr, *Vietnamese Anticolonialism*, p. 169.

[74] See for example, ibid.

[75] Chương Thâu, *Đông Kinh Nghĩa Thục* (Hanoi: Nxb Hà Nội, 1982), p. 39.

measures obviously followed the Meiji "modernization boom" of the early 1870s, and they appeared to be successful, albeit to a lesser degree, in Vietnam in Phan's time as well. The term "Tây Hồ style" (Viet. *mốt Tây Hồ*), i.e., "Phan Châu Trinh's style," was in vogue around this time and meant dressing in Western-style clothing that was made in Vietnam with local materials.[76] Ernest Babut, the French editor of the *Đại Việt* newspaper, frequently attended Phan Châu Trinh's speeches, and the two became close friends. One of the speeches Phan delivered at this time, "Hiện trạng vấn đề" (The Current Problems), was known throughout the country. The oration concluded with the now famous sentence: "Don't rely on foreign help, reliance on foreign help is foolish; do not resort to violence, violence is self-destructive" (Viet. *vọng ngoại tắc ngu, bạo động tắc tử*.)[77] Unfortunately, the Đông Kinh Nghĩa Thục was very short-lived: it was closed in February 1908 as a result of the tax-protest riots. Nevertheless, this school is remembered as a successful first step in the modernization movement. Phan Châu Trinh's influence and unyielding commitment to modernization and to the Đông Kinh Nghĩa Thục clearly established among the people his credibility as an enlightened thinker and a passionate and devoted reformer.

VIETNAM ERUPTS

When tax revolts erupted in Quảng Nam and other cities in central Vietnam in 1908, those who bore Phan Châu Trinh a grudge among the officials in the Huế court accused him, along with those who had initiated the movement for popular rights, of maintaining surreptitious contacts with Phan Bội Châu and inciting the public to join in revolt. Phan Châu Trinh was arrested and transported to Huế. When Phan Châu Trinh passed by the southeastern gate of the Huế citadel, he composed the following Chinese four-line poem:

> *Luy luy già toả xuất đô môn,*
> *Khẳng khái bi ca thiệt thượng tồn.*
> *Quốc thổ trầm luân dân tộc luy,*
> *Nam nhi hà sự phạ Côn Lôn.*

> Tied up by chains, I departed the imperial gate,
> Chanting in mournful tone, my tongue nevertheless still exists,
> The country is at the lowest ebb, people have to bear the burden,
> Who is going to fear Poulo Condore Island![78]

At first Phan Châu Trinh was condemned to death, but through the intervention of Ernest Babut, who was also a celebrity in the Ligue des Droits de l'Homme (League of the Rights of Man), his death sentence was commuted to life imprisonment on Poulo Condore Island. It is worth mentioning that Phan was

---

[76] Jamieson, *Understanding Vietnam*, p. 59.

[77] The text of "Hiện trạng vấn đề" was lost. Huỳnh Thúc Kháng, *Phan Tây-Hồ tiên sinh lịch sử*, p. 22.

[78] Huỳnh Thúc Kháng, *Thi tù tùng thoại* [Stories of Poetry Written in Prison] (Hồ Chí Minh City: Nxb Văn hóa Thông tin, 2000), p. 12.

among the first to become a political prisoner on the island.[79] Thanks to Babut's intervention, however, Phan Châu Trinh did not have to live in the prison and was allowed to lodge in An Hải fishing village. He received rather lenient treatment: he did not have to wear a prison uniform, eat prison meals, or engage in forced labor like the other prisoners.

About the time Phan Châu Trinh was sent to Poulo Condore Island, he heard of Trần Quý Cáp's tragic death in Nha Trang city.[80] Though at that point Phan did not know the details of his good friend's death, he must have been shocked by the news. Trần Quý Cáp and Phan were particularly close in temperament and both were very eloquent. Phan Châu Trinh and Trần had nourished a dream to work together, but after Trần's death Phan felt overwhelmed and desperate, like the proverbial *Tinh Vệ* bird hoping to fill the Eastern Sea with rocks it carried in its beak, he said. Phan Châu Trinh thus composed this poem:

> *Anh biết cho chăng hỡi Dã Hàng?*
> *Thình lình sóng dậy cửa Nha Trang.*
> *Lời nguyền trời đất còn ghi tạc,*
> *Giọt máu non sông đã chảy tràn.*
> *Tinh Vệ nghìn năm hồn khó dứt?*
> *Đỗ Quyên muôn kiếp oán chưa tan.*[81]

---

[79] Huỳnh Thúc Kháng, *Phan Tây-Hồ tiên sinh lịch sử*, p. 24.

[80] Trần Quý Cáp (1876–1908) was a native of Quảng Nam. His pen name was Thai Xuyên (Prime River), and his pseudonym was Dã Hàng (Lone Traveler). Trần Quý Cáp received his *tiến sĩ*, the highest degree, in the examination in 1904, at the same time as Huỳnh Thúc Kháng. He was known to be a deep thinker and was indignant at the whole situation in his country. After Trần Quý Cáp, Huỳnh Thúc Kháng, and Phan suspended their trip to the southern provinces in 1905 as a result of Phan's illness, Trần Quý Cáp went back to Thăng Bình in his home province to become a teacher. He used "New Books" in his teaching and hired other teachers to teach vernacular Vietnamese, *quốc ngữ*, and French to his students. Owing to his educational reforms, he was seen as a personal enemy of die-hard mandarins. He was removed to Khánh Hòa province because of that hostility. During the 1908 uprising, he was arrested and kept in Nha Trang (capital city of Khánh Hòa) prison. The Khánh Hòa magistrate (Viet. *án sát*), Phạm Ngọc Quát, wanted to show his superiors his efficiency in dealing with "new rebels," so he made an example of Trần Quý Cáp and sentenced him to be executed without a trial (Viet. *mạc tu hữu*). Trần Quý Cáp was guillotined immediately. It is important to note that Trần Quý Cáp's sentence was the same one dealt to the famed Yue Fei (1103–41; Viet. Nhạc Phi), one of China's most celebrated generals in the Southern Song (1127–1279; Viet. *Nam Tống*). Later on, the husband and wife of Qin Guei (1090–1155; Viet. Tần Cối), the minister who arranged Yue Fei's death, came to be despised and recognized as the prototype for traitors. Trần Quý Cáp's friends were well aware of the similarity. When Phan was released from Poulo Condore in June 1910, among the first things he did was to ask the authorities to punish Phạm Ngọc Quát. For further details, see Anh-Minh Ngô Thành Nhân, *Ngũ Hành Sơn chí sĩ hay là Những Anh hùng Liệt sĩ Tỉnh Quảng Nam* [The Men of Determination of the Land of Five-Mountains-Running-Continuously, or The Heroes of Quảng Nam Province] (Huế: Nxb Anh Minh, 1961).

[81] Tây-Hồ Phan Châu Trinh, *Tây-Hồ và Santé Thi tập* [Phan Châu Trinh and a Collection of Poems in Santé Prison], Lê Ấm sưu tập (Nhà in Lê Thị Đàm, 1961), trang 21. This poem is missing two lines. *Tinh Vệ* (C. *jingwei*) is a bird similar to a crow that lives on the seashore. It is said that the daughter of Viêm Đế (Emperor Yan) became a bird when she drowned in the sea. The bird carried stones in its beak hoping to fill the Eastern Sea. *Đỗ Quyên* (C. *dujuan*) is a cuckoo. It is said that Emperor Shu (Viet. Thục Đế) had an affair with the wife of one of his followers, and because of this action he was forced to give up the throne and left the

Alas! How would you feel, Wild Traveler [Dã Hàng, Trần Quý Cáp]?
The waves suddenly struck Nha Trang beach,
Heaven and earth remember my feelings now!
The blood has already been shed.
The *Tinh Vệ* bird will try its bid even if it takes a thousand years,
How can the *Đỗ Quyên* forget its vow?

After three years on Poulo Condore Island, Phan Châu Trinh was released in June 1910, again through the intervention of Babut and other French admirers. The colonial authorities tried to hold Phan under house arrest in Mỹ Tho, in the Mekong delta, but when he protested vehemently, the authorities gave in and agreed to allow him and his son, Phan Châu Dật, to depart for France.

Phan Châu Trinh also had two daughters, Phan Thị Châu Liên and Phan Thị Châu Lan, who remained in Vietnam.[82] Phan Châu Trinh's wife rarely appears in the documents. She was a traditional wife and ran the family rice farm in Quảng Nam while Phan was studying and later working in Huế. She died in 1911, almost immediately after Phan departed for Paris. Phan Châu Trinh also had other relationships. When he was living in Huế, he met an attractive girl from a well-to-do family. After some months of exchanging ideas on literature, they became interested in each other. Phan said to her, "Let me go home and ask my wife's opinion." When arriving in Quảng Nam, Phan saw his wife coming back from the rice fields, her hands and feet splattered with mud. She rushed to cook lunch. Seeing this, Phan realized that he had been living in a daydream, and he severed his relations with the lady in Huế.

Before leaving Vietnam, Phan Châu Trinh drafted "Pháp Việt liên hợp hậu chi Tân Việt Nam" (A New Vietnam Following the Franco-Vietnamese Alliance), in which he exposed the differences between the divergent political stances adopted by him and Phan Bội Châu, unquestionably the two most important Vietnamese political activists in the first quarter of the twentieth century. Although this work voiced opposition to the ideas of Phan Bội Châu and the vast majority of Vietnamese revolutionaries who would come after him, Phan Châu Trinh nevertheless was not to be accused of being "against the revolution," and his status as a forerunner of the revolution survives to this day. In this respect, his case is unique, indeed. Since this work is so important in placing Phan Châu Trinh's ideas within the context of those of his contemporaries, it is translated from literary Chinese into English and included in this volume.

---

country. He later regretted his actions and was reincarnated as a *Đỗ Quyên* bird. In Vietnam, the *Đỗ Quyên* bird is used as a trope to invoke one's love for one's country.

[82] This story about Phan Châu Trinh was related by his daughter Phan Thị Châu Liên. See Phan Thị Châu Liên, "Phan Châu Trinh Tiên sinh dật sự"[Episodes concerning Phan Châu Trinh] in Phan Châu Trinh, *Giai nhân kỳ ngộ diễn ca* [Chance Encounter with Elegant Females—Translated into Verses], ed. and trans. Lê Văn Siêu (Saigon: Hướng Dương, 1958), p. LXVIII. It is of interest to note that Madame Nguyễn Thị Bình, foreign minister at the Paris Conference during the late 1960s and early 1970s representing the former National Liberation Front of South Vietnam, was one of Phan Châu Trinh's granddaughters. After 1975, she was assigned to more or less ceremonial roles. During the early 1990s, for example, she was named vice president of Vietnam. At present, Madame Nguyễn Thị Bình is mainly occupying herself with educational matters.

It was unfortunate that Phan and Phan Bội Châu last saw each other in Japan and Hong Kong in 1906, and never met again, even when the two finally came back to Vietnam in the same year (1925), Phan Châu Trinh from France and Phan Bội Châu from China.

FOURTEEN-YEAR SOJOURN IN FRANCE

Phan Châu Trinh arrived in France in April 1911. At the beginning of his sojourn, he received money from the French government, but after a few years this funding was withdrawn because Phan often criticized French colonial policy. Yet he refused to succumb to pressure. Phan opened a business, retouching photographs to make his living and to support his son, while continuing to speak out to urge the French government to liberalize its colonial policy in Indochina. *Đông Dương chính trị luận* (On Indochinese Politics) and *Trung Kỳ dân biến thỉ mạt ký* (History of the Insurrection in Central Vietnam) were the two major pieces he wrote following his arrival in France. These works explored the social evils in Vietnam's feudal system, and the deplorable condition of the Indochinese people. Phan Châu Trinh maintained close contacts with prominent Vietnamese political activists living in Paris, most notably Nguyễn Ái Quốc[83] and Phan Văn Trường,[84] and collaborated with liberal French politicians and prominent personalities.

---

[83] Nguyễn Ái Quốc's (Nguyễn the Patriot) real name was Nguyễn Tất Thành; he was a Vietnamese Communist leader and a major force behind the resistance to French colonial rule. Nguyễn Tất Thành was born in 1890, in the village of Kim Liên, Nam Đàn prefecture, province of Nghệ An. His father, Nguyễn Sinh Sắc, was a mandarin who was a friend of Phan Châu Trinh. They both had earned a *phó bảng* degree in 1901 and shared a further connection because at the time their home provinces, Nghệ Tĩnh and Quảng Nam, enjoyed close cultural links since both had resisted the establishment (i.e., the imperial court in Huế). Nguyễn Sinh Sắc had resigned his position in protest against the French domination of his country. As a teenager, Nguyễn Tất Thành studied at the famous Huế high school. He then taught briefly in Phan Thiết. In 1911, he found work as a cook on a French steamer and visited various ports, including Boston, New York, and London. During this time, he wrote several letters to Phan Châu Trinh, who filled a role as an unofficial surrogate father. After living in London from approximately 1915 to 1917, Nguyễn Tất Thành moved to France and met with Phan Châu Trinh in Paris. While in France, Nguyễn Tất Thành maintained a close collaboration with Phan Châu Trinh, though their ages and politics were different. Nguyễn Tất Thành engaged in radical activities and helped found the French Communist party in 1920. He traveled to Moscow in late 1923 for training, and in late 1924 was sent to Canton (China), where he organized the Vietnamese exiles into a radical, militant movement. In 1927, he was forced to leave China when local authorities expelled Communists. Returning to China in 1930, he founded the Indochinese Communist Party and acted as representative of the Communist International. In June 1931, he was arrested in Hong Kong by the British. In 1933, reports circulated claiming that Nguyễn Tất Thành had died in prison, news that set off a wave of great mourning in Vietnam. However, most reliable accounts report that Nguyễn Tất Thành escaped and made his way back to the Soviet Union via Hong Kong. In 1938, he returned to China and served as an adviser with Chinese Communist armed forces. When Japan occupied Vietnam in 1941, he helped to found a new Communist-dominated independence movement, popularly known as the Vietminh, which became the dominant force for independence both during and after the war. In August 1942, Nguyễn Tất Thành adopted the well-known pseudonym Hồ Chí Minh (Hồ the Enlightened)—among the many pseudonyms that he used. When Japan surrendered in August 1945, the Vietminh seized power and declared the establishment of the Democratic Republic of Vietnam, and Hồ became president. The French were unwilling to grant independence to Vietnam, and in late 1946 war broke out. The war lasted for eight years. The Vietminh finally defeated French troops in the decisive battle of Điện Biên Phủ in 1954. At the Geneva Conference held

Following the completion of these political works, Phan Châu Trinh spent a great deal of time, probably during 1912–1914, translating into Vietnamese Liang Qichao's Chinese translation of *Kajin no kigû* (Chance Encounters with Elegant Females). *Kajin no kigû* is a political serialized novel that explores popular rights and revolution; it was first published in Japan from 1885 to 1897 by the Japanese ex-*samurai* Tôkai Sanshi. The novel was translated into Chinese by Liang Qichao during his voyage to escape from China to Japan in 1899. Phan did not read Japanese, so he read Liang's Chinese translation, a copy of which he probably acquired during his trip to Japan in 1906.[85]

Judging from the fact that Phan Châu Trinh chose this work to translate while he was in France, one could say that the impact of Phan's visit to Japan did not fade within a few years after his departure from that country, but lasted throughout his life. In taking up the translation work, Phan, a committed reformer, apparently intended to educate and inspire Vietnamese readers with a deep concern for liberty and freedom, a concern demonstrated by characters in the novel. Earlier, Liang Qichao had noted the crucial role that political novels exerted in the advancement of political awareness in Japan and remarked that they had "contributed to the successful outcome of the Meiji Restoration." He pointed out that the idea of freedom embedded in Western novels that were circulated through Japanese translations influenced the Japanese Movement for Freedom and Popular Rights in the early 1880s. The three major Japanese political novels in the Meiji period were Tôkai Sanshi's *Kajin no kigû*, Yano Fumio's *Keikoku bidan* (Statesmanship Stories; 1883) and Suehiro Tetchô's *Setchûbai* (Plum Blossoms in the Snow; 1885). Phan would have known the background to Liang's translation of

---

following this battle, however, Hồ was forced to accept that his government would only be given control of North Vietnam. In the early 1960s, Communist-led guerrillas mounted an insurgency against the US-supported government in Saigon. Since Hồ was now in poor health, his role became largely symbolic. On September 2, 1969, he died in Hanoi of heart failure. Hồ Chí Minh's public personality is best represented by his widely popular name, Uncle Ho.

[84] Phan Văn Trường (1878–1933) was a lawyer, journalist, and writer who participated in the democratic movement in Paris and Saigon. A native of Hà Đông (presently Hanoi), he ventured to Paris at the end of 1908 and became a lawyer in 1912. During that year, he met Phan Châu Trinh and became Phan's very good friend. In addition to this friendship with Phan Châu Trinh, Phan Văn Trường also enjoyed good relationships with prominent Vietnamese figures such as Nguyễn Ái Quốc, Nguyễn An Ninh, Nguyễn Thế Truyền, and others. In September 1914, he was arrested with Phan Châu Trinh under the charge that they were plotting against the French state. They were released in July 1915 since the French authorities did not have any evidence to support the accusation. Because he spoke out publicly in France to support the Vietnamese, Phan Văn Trường was well liked by his compatriots. He was among the first Vietnamese to study Marxism, although he was not identified as a Marxist *per se*. In 1924, he returned to Vietnam. There he collaborated with Nguyễn An Ninh in editing the journal *La cloche fêlée*, which since 1923 had openly questioned colonialism in Vietnam. When Nguyễn An Ninh was arrested in 1926, Phan Văn Trường replaced him as editor of the journal, which changed its name to *L'Annam*. He authored several books, including *Essai sur le Code Gia Long* (Essays on the Gia Long Code), which was the dissertation submitted for his doctor of law degree in Paris. Phan Văn Trường died in Hanoi in 1933. See Nguyễn Q. Thắng, *Từ điển tác gia Việt Nam* (Thành phố Hồ Chí Minh: Nxb Văn hóa Thông tin, 1999), pp. 1271–75.

[85] See Nguyễn Phan Quang and Phan Văn Hoàng, "Phan Châu Trinh dưới mắt Phan Văn Trường" [Phan Châu Trinh Seen Through the Eyes of Phan Văn Trường], *Nghiên cứu lịch sử*, 4, 275 (July–August 1994): 168.

Kajin no kigû when he undertook his own, and in many ways Phan's life mirrored that of Liang, as he, too, began to translate the novel after arriving in France.

Phan Châu Trinh's regard for Liang's translation was evident. After he arrived in France in April 1911 and completed his urgent tasks, such as writing to defend his friends who were still on Poulo Condore Island, Phan presumably began his translation of *Kajin no kigû*. Huỳnh Lý, a scholar of Phan Châu Trinh, suggests that Phan translated this work during 1912–13 when he was in Paris. He bases this judgment on the following considerations: (a) the manuscript was written by Phan in a notebook sold in Paris, brought back to Vietnam by Phan in 1925, and later found in the possession of Phan Thị Châu Liên, Phan's daughter; (b) after his release from Santé prison, Phan's French government pension was cut so he had to work very hard to support himself; therefore he would not have been in a position to work on the translation during this time;[86] and (c) a letter written by Nguyễn Tất Thành (Nguyễn Ái Quốc) to Phan in 1913 reads: "When you have translated the later chapters, please send them to me," and of all Phan Châu Trinh's works, *Giai nhân kỳ ngộ diễn ca* is the only one that was divided into chapters.[87] Huỳnh Lý's hypothesis appears to be sound, but I think that Phan may have worked on the translation into 1914, prior to his arrest. His translation in verse is a work of enormous scale: it consists of approximately 7,800 lines (about 2.5 times longer than *The Tale of Kiều*), which would require at least two and a half years' work.

Considering the time Phan Châu Trinh designated to the translation of this work, it is worth discussing further. *Kajin no kigû* was written by Shiba Shirô (Viet. Sài Tứ Lang; 1852-1922), who wrote under the *nom de plume* of Tôkai Sanshi (Viet. Đông Hải Tán Sĩ), literally the Wanderer of the Eastern Sea. As a youth, Sanshi fought on the losing Tokugawa side during the civil war prior to the Meiji Restoration; over the course of the war, he lost most of his family before he himself was arrested. Although he suffered bitter experiences with the new Meiji government, Sanshi was gradually integrated into the new regime. In 1879, he went to the United States to study, first attending a commercial college in San Francisco, and later studying political science and economics at Harvard and at the University of Pennsylvania, where he obtained a bachelor's degree in finance.

Returning to Japan in 1885, Sanshi published the first part of his *Kajin no kigû*, the preliminary idea of which had apparently taken root during his stay in the United States. He became a private secretary to Tani Kanjô, minister of agriculture and commerce, and accompanied the minister on a trip to Europe in 1886. During this trip, he managed to meet leaders of various nationalist movements, such as Arabi Pasha of Egypt, Osman Pasha of Turkey, and Lajos Kossuth of Hungary. In 1892, Sanshi was elected to the Diet, where he often voiced his opposition against the government's moderate policy vis-à-vis the West and called for "strong" and resolute diplomacy. He displayed great interest in the conflict between Japan and China regarding Korea and personally visited Korea after the Sino-Japanese War (1894–1895) to find ways to support the pro-Japanese faction there. Sanshi's nationalist inclination was vividly reflected in the later part of *Kajin no kigû*.

---

[86] Phan was arrested and imprisoned for ten months, from September 1914 to July 1915.

[87] Huỳnh Lý, *Thơ văn Phan Châu Trinh*, pp. 156–57. My discussion of Phan Châu Trinh's *Giai nhân kỳ ngộ diễn ca* in this section is based on materials in Vinh Sinh, "'Elegant Females' Re-encountered: From Tôkai Sanshi's *Kajin no kigû* to Phan Châu Trinh's *Giai nhân kỳ ngộ diễn ca*," in *Essays into Vietnamese Pasts*, ed. K. W. Taylor and John K. Whitmore (Ithaca, NY: Cornell University Southeast Asia Program Publications, 1995), pp. 195–206.

Kajin no kigû is a novel based on Tôkai Sanshi's experiences in the United States and Europe. It begins with the hero, Tôkai Sanshi himself, meeting two "elegant females." On this day, Sanshi climbs to the top of Independence Hall in Philadelphia to look at the cracked Liberty Bell and becomes fascinated with the history of the American struggle for independence against the tyranny of the king of England. As he pensively looks out the window, two graceful ladies approach; one of them is explaining to her companion the significance of historic sites such as Valley Forge, the Delaware River, and Bunker Hill, describing with intense feeling how the Americans triumphed in the War of Independence and successfully built a wealthy and powerful nation. A few days later, Sanshi meets the two women again. One is named Yûran (Viet. U Lan), a Spanish patriot and daughter of a noble whose life is being threatened because he is trying to free Spain from foreign intervention. The other is Kôren (Viet. Hồng Liên), an Irish patriot whose father died as a victim of tyranny. The fourth character who figures in this meeting is Fan Qing (Viet. Phạm Khanh), the Chinese butler of the two European ladies who turns out to be a Ming loyalist, who was once a gallant rebel fighting against the Manchus but is now living in exile. After hearing their stories, Sanshi confides that he, too, is a surviving victim of a lost cause and recalls the suffering and humiliation that he and his family experienced at the time of the Meiji Restoration. He feels that all four of them are in the same boat.

Following this dramatic *mise en scène*, the setting moves from the United States to Europe and Egypt, and an indistinct tender affection, it is hinted, develops between the two European ladies and Sanshi. What follows afterward is rather anticlimatic. There is no real plot; particularly through the second half of the novel, the reader is simply entertained with discourses on nationalist movements in Ireland, Egypt, Hungary, Poland, China, and India. Sanshi displays his sympathy for the conquered countries, a sympathy that springs from his own experiences as a young samurai whose domain was appropriated during the Meiji Restoration and from his concern for the precarious situation faced by those powers that are just beginning to modernize in the 1880s. At the same time, his nationalist penchant is equally obvious when he suggests that Japan's mission is to be leader of East Asia and to bring the latter to the realm of civilization through military expansion.

In spite of *Kajin no kigû*'s deficiency as a novel, it was widely popular among the Japanese reading public at the time. Even in remote villages, young men carried a copy in their pocket so that they could recite beautiful passages.[88]

Phan Châu Trinh also loved the story and expressed his opinion of the work in a poem, "Độc Giai nhân kỳ ngộ" (Upon reading *Giai nhân kỳ ngộ*):[89]

---

[88] Nakamura Tadayuki, "Chûgoku bungei ni oyoboseru Nihon bungei no eikyô, III" [The Influence of Japanese Literature on Chinese Literature, Part III], *Taidai bungaku* 8,2 (August 1943): 48.

[89] According to Phương Hữu, Phan Châu Trinh wrote this poem when he was in Japan. See *Phong trào Đại Đông Du* [The Great Đông Du Movement] (Sài Gòn: Nam Việt, 1950), pp. 16–17. In Phan's manuscript of *Giai nhân kỳ ngộ diễn ca*, at the top of every chapter Phan drew a small picture. These drawings remind one of similar pictures that appeared in the original Japanese edition of *Kajin no kigû*. One wonders whether Phan saw the original of *Kajin no kigû* when he was in Tokyo. See Phan Châu Trinh, *Giai nhân kỳ ngộ diễn ca* [Chance Encounter with Elegant Females—Translated into Verses], esp. small picture following p. LXV.

Vật cạnh phong trào hám ngũ châu,
Anh hùng tâm toái Tự do lâu.
Bạch đầu tráng sĩ chân ưu quốc,
Hồng tụ giai nhân giải báo cừu.
Đàm tiếu nhãn ky không nhất thế,
Tử sinh nhân tự túc thiên thâu.
Hào tình diệu luận phân phân thị,
Nhất độc linh nhân nhất điểm đầu.[90]

The scramble for survival is shaking the entire world,
With their hearts broken, heroes and heroines meet at Independence Hall,
Though his hairs have already turned grey, a man of high purpose shows
    concern for his country,
Fashionably attired, elegant women vow revenge for their lands,
Indignant at world affairs, they converse with spirit,
Indifferent to life and death, their names will go into history.
Their gallant spirit and felicitous words
Move everyone reading their story.

Liang's translation of *Kajin no kigû* has been recognized as significant because it marked an important point in the literary revolution in modern China. Much less well known is the fact that Phan Châu Trinh's Vietnamese retranslation of Liang's version was undertaken as part of his ongoing effort to educate his people about the ideas of popular rights. It is interesting that Phan translated about half of the novel, *Kajin no kigû*, into modern Vietnamese in verses. We can only guess why Phan did not translate further. Was it because he was so busy working for his living after his release from prison in 1915? Or did he find the political discourses by Sanshi in the second half of the novel not sufficiently inspiring to translate into verse? So far no clues have been discovered that might answer this question. What we may conclude with certainty is that Phan's impression after reading Liang's translation, as indicated in the above poem, was very positive, and the sections that he translated indeed represent the best part of the novel.

In comparing Phan Châu Trinh's translation with Liang's version, one first notes that, although by and large Phan apparently tried to be faithful to Liang's Chinese text, there were modifications that he seems to have made purposely. For example, where "the *Marseillaise*, the patriotic song of the French" is mentioned in Liang's version, Phan simply translated the title as "a patriotic song." Similarly, the first line of the *Marseillaise*, written as "the glory of France" in the Chinese translation, are changed to "the glory of the nation" in Phan's translation.[91] One of the most interesting alterations in the *Giai nhân kỳ ngộ diễn ca* appears in the poem sung by Kôren, expressing her wish to visit Japan. The poem in Sanshi's original text and in Liang's translation reads:

---

[90] Ibid., immediately following the "Contents" of the book.
[91] See Liang Qichao, *Jiaren jiyu*, in *Yinbingshi quanji* [Complete Works of Liang Qichao], Book 88, in *Yinbingshi heji* [Collected Works and Essays of Liang Qichao] (Shanghai: Chunghua Bookstore, 1932), p. 25.

> Where I am longing for now is the end of the Eastern Sea,
> I want to go there, yet the waterway is treacherous,
> At the end of the sea, there is Japan,
> Whose customs and manners are elegant,
> The imperial house reigns in an unbroken line,
> Its fame resounds through generations,
> The samurai treasure honor and take profit lightly,
> Self-denyingly, they revere their emperor.[92]

Phan Châu Trinh rewrote the above poem as follows:

> *Ta nhớ đâu, nhớ đầu biển Á,*
> *Muốn theo qua, sóng khỏa ngàn trùng;*
> *Bốn ngàn năm còn dõi giống Lạc Hồng,*
> *Kìa biển, kìa núi, kìa sông, kìa đô ấp;*
> *Từ Đinh Hoàng dựng cờ độc lập,*
> *Đến Nguyễn triều thâu thập cõi Nam Trung,*
> *Trải xưa nay lắm sức anh hùng,*
> *Liều trôi máu vẽ nên màu cẩm tú ...*[93]

> Where I am longing for is the end of the Eastern Sea,
> I want to go there, yet the rough waves are boundless,
> The vestiges of Lạc Hồng still remain, after four thousand years of history,
> In the mountains and in the sea, in the rivers, in villages, and in cities,
> Since Đinh Tiên Hoàng raised the flag of sovereignty,
> Till the Nguyễn dynasty extended to the Center and the South,
> There have been numerous heroic deeds,
> They risked their blood to add colors to this beautiful country ...

Finally, the most important revision that Phan Châu Trinh introduced to this text was to render his translation entirely in verse. Apart from the Chinese poems, which are scattered here and there in the text, and which he translated into different formats, Phan translated the main narration of the novel into six–eight couplets (*thơ lục bát*), the most popular form of poetry in Vietnam, in which the lines are alternately composed of six and eight words. This popular mode has been traditionally adopted by various Vietnamese authors to translate and adapt Chinese novels and plays to the Vietnamese cultural and social milieu.[94] Phan's *Giai nhân kỳ ngộ diễn ca* was the last attempt to use this popular medium to translate a Chinese text on an enormous scale.[95]

Judging it purely based on literary merit, Phan Châu Trinh's translation cannot be considered an outstanding work. Its quality is uneven. As has been pointed out, Phan's personality seems to have been reflected in his translation. His poetry is lively, passionate, and assured when calling for liberty and popular rights, or

---

[92] Tôkai Sanshi, *Kajin no kigû*, p. 55; Liang Qichao, *Jiaren jiyu*, p. 46.

[93] Phan Châu Trinh, *Giai nhân kỳ ngộ*, p. 275.

[94] Most notably *The Tale of Kiều, Nhị độ mai, The Tale of Hoa Tiên, The Tale of Phan Trần*, and *The Tale of Tây Sương*.

[95] Huỳnh Lý, *Thơ văn Phan Châu Trinh*, p. 155.

attacking inequality and oppression. His translation of the numerous classical Chinese poems in the text is impressive. Yet when it comes to narration, his poetry becomes somewhat pedestrian and too colloquial.[96] Part of Phan's problem in his translation could be attributed to the lengthy political discourses in the Japanese original. But more than anything else, Phan's decision to translate a political novel of this sort into verse was not a prudent choice.

As a political tract, *Giai nhân kỳ ngộ diễn ca* did not have significant impact. The picture of a world-wide struggle for independence from colonial powers portrayed in Sanshi's original Japanese text might have appealed to Liang when he translated this narrative at the end of the nineteenth century, but by the time Phan retranslated it, its connotations had changed and became more complex. Phan's version was first published after his death in 1926 in Hanoi by Ngô Đức Kế, but copies were immediately confiscated and burnt by the authorities, so it was not until 1958 that *Giai nhân kỳ ngộ diễn ca* was made available to the public thanks to the initiative of Lê Văn Siêu. Lê Văn Siêu, consciously or unconsciously, however, introduced the book as Phan's original work, not a translation of Sanshi's novel.[97]

If we consider Phan's translation in a historical context, the fact that leading intellectuals of China and Vietnam, such as Liang Qichao and Phan Châu Trinh, were engaged in introducing Tôkai Sanshi's political novel to their respective audiences is itself highly significant and bespeaks the earnest desire on the part of Chinese and Vietnamese intellectuals to derive lessons from Meiji Japan. *Giai nhân kỳ ngộ diễn ca* is indeed an eloquent testimony to the intriguing cultural interaction between East Asia and the West, and between Japan and China and Vietnam at the turn of the twentieth century.

In 1914, when the First World War broke out and Germany attacked France, Phan Châu Trinh refused to be conscripted for French military service. Arrested on the false charge that he had sought Germany's help to fight against France, Phan Châu Trinh was thrown into Santé prison, where political offenders were kept, and jailed for nearly ten months (September 1914–July 1915). Although Phan Châu Trinh was innocent, French authorities had reason to be suspicious of Vietnamese nationals. In the case of Phan Bội Châu, we know that he had requested permission from Germany, particularly during the First World War, to use the German foreign

---

[96] Huỳnh Lý, "Về quyển *Giai nhân kỳ ngộ diễn ca* của Phan Châu Trinh" [About Phan Châu Trinh's *Giai nhân kỳ ngộ diễn ca*], *Văn học* 1 (1969): 78–81. I thank Prof. K. W. Taylor of Cornell University for his help in locating this article.

[97] See Phan Châu Trinh, *Giai nhân kỳ ngộ*, ed. and trans. Lê Văn Siêu. In his introduction to the book, Lê Văn Siêu compared *Giai nhân kỳ ngộ* with *The Tale of Kiều*, a nineteenth-century Vietnamese classic by Nguyễn Du, finding *Giai nhân kỳ ngộ* to be the superior work. By doing so, he renewed the debate over *The Tale of Kiều* that had taken place in the 1920s and 1930s. On the one side, Phạm Quỳnh, an advocate of colonial interests and a highly capable scholar, applauded *The Tale of Kiều* as a work of national significance. Phạm Quỳnh's famous statement was, "As long as *The Tale of Kiều* lasts, our language will last; as long as our language lasts, our country will last." On the other side of the debate, Ngô Đức Kế and Huỳnh Thúc Kháng opposed French rule and for political reasons challenged Phạm Quỳnh's analysis. Lê Văn Siêu suggests that, at the time, Huỳnh Thúc Kháng was probably conscious of the existence of Phan Châu Trinh's *Giai nhân kỳ ngộ*. According to Lê Văn Siêu, *Giai nhân kỳ ngộ* represents "the spirit of indomitability" of the Vietnamese people and is indeed "comparable to the epic *Aeneid* of the Roman poet Virgil." In retrospect, it is clear that by misrepresenting *Giai nhân kỳ ngộ diễn ca* as Phan's original work and by unjustifiably drawing it into the old political debate over *The Tale of Kiều*, Lê Văn Siêu did more damage to Phan and his work than anything else.

offices in Peking and Bangkok as a base for the resistance effort against France. Germany was not the only foreign country that Phan Bội Châu petitioned. Before he returned to Vietnam in 1925, Phan Bội Châu believed that without China and Japan's assistance, Vietnam could not achieve independence from France. In Phan Bội Châu's mind, France was the only country that was plotting treachery against Vietnam. As Phan Châu Trinh maintained, Phan Bội Châu was anti-French, on the one hand, but foolishly reliant on German, Russian, Chinese, and Japanese assistance, on the other. Phan Châu Trinh's position was very different. He was wary of any foreign assistance in attaining Vietnamese independence, believing it would result in simply replacing one master with another. Phan Châu Trinh maintained this position until his death and always made his stand amply clear, so it is hard even to imagine him applying to Germany for help against the French.

Phan Châu Trinh refused to be subdued by false accusations, and he poured his energy into proving his innocence. In a letter to a prosecutor of the military court, Phan Châu Trinh wrote: "You are a tricky prosecutor. You used your ideas to send me to prison. From now on, I will use arguments to fight against your unfair and tricky opinions." In prison, Phan also composed about two hundred poems, which bear witness to his indomitable spirit and his composure in adversity.[98] After nine months in prison, thanks to the protests of Marius Moutet, Jules Roux, and other French admirers, directed to Prime Minister Poincaré, Phan Châu Trinh was released. Upon regaining his freedom, Phan Châu Trinh heard of the tragic news of the death of his son, Phan Văn Dật, who had been repatriated and succumbed to tuberculosis at the Huế hospital.

Life was difficult for Phan Châu Trinh after his release from Santé prison in 1915. Apart from working as a photo retoucher, he actively participated in political activities, mainly with Nguyễn Ái Quốc and Phan Văn Trường, and with liberal French politicians and prominent personalities. As an enemy of autocracy living in France—the country Phan Châu Trinh always saw as one of the most democratic countries in the world—Phan seems to have absorbed and relished the French political atmosphere. As a young official in Huế, Phan Châu Trinh had read Chinese reformist literature, including translations of Rousseau's and Montesquieu's philosophies. During his fourteen years in France, though he did not study French, he probably read further. The most important aspect of this period in his life, however, was the opportunity to experience everyday French life. This opportunity solidified his conviction in assigning top priority to the promotion of democracy and popular rights and to the improvement of the people's quality of life in his homeland. In 1930, an anonymous contributor to *Phụ Nữ Tân Văn* (Women's Newspaper) provided insight into the significance of Phan Châu Trinh's experience in France:

> So far as Occidental studies [Viet. *Tây học*] were concerned, though he was staying in France, Phan [Châu Trinh] never studied French. But there were occasions when Phan read Chinese translations of Montesquieu, Voltaire, and others. Also, thanks to the time he spent in France, his contacts with numerous people, and the things that he saw and heard, he grasped [Viet.

---

[98] These poems are collectively known as *Santé thi tập* (Anthology of Poetry Written in Santé Prison), included in *Tây Hồ và Santé thi tập* [Phan Châu Trinh and His Anthology of Poetry Written in the Santé Prison], ed. Lê Ấm (Saigon: Nhà in Lê Thị Đàm, 1961).

lãnh hội] the basics of Western studies and observed exhaustively the thinking and the circumstances of the Europeans. In short, regarding his engagement in Occidental studies or Chinese studies, Phan Châu Trinh did not study extensively [Viet. *không học nhiều*] but had broad experience and understanding [Viet. *có thức rộng*]. People need to study, but studying must be combined with experience and understanding; study without experience is not worthwhile. The fact that Phan's study surpassed that of other people is not because he studied a great deal, but because his knowledge, which combined study and experience, was abundant. Everything Phan said, every deed he acted upon, demonstrated this fact.[99]

When the international conference at Versailles was convened in 1919, at the end of World War I, Phan Châu Trinh, along with Nguyễn Ái Quốc and Phan Văn Trường, advocated a list of demands that included the following eight points:

1. Complete amnesty for all Indochinese political prisoners.
2. Reform of the justice system in Indochina and the introduction of laws similar to those in Europe.
3. Freedom of the press and of expression.
4. Freedom to form societies and meetings.
5. Freedom of emigration and overseas tourism.
6. Freedom to establish schools in different provinces to teach techniques and professions to the indigenous people.
7. Reform of the legal system.
8. Appointment of Indochinese representatives to work alongside the French parliament and to communicate Indochinese concerns.

These points were made in the form of a flyer and distributed to French and Vietnamese participants to raise their awareness of the alarming circumstances in the Indochinese colonies.

In 1922, Emperor Khải Định accepted the French government's invitation to attend the International Exposition in Marseille. Phan Châu Trinh had little respect for the emperor; he viewed him as the sovereign of a small nation, who wanted to use the power of France, the imperial state, to show off his prestige while wasting money without thinking of the future of those who were distressed at home. French newspapers also reported that the emperor's actions were "phony," not "fair and open."[100] In a letter that was drafted in classical Chinese using direct and scathing language, Phan Châu Trinh accused the emperor of seven offences. This letter, commonly known at the time as "Thư thất điều" (literally "The Letter of Seven Clauses"), stunned readers in both France and Vietnam and elicited strong responses. French readers generally applauded, particularly "the young and those absorbed in new ideas."[101] As the letter reveals distinctive aspects of Phan's views, particularly his Confucian ideas, its translation is included in this volume.

---

[99] *Phụ Nữ Tân Văn*, no. 44, March 20, 1930, p. 11, reprinted in Thanh Lãng, *13 Năm Tranh Luận Văn Học* [Thirteen Years of Literary Disputes], vol. 2 (Thành phố Hồ Chí Minh: Nxb Văn Học, 1995), pp. 37–38.

[100] Huỳnh Thúc Kháng, *Phan Tây-Hồ tiên sinh lịch sử*, p. 29.

[101] Ibid.

It is interesting that in June 1922, Nguyễn Ái Quốc also wrote a short, satirical play, *Le Dragon de bamboo* (The Bamboo Dragon), to ridicule Emperor Khải Định and the customs of the Vietnamese imperial court. *Le Dragon de bamboo* is about a toy dragon fashioned out of twisted bamboo by an antique collector. The stalks of bamboo take on the shape of a dragon, while retaining their essential qualities as bamboo; they are grasses proud to borrow the name and shape of a dragon. In short, the composite is a useless monster. Nguyễn Ái Quốc also used his position as editor of *Le Paria* (The Outcast), the organ of the Inter-colonial Union, as well as his access to *L'Humanité* and *Le Journal du Peuple,* to voice opinions on the occasion of the emperor's visit to Marseille.[102]

RETURN TO VIETNAM

In early 1925, after more than fourteen years living in France, Phan Châu Trinh returned to Vietnam. With the end of the First World War, Phan thought that if he had a chance to use his "hot blood to water the Vietnamese mountains and rivers, perhaps he would be lucky enough to reach those who may take over his cause." Phan discussed his plan with officials at the Ministry of Colonies and was told that if he returned, the Vietnamese mandarins would "devour" him. Phan replied: "If the Ministry of Colonies does not help them, it should be fine!"[103] His request for repatriation was heatedly debated in the French Chamber of Deputies. Thanks to the dedicated work on his behalf by Moutet, one of the deputies, in June 1925 Phan finally returned home.

Upon his return to Vietnam, Phan Châu Trinh decided to stay on in Saigon to rest, rather than traveling immediately to his home province of Quảng Nam. He intended to tour the country and then to build a print shop, a newspaper, and an agriculture society. Phan Châu Trinh also joined a campaign to demand the release of Phan Bội Châu,[104] who at the time was confined in Hỏa Lò prison, Hanoi, following his arrest by French agents in Shanghai and transportation back to Vietnam. After December 1925, Phan Bội Châu was released from Hỏa Lò prison, and he lived in Huế under house arrest until his death in 1940.[105] In contrast to his earlier career, Phan Bội Châu's last fifteen years in Huế were moderate and quiet. His most sympathetic and understanding friend was Huỳnh Thúc Kháng, the editor-in-chief of *Tiếng dân* (The People's Voice); for a time, Phan Bội Châu even took charge of a column providing advice to aspiring poets. Also, it was in Huế that Phan Bội Châu wrote his works *Tự phán* (Self-judgment), *Phan Bội Châu niên biểu* (The Autobiography of Phan Bội Châu), and *Khổng học đăng* (Light of Confucianism), among others.

Phan Châu Trinh was not well at this point; his tuberculosis had taken a turn for the worse. Nonetheless, his compatriots in Saigon were so eager to hear him, he

---

[102] The text of *Le Dragon de bamboo* is lost. The play was probably typewritten and not printed. See Thu Trang, *Nguyễn Ái Quốc tại Paris, 1917–1923* [Nguyễn Ái Quốc in Paris, 1917–1923] (Hanoi: Viện Văn hóa Nghệ thuật Việt Nam, 1991), pp. 196–206; and Chu Trọng Huyến, *Hồ Chí Minh thời trẻ* [Hồ Chí Minh in Youthful Time] (Vinh: Nxb Nghệ An, 2000), pp. 381–86.

[103] Ibid., p. 31.

[104] Ibid., pp. 31–32.

[105] Ibid., p. 32.

could not refuse.[106] Consequently, Phan Châu Trinh poured his remaining strength into preparations for two public lectures that would sum up the cultural and political views of a man who had dedicated his entire life to his people. The two lectures, entitled "Morality and Ethics in the Orient and in the Occident" (Viet. *Đạo đức và luân lý Đông Tây*) and "Monarchy and Democracy" (Viet. *Quân trị chủ nghĩa và Dân trị chủ nghĩa*), were delivered to packed halls, and reportedly the audiences felt as if "they acquired precious pearls" after they had heard these lectures. Huỳnh Thúc Kháng wrote, "It looked as if the sky that had been covered by dark clouds for many years was suddenly almost cleared by two rains. The sun rises on the East, shedding light at a corner of the horizon. The air is entirely different! Alas! Now reading these two speeches, whose nerves are not touched and whose are not feeling stronger than ever ... ?"[107] Phan Châu Trinh's lectures had served his purpose. People came to hear his message of popular rights and democracy, and saw why they were essential to the future of Vietnam.

At the end of December, Phan Châu Trinh planned to travel to Hanoi to deliver a speech at Hanoi University at the invitation of its students, and to Huế to meet Phan Bội Châu, who had recently been released.[108] However, he was forced to set aside these plans as his illness worsened. Until the last minutes of his life, Phan Châu Trinh continued to receive visitors. Among them, the one who must have given him a welcome surprise was Huỳnh Thúc Kháng. These two friends had not seen each other since Phan left Poulo Condore Island in 1910. As they were smiling at each other, Phan Châu Trinh said to Huỳnh Thúc Kháng: "That you and I can spend time together in this world for this brief moment is good indeed. We know each other so deeply, we won't need to talk for long!"[109] Phan Châu Trinh drew his last breath at the age of fifty-six on the evening of March 24, 1926.

The news of Phan Châu Trinh's death shocked the Vietnamese populace. The entire country went into mourning. His funeral in Saigon was reportedly attended by some sixteen thousand people. The memorial service was organized by well-known persons, such as the founder of the Constitutional Party, Bùi Quang Chiêu, the renowned lawyer, Phan Văn Trường, and the editor-in-chief of *Đông Pháp Thời báo* (Indochine Française Tribune), Trần Huy Liệu.[110] The women's delegation's banner was decorated with flowers and read, "The Nation was Relying on You" (Viet. *Quốc gia thử thân*). The *Đông Pháp Thời báo* published a picture of Phan Châu Trinh standing on the podium, with a caption reading, "Uphold Republicanism!" (Viet. *Thủ xướng cộng hoà*).[111] As well as the crowds of Vietnamese who attended the service, many Chinese, French, Cambodians, and Cham came to express their

---

[106] Ibid.

[107] Ibid.

[108] Huỳnh Thúc Kháng was known to have an elephantine memory and most reliable judgment. It was Huỳnh who said that Phan intended "to meet Phan Bội Châu to discuss things." Ibid., p. 32. In his eulogy for Phan Châu Trinh, Huỳnh Thúc Kháng also mentioned the following: "... When his [Phan Châu Trinh's] illness had become so critical, he still said he would go to Trung Kỳ to visit Sào Nam [Phan Bội Châu] to arrange things." See Thế Nguyên, *Phan Chu Trinh* (1872–1926) [Phan Châu Trinh (1872–1926)] (Saigon: Tủ sách Những "Mảnh Gương" Tân Việt, 1956), p. 60.

[109] Huỳnh Thúc Kháng, *Huỳnh Thúc Kháng tự truyện* [The Autobiography of Huỳnh Thúc Kháng], trans. Anh Minh (from the original literary Chinese) (Huế: Anh Minh, 1963), p. 47.

[110] Trần Huy Liệu was later a militant Marxist historian.

[111] Thế Nguyên, *Phan Chu Trinh*, pp. 53–54.

condolences.[112] Students from the South to the North voluntarily stayed away from classes to hold memorial services. The service in Huế was presided over by Phan Bội Châu, whose moving eulogy for Phan Châu Trinh expressed an honest appreciation of the latter's determined struggle throughout his life for democracy and popular rights. It is possible to say that the "funeral of Phan Châu Trinh and the campaign shortly before that to demand Phan Bội Châu's release may be regarded as the first widespread, public, and powerful expressions of nationalism that modern Vietnam had ever witnessed."[113] Phan Châu Trinh was buried near Tân Sơn Nhứt airport, in the suburb of Saigon.

Phan Bội Châu was deeply affected by Phan Châu Trinh's death. After he settled down under house arrest in Huế, there was a significant change in his thought, as he grew more inclined to favor peace and moderation. Phan Bội Châu wrote the following couplet (Viet. *câu đối*) for Phan Châu Trinh:

> *Thương hải vi điền, Tinh Vệ hàm thạch,*
> *Chung Kỳ ký một, Bá Nha đoạn huyền.*

> The blue sea has become a rice field, the *Tinh Vệ*[114] bird dashes against the rocks,
> Now that Chung Kỳ died, Bá Nha[115] broke his harp.

A very moving couplet indeed. But one should note that Phan Bội Châu exaggerated the closeness of his relationship with Phan Châu Trinh. Indeed, the two had not met each other for twenty years, and Phan Châu Trinh had felt betrayed in 1908, when he and many of his friends were either sent to Poulo Condore Island or killed as a result of their suspected association with Phan Bội Châu and his militant policies, which had been broadcast from the safety of Tokyo. Phan Châu Trinh's feelings of betrayal at the time were voiced in "A New Vietnam," translated and included in this monograph. Phan Châu Trinh may have forgiven Phan Bội Châu, and he did intend to see him before he died in 1926, but it is important to note that he still criticized Phan Bội Châu's militant approach in his lecture, "Morality and Ethics in the Orient and the Occident," presented in November 1925.

In March 1927, on the first anniversary of Phan Châu Trinh's death, Phan Bội Châu wrote the following lines:

> Alas! Would he be willing to forgive me? When I sent him off from Hong Kong, on his return to Vietnam from Japan, he held my hand and told me his last feelings. "From the nineteenth century onward, the countries in the world have competed against one other more fiercely than ever. The fate of a country must be left in the hands of a large number of people. I have not

---

[112] Ibid., p. 33. It is interesting to see that, in March 1926, the Cham still figured as a distinct, separate group, unlike now.

[113] "Introduction" by Vinh and Wickenden in *The Autobiography of Phan-Bội-Châu*, p. 23.

[114] *Tinh Vệ* (C. *jingwei*), see footnote 81, above.

[115] Chung [Tử] Kỳ and Bá Nha were close friends during the time of the Spring and Autumn Warring Period (770–403 BCE). Bá Nha knew that Tử Kỳ appreciated his harp playing more than anyone else, so when Tử Kỳ died, he broke his harp and vowed not to play again.

seen any country survive in which the people's rights were lost. How can you uphold monarchism at this moment?" When he said that, I did not have a reply for him. Today more than twenty years have passed, and the more I think about what he said, the more I feel he is right. I know that what I considered or what I examined is nothing as compared to his thought! If he were still alive, we would ask him to lead us. Nowadays, those who worship him, those who love him—aren't they only watching his statue, or picking up sentences from his writings, and imagining that they are patriotic? We must know that Hy Mã's [Phan's] name will last forever because he had real principles and real spirit.[116]

In *The Autobiography of Phan Bội Châu*, written about two years later, Phan Bội Châu confessed:

Alas! My history is a history of failures without one single success. For some thirty years, while I roamed hither and yon, calamity struck those involved with me throughout the land—association with me brought imprisonment, and ill effects spread among my compatriots. In the depths of each night I have beaten my breast and gazed up at heaven and wiped away my tears. I have been stumbling and falling for twenty years and more.[117]

Huỳnh Thúc Kháng wrote about Phan Châu Trinh's life:

Tiên sinh[118] was not only a patriotic man of high determination (Viet. *chí sĩ*), he was also Vietnam's first revolutionary politician (Viet. *nhà chính trị cách mạng đầu tiên*). Shouldering the burdens of his country and loving his people, *Tiên sinh* was an intellectual who charged upon the enemy alone for over twenty years. He survived numerous dangers and tasted bitter experiences. *Tiên sinh* still carried his message, although distress hung on him, he would not stop. He could not be bought with name nor money and difficulty would not change his position. Even when a sword was held to his neck and a gun was held to his stomach, he would not change his position. Compared to Sào Nam,[119] his will was equivalent, his passion was equivalent, his capacity was equivalent, but his circumstances were more difficult and his heart was much tougher.[120]

---

[116] Phan Bội Châu, *Tiếng dân*, March 24, 1927. Reprinted in *Tân dân*, March 24, 1949 (Hanoi).

[117] Phan Bội Châu, *The Autobiography of Phan-Bội-Châu*, p. 43.

[118] Normally translated as "Sir" or "Teacher," it is an honorable term of address.

[119] Sào Nam was another of Phan Bội Châu's pen names. Sào Nam means "bird nest" in the South and referred to Phan Bội Châu's longing for Vietnam.

[120] Huỳnh Thúc Kháng, *Phan Tây-Hồ tiên sinh lịch sử*, pp. 33–34.

Part III
"A New Vietnam" (1910–1911)[121]
Phan Châu Trinh's Views of Phan Bội Châu

"A New Vietnam Following the Franco-Vietnamese Alliance" (Viet. *Pháp Việt liên hợp*[122] *hậu chi Tân Việt Nam*) was drafted in classical Chinese by Phan Châu Trinh.

The manuscript of "A New Vietnam" was in very rough form, written when Phan Châu Trinh was in Mỹ Tho city sometime after he was released from Poulo Condore Island and before he went to France (June 1910–April 1911). For this reason, the first section of it is somewhat unfinished, tangled with circular arguments. In this section, Phan Châu Trinh presented his unique interpretation of Vietnamese history, in which he identified the development of Vietnam's national traits. Before translating this section into English, I decided that I would not edit the text substantially because I did not wish to change the manuscript's original form and flavor and risk losing the obvious development of Phan's thought at such a critical period in his life. Fortunately, in the second part, which deals with Phan Châu Trinh's understanding of the dispute between himself and Phan Bội Châu, and which provides an important account of the 1908 Trung Kỳ tax protest and insurrection, the writing is fluent and very passionate. One has the feeling that Phan Châu Trinh had contemplated these issues and their place within Vietnamese history during the solitary evenings he spent while confined for three years (1908–10) in An Hải, a fishing village on Poulo Condore Island. Note that the remaining three articles in the monograph reflect Phan Châu Trinh's matured articulate and passionate style.

This work has been translated twice in the past, but both translations contain errors.[123] Phan Châu Trinh brought the manuscript back to Vietnam when he repatriated in 1925. Neither of the previous translators of "A New Vietnam" indicated when Phan Châu Trinh wrote this work and until now this question has gone unanswered. However, a careful reading of the manuscript provides clues to this mystery.

At one point, Phan Châu Trinh states he was "placed in a corner under surveillance":

---

[121] Phan Châu Trinh's draft consists of forty-two pages in classical Chinese, of which the first thirty-one pages contain the argument's main gist. There are passages in which the characters are small and written in cursive. Two *quốc ngữ* versions are available in translations, but because these translations are imprecise, I have used the original in classical Chinese. I obtained a copy of Phan Châu Trinh's "Pháp Việt liên hợp hậu chi Tân Việt Nam" through the kind help of the late Mr. Nguyễn Văn Xuân and one of Phan Châu Trinh's granddaughters, Mrs. Lê Thị Kinh (Phan Thị Minh).

[122] The title in the Nguyễn Văn Dương and Nguyễn Q. Thắng editions of Phan Châu Trinh's works is misspelled as "*liên hiệp*." It should be "*liên hợp*," as Phan Châu Trinh wrote in the original. "Việt Nam" is originally written in literary Chinese by Phan Châu Trinh; he did not use "An Nam." Phan Bội Châu also used "Việt Nam" very early, at least by the time he wrote *Việt Nam quốc sử khảo* [A National History of Việt Nam] (1906). See Nguyễn Q. Thắng, *Phan Châu Trinh: Cuộc đời và tác phẩm* [Phan Châu Trinh: Life and Works], and Nguyễn Văn Dương, ed., *Tuyển tập Phan Châu Trinh* [Selected Works of Phan Châu Trinh].

[123] See Nguyễn Văn Dương's and Nguyễn Q. Thắng's translations. Nguyễn Q. Thắng, *Phan Châu Trinh: Cuộc đời và tác phẩm*, and Nguyễn Văn Dương, ed., *Tuyển tập Phan Châu Trinh*.

> Although I was favored with release, I am placed in a corner under surveillance.[124] My activities are being watched, and I cannot speak from the bottom of my heart. I feel ashamed for having offended my late friend.

> My late friend is Dr. Trần Quý Cáp, an erudite scholar and also a man of principle. He looked on the advocacy of violence with unconcealed aversion. He wrote an essay entitled "[A Scholar's] Argumentation for Self-rule" [Viet. (*Sĩ phu*) *tự trị luận*] to rebut Phan Bội Châu. For unknown reasons, he was murdered in Khánh Hòa.[125] Alas! How lamentable it is![126]

Later in the text he wrote: "Released from Poulo Condore Island, I was put in a room in the government-controlled residence in Mỹ Tho, Sài Gòn, without knowing a person."[127] Based on these passages, one can determine that Phan Châu Trinh wrote "A New Vietnam" in Mỹ Tho city sometime after he was released from Poulo Condore Island and before he went to France. Of Phan Châu Trinh's many manuscripts, "A New Vietnam" is the only manuscript in which the Chinese characters are very small, with many sections crossed out and revisions crammed in between the lines. It is also difficult to read because the paper used for the manuscript is of mixed and often poor quality. This evidence implies that Phan Châu Trinh was working under extraordinary circumstances in a difficult place, which again points to Mỹ Tho city as the location for the composition of this work.

Phan Châu Trinh wrote this piece to delineate clearly the differences between his position and that of Phan Bội Châu, and to defend his friends who were in prison following the riots in Trung Kỳ in 1908. Phan Châu Trinh's friend, Huỳnh Thúc Kháng, placed this work within the intellectual context of early twentieth-century Vietnam:

> At the time, as Sào Nam [Phan Bội Châu] raised anti-foreign sentiments, everyone in the country followed him. Anti-foreignism is clear and easy to understand; moreover, it feeds the habit of the people throughout history, therefore many people like it. The popular rights and self-rule theory is new. It has not been used in history, and, moreover, it hurts the mandarin class, therefore many people do not like it, and no one asks anything about it. Only a very few who have obtained "New Studies" would think that it suits the time. In "A New Vietnam Following the Franco-Vietnam Alliance," he [Phan Châu Trinh] talks about it very clearly.[128]

In this important work, Phan Châu Trinh highlighted the crucial difference between his understanding of Vietnam's history and current temperament and that of Phan Bội Châu. Rather than accepting the traditional interpretation of the past,

---

[124] Phan Châu Trinh was kept in Mỹ Tho city, located in the Mekong delta region.

[125] At this point, Phan Châu Trinh had not heard about the details of Trần Quý Cáp's execution, of which he became aware shortly before he left for France.

[126] "Tân Việt Nam," p. 15.

[127] Ibid., p. 34.

[128] Huỳnh Thúc Kháng, *Phan Tây-Hồ tiên sinh lịch sử*, p. 35.

as had Phan Bội Châu and the majority of contemporary intellectuals, Phan Châu Trinh reexamined Vietnam's history. Although his account was not entirely accurate,[129] it was a notable departure from the contemporary state of historical scholarship, and it allowed him to view the nation's past and present place within the world from a unique perspective.

Phan Châu Trinh began by examining the beginning of Vietnamese history in the Red River valley, which at the time was completely "independent from the outside world." According to Phan, China extended its rule to Vietnam at the time of the First Emperor (Qin Shihuang) (221 BCE). Under a millennium of Chinese reign, however, the Vietnamese retained their spirit—"deep in thought, independent, and indomitable." When China became embroiled in turmoil during the tenth century, the Vietnamese made use of the opportunity to rise in arms, with Đinh Tiên Hoàng (r. 968–979) as their leader, and began the "era of independence forever." According to Phan Châu Trinh, since Đinh Tiên Hoàng's times, the Vietnamese were aware that the greatest degree of independence could be achieved only by using diplomatic means to avoid fighting imperial China:

> For this reason, after the war was over, we sent silver and silk so that the other side would not feel humiliated, ... the enmity would disappear and the harmony among the two peoples would be born. In the meantime, we would have time to organize ourselves, arrange our armaments, and politically reorganize so that we could build our country. Alas! In the olden days the caliber of our people was so sharp and their vision so penetrating![130]

Phan Châu Trinh interpreted Vietnam's feudal relationship with China as a "diplomatic way." At the time, the Vietnamese court viewed "the conferring of a title as little more than a game [Viet. *hý*] rather than an honor." This was the policy of *"viễn giao cận công"*—"when a country is farther away, we should be cordial; but if the country is nearby, we should maintain an offense." Thanks to this policy, Phan Châu Trinh argued, "we didn't have to worry about the North," and "used internal power to expand in the South." In Phan Châu Trinh's view, the fact that "today Vietnam has a tiny, long piece of land on the world atlas is owing to this endeavor." Sadly, Vietnamese in later times misunderstood the intentions of the first generations and veered from earlier national policies: "They neglected their armaments and domestic affairs, and considered the giving of silver and silk more important than building a domestic fortress." China used this opportunity "to put on a mask [Viet. *giả diện*]—behaving like a celestial court but using many cunning tricks."[131] According to Phan Châu Trinh, "the tendency of relying on China must

---

[129] For example, the actual period of direct Chinese rule lasted just over a millennium, from the Han dynasty to the end of the Tang dynasty (from 111 BCE to 939 CE). As well, Đinh Tiên Hoàng never fought the Chinese; instead, in the key battle that occurred by Bạch Đằng River in 938, the Vietnamese forces were led by Ngô Quyền. It is true that, with the Bạch Đằng victory, the Vietnamese conclusively defeated Chinese forces and gained independence. Ngô Quyền took the title of king and established his capital at Cổ Loa in 939. For a detailed discussion of Vietnam's early history, see Keith Weller Taylor, *The Birth of Vietnam* (Berkeley, CA: University of California Press, 1983).

[130] "Tân Việt Nam," p. 2. I have cited from the literary Chinese manuscript.

[131] Ibid., p. 4.

have occurred at the end of each dynasty, particularly the Trần [1225–1400] and Lê [1428–1788] dynasties, and under our [Nguyễn] dynasty it is even more conspicuous."[132] Phan Châu Trinh saw that, in the past, Vietnam's ancestors considered receiving titles from China as something which they had no choice but to accept. If they could outwit the Chinese they did so with pride. In later years, however, envoys to China from Vietnam so admired things Chinese that they were happy to relate any story of the Chinese intellectuals to Vietnamese friends. "This simply shows the decline of the intellectual level of the Vietnamese," Phan Châu Trinh suggested. He ridiculed those who learned to write Chinese only in order to pass examinations and condemned their writing for being empty as "eight-legged essays" (*bát cổ văn*),[133] a strict writing form that inhibited independent or creative thought. Typical of these persons, according to Phan Châu Trinh, would be Phan Bội Châu.

Significantly different from Phan Bội Châu, Phan Châu Trinh promoted nonviolent and legal means to achieve national independence. As noted above, he recommended that Vietnam move gradually toward national autonomy and modernization, and that it follow the example of France when appropriate, as expressed in the slogan, "relying on France to look for progress" (Viet. *ỷ Pháp cầu tiến bộ*). In spite of Phan Châu Trinh's moderate position, after the 1908 insurrection in Trung Kỳ and the Hanoi mutiny, he was suspected of working with Phan Bội Châu. As a result, his friend Trần Quý Cáp was murdered in Khánh Hòa, and Huỳnh Thúc Kháng, Ngô Đức Kế, and others were exiled to Poulo Condore Island by the colonial authorities. Phan Châu Trinh clearly felt that he had an obligation to clear their names.

In the judgment of Phan Châu Trinh, "the insurrection and mutiny followed strictly to the letter that which Phan Bội Châu indicated in his writings."[134] The insurrection ended in disaster for the reform movement because the Vietnamese mandarins overreacted, and the two factions—which would evolve into the Revolutionary Party of Phan Bội Châu and the Self-rule Party of Phan Châu Trinh[135]—fought against each other. "The mutiny was an outcome of the insurrection," he argued, and added that once "self-rule was defeated by revolution, people would follow the anti-French."[136] For this reason, Phan Châu Trinh reluctantly admitted that violence was "inevitable" and "indispensable."

As Phan Châu Trinh explained, these reform factions were not always so sharply divided. At first, there had been no parties but only two reformers with two opinions vying against one another. Phan Bội Châu was for violent resistance, but when Phan Châu Trinh met him in 1903 and dismissed that approach, Phan Bội Châu at that time agreed with him. Both would call for the abolishment of the examination system and various reforms (Viet. *biến pháp*). But then Phan Bội Châu refused to sign his name to this compromise agreement because he wanted the opportunity to write the doctorate examination (which he failed), and the literati

---

[132] Ibid.

[133] Ibid.

[134] Ibid. p. 31.

[135] "Self-rule" (Viet. *tự trị*) has several connotations in this context. Apparently, Phan Châu Trinh envisioned self-rule as a political condition that would allow the Vietnamese to govern themselves, but would not preclude some connections with France.

[136] "Tân Việt Nam," p. 31.

followed suit, dismissing the reform agenda, because Phan Bội Châu was highly influential among them. After this, Phan Bội Châu went to Japan. As a result of these disagreements, two parties emerged: the Revolutionary Party founded by Phan Bội Châu, with branches both inside and outside Vietnam, and the Self-rule Party initiated by Phan Châu Trinh, which encompassed members inside and outside Vietnam in a single organization. Phan Châu Trinh summarized his relationship with Phan Bội Châu:

> The history of Phan Bội Châu is a sorrowful and gloomy history. It is a history full of hardship and challenge. His history is also the history of my life. His temperament is identical to mine, his aspiration is identical to mine, and his circumstances are identical to mine. Only his opinion is not identical to mine, and his conviction is just as different. That is why at the outset we were fond of one another, but eventually we parted from one another. At the beginning, we were friends, but later we were enemies. It was because of him that I paid no attention to suspicion and obstacles, and that I followed him to meet him abroad. It was because of him that I risked my life and paid no regard to taboos to appeal to the people inside the country. It was because of him that I failed—being beaten to the ground. I had no one left with me, my comrades and friends were murdered or imprisoned, and even now I am still being suspected and cannot speak my mind.[137]

To Phan Châu Trinh, Phan Bội Châu was "a person of unparalleled will, power, energy, patience, and audacity." Phan noted, "if he believes in something, he adheres to it and never abandons it, ... even thunder cannot change his mind." But, in his opinion, Phan Bội Châu also had serious shortcomings: "Besides having shallow knowledge, he is ignorant of the world trends and is fond of using intrigues, fooling himself and the people," "he is also stubborn and is not willing to alter his views," and "thoroughly conservative, he adamantly refuses to read New Books." In fact, Phan Châu Trinh regarded Phan Bội Châu as a man of the past, not a man for the Vietnam of tomorrow:

> Phan Bội Châu is the person who exemplifies our national traits [Viet. *tập quán dân tộc*], shaped throughout the history of the Vietnamese people over the last millennium. If one does not know the real nature of the Vietnamese, just look at him. Our people have abundant anti-foreignism, and in him, anti-foreignism reaches an extreme. Our people like to rely on foreigners, and in him, reliance on foreigners goes to extremes. Our people lack the spirit of independence, and in him, this lack is even more conspicuous. His disposition and standards fit well to the dispositions and standards of our people.[138]

In short, Phan Châu Trinh was adamant in criticizing Phan Bội Châu's fervent anti-French-at-any-cost approach and his one-sided favorable attitude toward Japan, which Phan Châu Trinh believed blinded him to the nature of Japan's own

---

[137] Ibid., p. 27.
[138] Ibid., p. 18.

imperial ambitions. Phan Châu Trinh was no less straightforward and clear-cut in speaking about popular rights (Viet. *dân quyền*) and self-rule (Viet. *tự trị*). He knew that, compared to Phan Bội Châu's anti-French fervor, his ideas were bound to meet with failure because the theories were new. He persevered nevertheless. It is possible to say that Phan Châu Trinh was ahead of his time indeed.

As noted above, "The New Vietnam" was written just after Phan Châu Trinh was released from Poulo Condore Island and was temporarily staying in Mỹ Tho city before going to France. His best friend Trần Quý Cáp had been murdered in 1908, and most of his comrades were still imprisoned on Poulo Condore Island. Phan Châu Trinh's feeling that he had been betrayed by Phan Bội Châu was real and acute at the time. Phan Bội Châu was expelled from Japan in 1909, after which he traveled to Siam and directed the anti-French movement from there. But Phan Châu Trinh, interned on Poulo Condore Island at the time, was not aware of these developments. In fact, after his visit to Japan in 1906, the two never saw one another again. Did Phan Châu Trinh intend to meet with Phan Bội Châu in Huế if he had a chance to go to Hanoi in 1926? That is difficult to say, but Phan Châu Trinh's most reliable biographer, Huỳnh Thúc Kháng, noted that Phan Bội Châu hoped to meet with Phan Châu Trinh prior to his death.[139] It is also clear that Phan Bội Châu's life from the end of 1925 to his last minutes in Huế, in 1940, demonstrated a change in attitude from revolutionary to moderate. Sadly, the meeting between the two men was never to take place, for Phan Châu Trinh died in March 1926, before the two had an opportunity to reconnect.

CONFUCIAN IDEAS AND "POPULAR RIGHTS": PHAN CHÂU TRINH'S "LETTER TO EMPEROR KHẢI ĐỊNH," 1922

The opportunity for Phan Châu Trinh to express publicly his notions concerning popular rights came when Emperor Khải Định paid an official visit to the Marseille Exposition in 1922 at the invitation of the French government. Phan Châu Trinh's letter to the emperor, formally called "Việt Nam quốc dân Phan Châu Trinh ký thư ư Việt Nam đương kim Hoàng đế" (A Letter by Phan Châu Trinh, a Vietnamese Citizen, Addressed to the Current Emperor of Vietnam), was written in classical Chinese, and translated in French and Vietnamese for circulation.

According to Phan Châu Trinh, Emperor Khải Định was guilty of seven offences against the Vietnamese people: reckless promotion of autocracy, unfair rewards and penalties, reckless demands that his subjects kowtow to him, reckless extravagance, improper dressing, unjustified travels, and shady dealings associated with his visit to France. Phan Châu Trinh added,

> I am a Confucianist, I do not observe the autocratic etiquette of avoiding your personal name, a practice created in the time of the First Emperor of Qin. This practice, already abolished in Japan, is still observed only in Vietnam. Today, I address this letter to Bửu Đảo, your personal name, as an expression of my protest.[140]

---

[139] Huỳnh Thúc Kháng, *Phan Tây-Hồ tiên sinh lịch sử*, p. 32.

[140] The *quốc ngữ* translation of this letter may be found in the following: (a) Trần Gia Thoại, ed., *Tâm sự nhà chí sĩ Phan Châu Trinh* [Phan Châu Trinh's Intimate Feelings as Reflected in his Poetry (and Prose)] (Đà Nẵng: Nhà sách Nguyễn Hữu Uẩn, 1958), pp. 71–107; (b) Thái Bạch, ed., *Thi văn quốc cấm thời thuộc Pháp* [Poems and Prose Prohibited During the French

As Phan Châu Trinh intended to reproach autocracy and promote popular rights, it is not surprising that he considered "reckless promotion of autocracy" the most serious offence. He accused the emperor of regarding himself as "a deity or a sage, sitting on the heads of the people without any compunction." He added, "obviously this attitude is against the principles of Confucius and Mencius."

Phan Châu Trinh referred to Western common political practice, declaring directly: "Whoever considers his country as private property, will be treated as a robber or a thief; whoever uses brute force to suppress his people, will be treated as a traitor and will be punished by the law of the land." He criticized the emperor for having said "our country holds Confucianism in reverence," while in practice, since his enthronement, he had issued decrees "to suppress the people and to promote autocracy." Phan Châu Trinh recalled a passage in which Duke Ting asked, "Is there such a single saying that can lead a country to prosperity?" and went on to explain:

> Confucius answered, "A saying cannot quite do that. There is a saying amongst men: It is difficult to be a ruler, and it is not easy to be a subject either." Mencius said, "The people are of supreme importance; the altars to the gods of earth and grain come next; last comes the ruler," and there are countless sayings to the same effect. If you open the *Five Classics* and the *Four Books*, is there anything that says autocracy should be promoted? As your [the emperor's] position is above everyone, your heart should be below everyone—that is the essence of Confucianism.[141]

Phan Châu Trinh compared Emperor Khải Định, as a promoter of autocracy, to Jie and Zhou, two notorious tyrants in Chinese history who had been removed because they acted against the Mandate of Heaven and in opposition to the will of the people. This was the essence of Confucianism, Phan Châu Trinh argued:

> Confucius has commented: "Tang chased out King Jie, King Wu defeated King Zhou, each of these responding to the Mandate of Heaven and following the will of the people." Mencius also said: "I have heard of the cutting-off of the head of the fellow Zhou, but I have not heard of the putting of a sovereign to death." Are not these most appropriate sayings of genuine Confucians?[142]

Phan Châu Trinh continued to question the motives of the emperor:

> The Classics and the Books are still here, all compiled from the sayings of Confucius and Mencius. How is it possible for you to deceive yourself and then go on to deceive others? When at this point you issue such a decree [for the promotion of autocracy], are you not yourself acting against

---

Colonial Era] (Saigon: Nhà sách Khai Trí, 1968), pp. 432-55; and (c) Nguyễn Văn Dương, ed., *Tuyển tập Phan Châu Trinh*, pp. 590–619.

[141] "Thư kể tội Khải Định," pp. 435–36.

[142] Ibid., p. 436.

Confucianism? Is there any king who, acting against the national religion [Viet. *quốc giáo*], can stay on the throne for a long time?

With respect to the promotion of autocracy in the West, Phan Châu Trinh gave the example of Louis XIV, who declared, *"L'état, c'est moi."* Phan Châu Trinh noted, "The French people all consider Louis to be a traitor; even now historians are infuriated at him." According to Phan Châu Trinh, "if a ruler follows the people, then he will be prosperous, but if he goes against them, then he will disappear." This fact was also reflected in the spirit of "our country's Confucianism." For example, Phan Châu Trinh argued, "Confucius said: 'If a ruler dislikes the things that the people like, and wishes for the things that the people hate, then disaster will come upon him immediately.' Again, he said: 'Barbarian tribes with their kings are inferior to civilized states without any kings.'"[143]

Phan Châu Trinh then mentioned the case of Japan, "which originally shared the same culture with us," but after the Diet was established (1890), "all matters were decided by the people, and the Emperor was not allowed to make decisions by himself. Nowadays it [Japan] has become prosperous, standing at the top of the countries in East Asia."

"Unfair rewards and punishments" was another offence for which Phan Châu Trinh condemned Emperor Khải Định. Not surprisingly, Phan Châu Trinh cited Confucius and Mencius to prove his point:

Confucius said: "When punishments do not fit the crimes, the common people will not know where to put their hand or foot." Mencius also said: "If those above do not follow a straight path; if those below do not observe the law, there has never been a country that has not been lost."[144]

Phan Châu Trinh held that

... in ancient times, rewards were conferred at the court to show that the entire country provided the reward. Punishment was carried out in the marketplace to show that it was punishment by the entire country. But if rewards and punishments have lost all their fairness, why should the people need to have a king and officials?[145]

Phan Châu Trinh compared Li Wang of the Zhou dynasty, who enacted a decree banning people from criticizing him, with Emperor Khải Định, who "keeps a platoon of secret soldiers, more than forty, who go morning and evening to spy in the villages and in the cities, to see if there is anyone criticizing him." According to history, Li Wang paid no attention to the advice of Shao Kung, his wise advisor, and was eventually killed by the people. "Why do you not take it as an example?" Phan Châu Trinh argued.[146]

---

[143] *The Analects,* Book III, p. 5.
[144] "Thư thất điều," p. 84.
[145] Ibid.
[146] Ibid., p. 86.

Phan Châu Trinh next upbraided the emperor for asking his subjects to kowtow to show their obedience on the grounds that this practice flouted human dignity:

> Where one man sits on high, and many sit beneath wearing court robes and hats performing kowtow, not only does this take no account of human dignity, it also serves only to make the one above feel more arrogant and the ones below lose their esteem. This protocol is extremely barbarous. [147]

According to Phan Châu Trinh, Governor-General Beau and Governor-General Sarraut had issued laws to ban kowtow. By now,

> Cochinchina and Tongkin have abolished this practice, so why do you persistently cling to this barbaric custom? Not only have you not abolished it, you are even trying to extend it ... Every time there is a kowtow session at the court, you let in people to take photographs to sell all over the country, and these photographs now have been circulated throughout the world.[148]

In the concluding part of the letter, Phan Châu Trinh declared:

> These thousand words that I have written without stopping are not to attack you in person but to attack a tyrant. It is not for self-interest that I have done this, but for the overthrow of tyranny and the promotion of liberty on behalf of my twenty million compatriots.[149]

A disciple of Mencius, Kungtu, put the question to his master: "Master, the people outside our school all speak of you as being fond of disputing, I venture to ask whether it be so." Mencius replied: "Indeed I am not fond of disputing, but I am compelled to do it." Phan Châu Trinh cited Mencius's reply and said: "My innermost feelings also are just so."[150]

It is significant that "Letter to Emperor Khải Định" was the last document Phan Châu Trinh wrote in literary Chinese. The two speeches he delivered in Saigon after he was repatriated in 1925 he wrote in *quốc ngữ*. This shows that, even while living abroad, Phan Châu Trinh still kept abreast with the linguistic developments taking place in Vietnam. Given the clarity of his later works, written in *quốc ngữ*, one tends to forget that he was a scholar who had trained in literary Chinese; we should not underestimate the effort he expended to learn the new form.

MONARCHICAL AUTOCRACY AND DEMOCRACY

After returning to Vietnam in 1925, Phan Châu Trinh delivered two well-attended public lectures, "Morality and Ethics in the Orient and the Occident" and

---

[147] Ibid.

[148] Ibid., p. 87.

[149] Ibid., pp. 105-06.

[150] Ibid., p. 106.

"Monarchy and Democracy." These lectures demonstrate his determination to voice his ideas about popular rights and democracy, and they represent the full maturing of his thought on these topics.

Confucianism, in particular Mencius's thought, remained at the core of Phan Châu Trinh's moral and political understanding. While most of his contemporaries among the literati continued blindly to accept the orthodoxy of Song Neo-Confucianism, he argued that the ideal model of Confucianism was rather to be found in the golden age, which spanned from "Yao and Shun to King Wen and King Wu—this age being just like serene spring air and tender sunlight, anyone would praise it." Phan Châu Trinh saw Confucius and Mencius as the guiding philosophers, and Yao and Shun, Yu, Tang, King Wen, and King Wu as the ideal practitioners, "who set an example that rulers of later generations would call Confucianism." In particular, he was influenced by Mencius's ideas about the subjects' duty to a just ruler and their rights to oppose an evil or corrupt ruler.

Phan Châu Trinh argued, however, that from the Qin dynasty (221–206 BCE) onward, even though the East Asian countries believed they were practicing Confucianism, in reality "they had strayed from its underlying principles, just one or two things remained in the family traditions," and apart from those surviving remnants of tradition, "the absolute monarchs relied on Confucianism only to exert pressure upon their peoples." Among the East Asian countries, in Phan Châu Trinh's view, only the Siamese and Japanese monarchs could be called "true kings" because both countries had adopted a "limited monarchy" (Viet. *quân dân cọng trị*), or "constitutional monarchy." Equality was observed in those countries "because from the king to the people, self-regulation was viewed as basic." This, argued Phan Châu Trinh, was the lesson that Confucius taught his disciple Cheng in *The Great Learning*.[151]

Phan Châu Trinh was also critical of the Vietnamese Confucian scholars who supported the emperor and of their role in perpetuating his regime and thus preventing Vietnam's development as a democratic state. The problem, he argued, was based on a faulty interpretation of Confucianism: [While] "Confucius handed down the doctrines of Yao and Shun as though they had been his ancestors" (Viet. *tổ thuật Nho giáo*), the Confucian scholars in Vietnam,

> ... in particular those who are *cử nhân* or *tiến sĩ* graduates, do not understand Confucianism whatsoever; nonetheless, every time they open their mouths they bring out Confucianism to support their denunciation of modern civilization—a kind of civilization that they do not understand at all.[152]

According to Phan Châu Trinh, the First Emperor of China was the one who laid the foundation for repressive monarchical autocracy. He noted that emperor's many oppressive initiatives: the burning of books, the massacre of intellectuals, the conscription of people, the construction of the Great Wall, the building of Afang

---

[151] Phan Châu Trinh, "Đạo đức và luân lý Đông Tây." The text of this lecture is included in Thế Nguyên, *Phan Chu Trinh*, p. 154. The source for this argument can be found in *The Great Learning*. See *Han-Ying Sishui*, trans. James Legge, annot. Luo Zhiye, pp. 2–5.

[152] Phan Châu Trinh, "Quân trị chủ nghĩa và dân trị chủ nghĩa." The text of this lecture is included in Thái Bạch, ed., *Thi văn quốc cấm thời thuộc Pháp*, p. 458.

palace to house the imperial concubines, the restriction of the term "Zhen," (I, We; Viet. *Trẫm*) which was to be used by the emperor only, and the employment of the title "Wang" (king; Viet. *Vương*), which had been highly respected by Confucianism, "to give to his followers."

The Confucians in Vietnam had contradicted themselves because "they loved Confucianism and deeply hated the Qin ... [since] the Qin had betrayed Confucianism," yet in practice, no matter "how evil their own king was, they still compared him with Yao, Shun, Yu, Tang, Wen, and Wu, but never would they compare him with the Qin Emperor." In Phan Châu Trinh's evaluation, the Chinese dynasties that followed were even worse:

> ... the policy of the Han dynasty did not have any aspect that could be called generous or fair, yet the Han was still better than the Tang, the Tang was still better than the Sung, the Sung was still better than the Yuan, the Yuan was still better than the Ming, and the Ming was still better than the Qing![153]

Phan Châu Trinh held that absolute monarchy in East Asia had been maintained by extolling heretical precepts (Viet. *tà thuyết*), such as "from the moment one comes into the world, one must fulfill one's duty as a subject toward the king" (Viet. *lọt lòng mẹ ra đã phải chịu nghĩa vua tôi*). Drawing on Mencius, Phan Châu Trinh argued that many were not aware of the fact that the relationship between the king and his subjects (Viet. *quân thần*) was a mutual one, as indicated in the saying *"quân thần dĩ nghĩa hiệp,"*[154] i.e., "in the relationship between the king and his subjects, duty [Viet. *Nghĩa*] must be foremost." The contemporary Vietnamese "autocratic court" demanded duty from its subjects, but ignored its own share of responsibility. It even punished those who were frustrated with officialdom and wished to resign their positions by making a law against "having talents but not allowing the king to use them" (Viet. *hữu tài bất dĩ quân dụng*),[155] and a law against "wheedling the king" (C: *yaochun*; Viet. *nũng vua*),[156] that is, having talents but forcing the king to beg for one's services.

To Phan Châu Trinh, "monarchical autocracy" (Viet. *quân trị*) was "rule by one man" (Viet. *nhân trị*). In a country that adopted autocracy, since laws were deliberately "made by the king and those who were completely unaware of anything," if that country were fortunate enough "to have a wise and heroic king, who understood the relationship between the people and their country, and was able to punish corrupted officials" so that people could live in peace and be content with their occupation (Viet. *an cư lạc nghiệp*), then it could enjoy prosperity and

---

[153] Ibid., p. 111.

[154] The original sentence might be *"quân thần hữu nghĩa,"* which can be found in *Mencius* (Teng Wen Gong, Book Two): "affection between father and son, duty between sovereign and subjects" (Viet. *phụ tử hữu thân, quân thần hữu nghĩa*). The source for the argument that the relationship between the sovereign and his subjects is mutual can be found in *Mencius* (Li Lou, Book One): "If you want to be a ruler, you must enact the way of a ruler fully. If you want to be a subject, you must enact the way of a subject fully."

[155] According to Phan Châu Trinh, this law was created by Emperor Hongwu (1368–98) of the Ming dynasty.

[156] According to Phan Châu Trinh, this law was created by Emperor Qian Long (1736–95) of the Qing dynasty.

peace as long as that king was on the throne. But if the king was "a despot, who lived with concubines and eunuchs, knew nothing of national affairs, and left his country's governance to his deceitful ministers [Viet. *ninh thần*], his country would certainly collapse because of the king, its ruler, being negligent."[157] For this reason, Confucius said: "The government of King Wen and King Wu is displayed in the records ... Let there be the men and the government will flourish; but without the men, the government decays and ceases" (Viet. *Văn Võ chi chính bố tại phương sách, kỳ nhân tồn tắc kỳ chánh cử, kỳ nhân vong tắc kỳ chính tức*).[158] Xunzi, on the other hand, said: "*hữu trị nhân, vô trị pháp*," literally "there are men who are able, but there are no laws that are able"[159]—implying that there are men who are capable of governing their country, but there are no laws which by themselves could govern the country. In his discussion, Phan Châu Trinh quoted Mencius, who he felt encompassed both Confucius and Xunzi: "Virtue alone is sufficient for the exercise of government; laws alone cannot carry themselves into practice" (Viet. *Đồ thiện bất túc dĩ chính vi chính, đồ pháp bất năng dĩ tự hành*).[160]

According to Phan Châu Trinh, laws imposed by autocratic rulers lead to arbitrariness, while those based on popular rights and democracy open the way to freedom and equality. Referring to the righteous emperors ruling prior to the Tang and Song dynasties, Phan Châu Trinh wrote,

> ... able kings and generals did their best to prevent "*quân trị*" [monarchical autocracy] from being "*nhân trị*" [rule by one man], but without any success. This is because the laws were made by the kings, and the laws were also abolished by them.

Nhân trị, to him, was "a form of government that may be liberal or harsh, entirely depending on the joyful or sorrowful, loving or unloving mood of the king, and in which the laws exist for nothing." To illustrate, Phan Châu Trinh cited the case of "Gia Long [r. 1802–20], who adopted the law enacted during the time of [China's] Qian Long of the Qing dynasty to govern the Vietnamese." This law stipulated that

> ... without acquiring military merits, one cannot be given the rank of marquis, or count [Viet. *phi quân công bất hầu*] ... Nguyễn Văn Thành [1757–1817] was given the rank of marquis and was even promoted to Military Secretary (Viet. *Trung quân*) because Gia Long was fair in his assessment of

---

[157] Phan Châu Trinh, "Quân trị chủ nghĩa và dân trị chủ nghĩa," p. 117.

[158] This passage is cited from *The Doctrine of the Mean* (Viet. *Trung dung*), chapter 20. The English translation used here is cited from James Legge, trans., *The Doctrine of the Mean*, revised and annotated by Liu Zhongde (Hunan: Hunan Publishing House, 1992). In Phan Châu Trinh's rendition into modern Vietnamese, he translated "*jiren*" (Viet. *kỳ nhân*; that man/those men) as "men skilled in politics" (Viet. *người chính trị giỏi*). His emphasis is thus on political skills rather than on virtue. In the context of the original passage, "*jiren*" might be interpreted to refer to those who possessed both virtue and ability, and in that text, it is only on such a basis that a government patterned after the regimes of King Wen and King Wu might be attempted.

[159] The source for this quotation can be found in Xunzi, "Jundao" (The Way of the Sovereign).

[160] The source for this quotation can be found in *Mencius*, Book 7 (Li Lou, Part I).

the military achievements that Nguyễn Văn Thành had accumulated since his youth.

Afterwards, however, when "Nguyễn Văn Thành's son[161] composed a poem just for pleasure, though in retrospect it was quite innocent, Gia Long ordered the execution of all Nguyễn Văn Thành's three families."[162] Phan Châu Trinh concluded: " ... because Gia Long was so infuriated, he ordered the murder, and this had nothing to do with the law."[163]

Comparing the two principles of "*quân trị*" (monarchical autocracy) and "*dân trị*" (democracy), Phan Châu Trinh asserted that "democracy is better by far than autocracy." To govern a country on the basis of "the personal opinions of one individual or of a court makes the people of that country not much different from a herd of goats; their prosperity and joy, or their poverty and misery, are entirely in the hands of the herder." In contrast, Phan Châu Trinh argued "democracy is *pháp trị*" (government by laws),[164] which requires democratic participation. He pointed out that, in Europe, some countries had retained their monarchy, but that they had all developed a democratic element in their parliaments. It was only in Vietnam that people remained unconcerned about the evils of autocracy: "The six provinces [of Cochinchina] have been in the hands of the French for sixty years ... Within the learned circle, the term 'République' is continually bandied about, but no one investigates its meaning and compares it with the autocracy in our country!" So far as people in rural areas were concerned,

> ... not only do they know nothing about democracy, they worship the king "in their heads" as if he were a deity or a sage ... not only do they dare not think about the question of whether or not we should have a king, but also they believe that if anyone did raise questions, he would be struck by a thunderbolt, buried under rocks, trampled by elephants, or torn apart by horses.[165]

According to Phan Châu Trinh, the Vietnamese "know of their family but not their country ... probably because the venom of autocracy has fatally poisoned the patriotism of our people." Consequently, he believed that an active, responsive patriotism could not be achieved unless people realized that Vietnam was indeed their country. To that end, he argued,

---

[161] His name is Nguyễn Văn Thuyên, a *cử nhân* graduate who loved to make contact with literary men in all parts of the country. In a poem sent to two literary figures in Thanh Hóa, he expressed his admiration for their literary talent and his wish to make their acquaintance. The letter was intercepted by an ally of Lê Văn Duyệt, Nguyễn Văn Thành's archrival. It is said that Lê Văn Duyệt reported the letter to Emperor Gia Long, and, using it as evidence, accused Nguyễn Văn Thành of being involved in a treasonable plot and his son of writing this letter to gather supporters.

[162] By three families, Phan meant Nguyễn Văn Thành's family, his father's family, and his son's family.

[163] Phan Châu Trinh, "Quân trị chủ nghĩa và dân trị chủ nghĩa," p. 119.

[164] Ibid., p. 126.

[165] Ibid., p. 121.

... probably one day the Vietnamese people will find that in this land that has been handed down to them over thousands of years, much still remains of their interests, much is still to be found of their rights; and they will realize that those who have been called kings and officials since the olden days are, after all, just their representatives acting on their behalf, and if they cannot do a good job, there is nothing wrong with chasing them away.

Phan Châu Trinh asserted that only when the people began to see things in that light would they learn to love their country, and "only when they know how to love their country might one hope for their self-determination and independence; otherwise they would have to remain slaves from generation to generation."[166]

Phan Châu Trinh's understanding of Confucianism, popular rights, and early East Asian history shaped his opinion of the monarchical system and his belief that a nation could not be strong and be ruled with justice unless the people were educated and enjoyed popular rights. Considering this line of thought, it is not surprising that he favored democracy over monarchical autocracy.

CONCLUSION

The four essays in this volume show no change in the fundamental direction of Phan Châu Trinh's thought, but reflect the maturing of his thinking about modernization and popular rights. In these works, Phan Châu Trinh focused on the necessity to strengthen Vietnam through modernization as a prerequisite to any plan for independence. Consequently, he called for modernization of education and the economy, and the creation of schools, academic institutions, and commercial societies to "invigorate the people's spirit." Phan Châu Trinh also argued for introducing popular rights and democracy, along with addressing the need to improve the well-being of the people. He clearly identified himself as a Confucian—to be precise, a pre-Qin Confucian. He is more in tune with Mencius, identifying himself with the people and their well-being. In talking about Japan, Phan Châu Trinh had no illusions about the expansionist aspect of Japanese imperialism, but, at the same time, he was convinced that Japan's modernization experience provided a meaningful example for Vietnam. Consequently, in his writings, Phan Châu Trinh concentrated on the positive aspects of Japanese modernization and argued that Vietnam should follow its example while making gradual progress within the French colonial system.

Within the context of Vietnamese history exclusively, Phan Châu Trinh's ideas were unique compared to those of his contemporaries. If we use a broader perspective that includes China and Japan, however, we see that during this period Phan Châu Trinh did not belong to a minority of Asian intellectuals; instead, he may be placed within the vast majority. Liang Qichao and Kang Youwei of China, or Nakae Chômin of Japan, were just a few examples of leading East Asian intellectuals who focused on modernization. Phan Châu Trinh's ideas and plans for modernization and democracy indeed provided a comprehensive strategy for meeting the challenge of his contemporary world, and much of his analysis still holds true today in a world transformed by increasing globalization.

---

[166] Ibid., p. 123.

Part VI
The Texts

The Vietnamese language underwent important, radical changes in the first quarter of the twentieth century. The written language of Vietnam changed from literary Chinese to the Vietnamese *quốc ngữ* (national language), which used romanized characters and which has remained in use ever since. Though literary Chinese was in the process of becoming obsolete during Phan Châu Trinh's lifetime due to the cancellation of the Chinese-style examinations, the changes took about three decades to take effect among the populace. The shift from classical Chinese to romanized Vietnamese is apparent in the two last essays translated for this volume.

As an intellectual who was active during this turbulent time, Phan Châu Trinh developed the exceptional ability to write well both in literary Chinese and in *quốc ngữ*, or romanized Vietnamese, a feat that few contemporaries were able to match. Phan Châu Trinh was a master at expressing himself in literary Chinese, and his literary Chinese prose and poetry have more flavors and complexity than those of his contemporaries. Phan Châu Trinh's ability to write fluently in *quốc ngữ* as well distinguished him from most Vietnamese literati of the time. For example, Phan Bội Châu was unable to write in *quốc ngữ*, although he was very capable in literary Chinese and *chữ Nôm*.[167] Because of the structure of the language, Phan Châu Trinh's *quốc ngữ* was less picturesque than his classical Chinese, nevertheless it succinctly expressed his ideas to his audience. The four texts in this volume can be separated into two types. The first two texts, (1) and (2), were written in literary Chinese, and the remaining two, (3) and (4), in *quốc ngữ* style.

Text (1), "A New Vietnam," is difficult to decipher because Phan Châu Trinh's writing is small and rough. He wrote it in Mỹ Tho city during the nine months after his release from Poulo Condore Island and prior to going to France. Until now, no one has been able to identify exactly when this text was written, but as mentioned, evidence within the document demonstrates that it must have been composed in Mỹ Tho. In its original form in literary Chinese, the first thirty-one pages of the manuscript contain the most important passages, and the discussion is not redundant. These pages were selected for English translation for that purpose.

---

[167] *Chữ Nôm* is the ideographic script indigenous to Vietnam. While *chữ* unquestionably means "character/script," it is not certain whether "*Nôm*" implies "Southern" or "popular/native" script, as some scholars would argue. It is important to note that this mode of writing might have evolved over a long time—even centuries—before *chữ Nôm* script emerged in the twelfth century. A demotic script, *chữ Nôm* uniquely combined and rearranged elements of Chinese characters (Viet. *chữ Hán/chữ nho/Hán tự*), expressing phonetic components of Vietnam's national language. Generally speaking, there are three major elements in *chữ Nôm*: phonetic loans, semanto-phonetic compounds, and semantic compounds. It should be emphasized that during the Hồ Quý Ly (r. 1400) and Quang Trung (r. 1788–92) dynasties, *chữ Nôm* received much attention as the national language, but for the rest of the time, literary Chinese was still used for official purposes, particularly in the examination system (Viet. *khoa cử*) from the late eleventh century to 1919. *Chữ Nôm* existed and developed parallel with literary Chinese, which was formally adopted in the examinations, until the early twentieth century, when both were supplanted by the Roman alphabetical script, *quốc ngữ*.

The manuscript used for my translation of the "Letter to Emperor Khải Định," text (2), is neatly written in literary Chinese. French and Vietnamese translations of this work are also available. The translation of the letter included in Trần Gia Thoại's book is excellent because Phan Châu Trinh did the translation by himself for most parts of the letter. For that reason, although I used mainly Phan's original work in literary Chinese for my English translation, footnotes will cite Trần Gia Thoại's book for the convenience of the readers.

Texts (3), "Morality and Ethics," and (4), "Monarchy and Democracy," are available in *quốc ngữ*. Readers who encounter Phan Châu Trinh's *quốc ngữ* for the first time should be warned that some of his word usage is now out-of-date due to the fact that these essays were designed to be presented orally and the Vietnamese language has changed since they were drafted. The value of Phan Châu Trinh's writings is, nevertheless, extraordinary; this becomes clear if we consider that these speeches in *quốc ngữ* were composed in late 1925, when as yet no significant Vietnamese literature had been published in the new script.

As one of the last turn-of-the-century Confucian scholars, who arguably could be considered the most eloquent Vietnamese author of beautiful Chinese poems and tasty Chinese prose, Phan Châu Trinh was also among the first to express his ideas in *quốc ngữ*. By virtue of this effort, he served as a bridge spanning the two eras. Most importantly, however, Phan Châu Trinh must be remembered as an enlightened thinker, and the first and the most eloquent proponent of democracy and popular rights in Vietnam.

A NEW VIETNAM FOLLOWING THE FRANCO-VIETNAMESE ALLIANCE

[Drafted in literary Chinese from June 1910 to April 1911 in Mỹ Tho city, following Phan Châu Trinh's release from internment on Poulo Condore Island and prior to his departure for France.]

DISTINCTIVE FEATURES OF THE VIETNAMESE PEOPLE

History of the relationship between Vietnam and China

Our nation, Vietnam,[1] is located in the South of East Asia, with a long and slender shape. Viewed from an East Asian perspective, China is like the upper part of a human body and Vietnam is like its right arm, stretching to the south. Our people originated and spread out several thousand years ago within the mount Tản Viên region[2] and the Red River basin, like those living in an Arcadia[3]—knowing nothing about the existence of the Xia [Viet. *Hạ*; 2205–1766 BCE?][4] and the Shang [Viet. *Thương*; 1766–1122 BCE] dynasties, let alone the times of Yao [Viet. *Nghiêu*; r. 2357–2256 BCE] and the Shun [Viet. *Thuấn*; r. 2255–05 BCE].

Although our people belong to the Yellow race, we originated and evolved independently in the south of East Asia, and our close ties with China only emerged during the Qin (Viet. *Tần*)[5] and the Han (Viet. *Hán*)[6] dynasties. Ever since, there has been exchange between the two peoples, and the origin of what eventually would become our nation began to take shape. We have nonetheless developed distinctive characteristics in the course of our history, which are now ingrained. Over the last thousand years, however, there have been historians among our people who have

---

[1] It is interesting to note that the term Phan Châu Trinh used in his original text, in literary Chinese, was "Việt Nam" and not "An Nam." In most documents of this period, the term "An Nam" was used, and "Việt Nam" was not commonly adopted as the name of the country until sometime in 1945. Thus, Phan Châu Trinh and Phan Bội Châu, who also used the term as early as 1906 (Phan Bội Châu wrote *Việt Nam quốc sử khảo* when he was in Japan), were clearly ahead of their time.

[2] Presently Mount Ba Vì.

[3] Taoyuan (Viet. *Đào viên*) in the Chinese original. This term is taken from a story of a man who crossed through a peach orchard and discovered a secluded valley in which people were living in peace, blissfully ignorant of passing events and changes of dynasty.

[4] The Chinese dynasties mentioned here represent the "golden age" of Chinese history and thus have heavy symbolic, as well as historical, significance.

[5] 221–207 BCE.

[6] Former Han, 206 BCE–8 CE and Later Han, 25–220 CE.

worshipped China to the extent that they have promulgated a mentality that lacks confidence in our people. They do not believe that we can stand on our own. In their view, China is seen as our father, and our people should willingly assent to be its children. Exposed to these opinions, we have become accustomed to the habit of being dependent. From this point forward, we must regain our senses in order to see past and overcome this irrational reliance.

When the First Emperor of the Qin dynasty, who aspired to bring the entire world under his rule, amalgamated the Six States, his abundant might was extended, for the first time, to the cradle of our people. This area, formerly called Giao Chỉ[7] and currently corresponding to the five provinces of Bắc Kỳ, fell under China's rule for more than 1,500 years,[8] even though the distant ancestors of our people had tirelessly worked to maintain control over their own lands.

What were the feelings of our people at that time? Though they had just escaped from the barbaric stage, they were still at the early phase of state formation and were unaware of what the Europeans now call nationalism (Viet. *dân tộc chủ nghĩa*). But nationalism is rooted in human nature; consequently, barbaric, semideveloped, and civilized peoples all have this distinctive feature. From time immemorial our ancestors have gone through every kind of hardship to set up a land that their descendants could rely on, and their descendants would, in turn, do the same thing for their own descendants. For this reason, this same land is where our descendants will continue to sing, cry, gather, and live their lives.

The people between the basins of the Yellow River (Viet. *Hoàng Hà*) and the Yangzi River (Viet. *Dương Tử*), however, without good reason, relied on force to intimidate the weaker. Their greed was limitless: without good reason, they confiscated other peoples' land; without good reason, they put other peoples under their yoke and took control of their lives; and without good reason, they committed genocide against other peoples. (At the time, the Chinese took our resources to China to add to their monarch's private property. It was different from the civilized European countries of the present day, which take our resources to incorporate into their colonial enterprises. If the resources were insufficient, the colonial authorities would ask the colonies to provide more resources to meet the mother country's needs. The reader should not be confused here.)

The situation at the time could be compared to people living in the same house with someone who was greedy and used violence to take away a plate of soup and a bowl of rice from the weaker, flayed them, and swallowed them alive, sat at a high place, ate heavily, and chanted songs, and left the children of the household in a corner or squeezed into a dark room, without hearing the songs, and no one cared if they were hungry and cold.[9] Alas! Human beings are neither sticks nor stones, how could our ancestors stand those circumstances?

But the ancestors of our people were unyielding. They refused to submit themselves to the aggressors even though they were forced to be under their rule a

---

[7] The early kingdom of Nanyue/Nam Việt included land on both sides of the present border. It was subsequently split into "Giao Chỉ" and China proper. It is said that Zhao Tuo (Viet. Triệu Đà) ruled this land for seventy years before he died in 137 CE. See Keith Weller Taylor, *The Birth of Vietnam* (Berkeley, CA: University of California Press, 1983), pp. 25–27.

[8] The actual period of direct Chinese rule was just over a millennium, from the Han dynasty to the end of the Tang dynasty (from 111 BCE to 939 CE).

[9] "The weaker" and "the children" used in this passage seem to be the metaphors for the smaller states, located on the periphery of ancient China.

hundred times. They were not timid, cowardly, or spiritless beings. They adopted purposeful measures. At times, they acted deferential, at times, they were combative. When the aggressors were malicious, they resisted. When our ancestors lost, the aggressors even exterminated the animals. When our ancestors triumphed, the rivers turned red with the aggressors' blood and their bones formed mountains. Using their greater strength in numbers, the aggressors charged with irresistible force, like a heavy cooking-stove pressing on a fragile egg, making it impossible for our people to fend off their assault. Against their enormous might, our people staged one uprising after another, during which so many of us were slaughtered. Resentful feelings were all the more intensified after each uprising and became embedded and seared in our people's minds. At the same time, some of our distinct traits, such as our indomitability, were nurtured. Our ancestors vowed to risk their lives to defend the fields and to dye the mountains and rivers with the aggressors' blood. Our history is the most sorrowful and inspiring of tragedies. For more than one thousand years, we have been engaged in a struggle, an evolutionary struggle (Viet. *thiên diễn giới*),[10] i.e., "survival of the fittest" (Viet. *ưu thắng liệt bại*), against a Chinese nation a thousand times larger than our own. When the aggressors perished, we survived; when the aggressors advanced, we retreated, but only when the enemy perished could our nation truly live.

Why was it that eventually, after more than one thousand years, we were able to gain our independence? At the time of the disunity of the Five Dynasties period [Viet. *Ngũ Đại*; 907–960 CE], the Later Zhou [Viet. *Hậu Chu*; 960–961] and the Song [Viet. *Tống*; 960–1125] fought against one another, China's power was sluggish, and its long whip could not reach our country. It was then that Đinh Tiên Hoàng[11] [r.

---

[10] *Thiên diễn giới* or *vật cạnh* (as in the first line in Phan Châu Trinh's poem "Impressions upon reading *Kajin no kigû*": Viet. *"Vật cạnh phong trào hám ngũ châu ... "*: The scramble for survival is shaking the entire world ...) are Sino-Vietnamese translations of the phrase "evolutionary struggle." Phan's terminology follows an earlier Chinese translation of the terms by Thomas Henry Huxley's famed translator Yan Fu (1853–1921). Since Chinese (and Korean and Vietnamese) scholars eventually switched to Japanese translations of this term (J. *shinkaron*: *tiến hóa luận*) around the middle of the twentieth century, Phan's use of the earlier Chinese terminology places him within the earlier generation of Vietnamese scholars and suggests that he probably first read this work while in Huế. For a discussion of Yan Fu, see Benjamin Schwartz, *In Search of Wealth and Power: Yen Fu and the West* (Cambridge, MA: Harvard East Asian Series, 1964).

[11] Phan Châu Trinh implies that Đinh Tiên Hoàng led the Vietnamese in a struggle for independence against the Chinese. Phan was mistaken in this respect. The Chinese had been driven out of Vietnam prior to Đinh Tiên Hoàng's time, and he did not create the first dynasty, but was the first to call himself emperor. Nevertheless, Đinh Tiên Hoàng was an important historical figure because he successfully consolidated authority over the warlords. He was born in Hoa Lư, Gia Viễn prefecture, province of Ninh Bình, and his real name was Đinh Bộ Lĩnh. He was son of Đinh Công Trứ, governor of Hoan Châu. It is said that, as a child, when he played with village children tending the water buffaloes, Đinh Bộ Lĩnh asked the children to carry him as their leader and used the reed flowers as flags to conduct war games. When Đinh Bộ Lĩnh grew up, thanks to his strength and talent, he was asked by the warlord Trần Lãm to direct his army. Upon Trần Lãm's death, Đinh Bộ Lĩnh took his army to go back to Hoa Lư and recruited more talented people. In 968 CE, he was able to unify all the warlords under his command and called himself Đại Thắng Vương (Great Vanquishing King). He named the country Đại Cồ Việt (Great Việt) and placed the capital at Hoa Lư. He and his eldest son were assassinated in 979. It is significant to note that Phan Châu Trinh always gave Đinh Tiên Hoàng a crucial place in Vietnamese history. Phan translated *Encounter with Elegant Females, Translated into Verses*, perhaps between 1912 and 1914 in France, because of his desire to educate the Vietnamese people about patriotism. In one section, Phan even changed the

968–79] raised his revolutionary army in Hoa Lư, hoisting the flag of independence and beating the drum of freedom. The indomitable spirit of resistance, a national trait of the Vietnamese people nurtured by a thousand years of foreign invasions, finally resulted in a lasting independence.

Alas! Even though Giao Chi is a tiny land, smaller than a big province in China, China has always had an insatiable covetousness and has looked for a chance to assimilate it. But our ancestors, without fear of the disparity in civilization and strength, risked their lives to resist the enemy and were unwilling to move back even a single step. By succeeding in the struggle for survival until today, we were able to exist as a great country in the South. Alas! Was our survival a matter of fortune (Viet. *thiên hạnh*)?[12] Or was it the result of Heaven's intervention (Viet. *thiên trợ*)?[13] Since it is not conceivable to attribute this feat of survival to these factors, we can say firmly that it was due to nothing but the special qualities of the inhabitants of our motherland, such as calm resoluteness, perseverance, self-reliance, and indomitability. Our country traditionally belonged to the same country as Guangdong (Viet. *Quảng Đông*) and Guangxi (Viet. *Quảng Tây*). The name of Vietnam was adopted after China had assimilated Guangdong and Guangxi. Our people, relying on the land of Giao Chi, resisted China's rule to preserve our independence and eventually were able to create on our own a separate nation. There were so many inconceivable factors in our search for national independence.

Even two thousand years ago, our people already possessed these great traits. If it were possible to adopt the present-day vigorous and forward-looking European political theories to modify and enhance these traits, the splendor of our people's future would then be immeasurable! The fortunes of our country, however, have gone unexpectedly from bad to worse. Errors were made, not only in political governance but also in education and diplomacy, and at present the country has been drifting into deeper water and cannot save itself. Who is to take the blame? Who is to take the blame?

Đinh Tiên Hoàng inaugurated a great undertaking a thousand years ago. Domestically we relied mainly on our own resources. But since the aggressor would amass forces and come back to strike us again and again,[14] and since we did not have much to rely on, we had to use diplomatic means. Even in our victory, jade and silk were brought to China as tribute for two reasons: first, to lessen the humiliation felt by the other side; and second, to moderate our people's excessive pride in victory, so that the people on both sides would not dwell on triumph or defeat. We therefore had time to strengthen our unity, prepare our armaments, renovate our political governance, and consolidate the foundation of our government. The forefathers of our country possessed unsurpassed ingenuity and vision! One cannot dream of seeing these things among the later weak-kneed scholars who have been trained in eight-legged essays and who care only for their personal life. Thus the achievement

---

Japanese name of the protagonist, Tôkai Sanshi, to Đinh Tiên Hoàng. See Vĩnh Sính, "'Elegant Females' Re-encountered: From Tôkai Sanshi's *Kajin no kigû* to Phan Châu Trinh's *Gian nhân kỳ ngộ diễn ca*," in *Essays into Vietnamese Pasts*, ed. K. W. Taylor and John K. Whitmore (Ithaca, NY: Cornell Southeast Asia Program Publications, 1995), pp. 195–206.

[12] A term used in *Zhuangzi*, "Yufu." See *Kadokawa Daijiten* (Kadokawa Great Dictionary of Etymology), ed. Ozaki Yujirô et al. (Tokyo: Kadokawa Shoten, 1992), p. 421.

[13] A term used in *Yijing* (The Book of Divination), "Jici," Part I. See ibid.

[14] "*Juantu chonglai*" (Viet. *Quyển thổ trùng lai*), a term used in Du Mu's (Viet. Đỗ Mục; 803–852) poem "Ti Wujiangting shi" (Viet. *Đề Ô-Giang-Đình thi*; At the Wujiang Pavilion).

gained by our forefathers has in later generations become a sad story of failure. For generations our country entered into a tributary relationship with China because that was our foreign policy. We saw it as a game, not an honor. Those who lost self-reliance and relied on China appeared much later, when our monarchs became irresolute and our ministers became deceitful. At this time, armaments were not consolidated, and people came to look at China as their father country and forgot its fierce wickedness. During the later years of the Trần and Lê dynasties, there was this tendency, but it became increasingly conspicuous during the current dynasty. Those envoys who went to China in the olden days would have been gratified at humiliating the Chinese; in contrast, our envoys of later generations took pride in receiving a poem, an essay, or a song from the Chinese scholars and were proud to show it off to their colleagues upon their return. This is yet another indication of the degeneracy of our scholars.

From the former Lê dynasty (980–1005 CE) to the current Nguyễn dynasty (1802–1945), through the intermediate Lý (1010–1225), Trần (1225–1400; 1407–1413), and Lê (1418–1527; 1533–1789) dynasties, our policy vis-à-vis China has been "to maintain good relations with China and to attack nearby [Southern] neighbors." If there was no need to be concerned with the North, armaments could be directed to the South, to assimilate Champa (Viet. Chăm-pa / Chàm) and seize Chenla (Viet. Chân Lạp).[15] By exerting our inner power (Viet. *nội lực*), our people were able to expand and spread out along the Southern coast. In the process, Cambodia and Laos came under our sphere of influence. That our country now occupies a place on the map of the world is thanks to that foreign policy.

Unfortunately, later generations[16] adopted an erroneous policy. Relying heavily on China, they did not conduct military drills and revitalize domestic concerns. They considered the offering of jade and silk as tribute to be more essential than fortifications and came to see dependence on China as a national policy. China took advantage of this, disguising its intentions with a mask and surreptitiously designing malicious schemes. For instance, the Ming used the excuse of restoring the Trần dynasty in our country to attempt to turn it into one of its provinces, eventually even supporting the leader of the rebellion, the Mạc clan, traitors of our imperial court. Similarly, the Qing (Viet. *Thanh*) feigned assistance to the Lê dynasty as a pretense to occupy our country, but after their defeat, they angrily arrested the Lê

---

[15] The kingdom of Champa existed in central Vietnam from the second to the seventeenth centuries, when it eventually fell to the Vietnamese. The Chams were of Malayo–Polynesian origin and were influenced by Indian culture. Champa was preceded by Linyi (Viet. *Lâm Ấp*), in existence from 192 CE; nevertheless, the historical relationship between Champa and Linyi is unknown. The second half of the eighth century was a crucial period in Champa's history: the political center shifted farther south and the capital was moved from the neighborhood of Huế to Vijaya (Viet. *Bình Định*). At the same time, the Chinese begin to refer to Champa as Huanwang (Viet. *Hoàn Vương*) instead of Linyi. Toward the beginning of the ninth century, Champa started a series of offensives against China to the north and Cambodia to the south. Eventually, Champa began a gradual decline under pressure from the Vietnamese, and in the seventeenth century Champa was largely absorbed by Vietnam. In 1832, the Vietnamese Emperor Minh Mạng finally annexed the last vestiges of Champa. Today, the Chams still form small minorities in Vietnam, though the majority have integrated with the Vietnamese. In Cambodia, a rather large Cham community still exists. Whereas most of the Chams in Vietnam are Hindus, those of Cambodia are Muslim. "Chenla" refers to present-day Cambodia.

[16] Though Phan Châu Trinh does not specify, he seems to be referring to Vietnam under the imperial dynasties after the sixteenth century.

king and his vassals and forced them to shave their heads [after taking them back to China]. Altogether, for approximately one thousand years, our people have been outraged. The current dynasty has not pondered things carefully and has followed the path of an overturned chariot. It has not fostered our self-reliance and has entrusted its fate to China.[17] It has made every effort to secure China's support, considering China to be as unshakable as Mt. Tai (Viet. *Thái Sơn*).[18] When, all of a sudden, Vietnam had to face powerful France, it had to surrender. It feared the tiger devouring it, yet had to offer its flesh to someone else. It is a painful story.

Nowadays, a distinguished person in our country claims that he is a patriot but flees overseas and behaves like a powerless lion.[19] He does not know how to appeal to our people to expend their domestic strength, and he has no course of action. He adores the Island Country's[20] brute force and has made irresponsible statements without contemplating the cost and injury to our country. He wanted to look for help from this utterly unprincipled (Viet. *bất nhân lý*) third country—whose words are benevolent like Buddha's, but whose heart is venomous like a poisonous snake (Viet. *khẩu Phật tâm xà*). He found pleasure in entrusting to it our entire national life, without realizing that if it does not have power it will shelve our request without responding to it, and if it indeed has power then it does not have to wait until we make our request. Look at Korea; there are all sorts of political parties allying themselves either with Russia or Japan; today, its queen has been murdered, the king is imprisoned, and the slaughter is endless. The request for Japanese assistance has thus been answered, but where is the profit? Even worse, in our country, the public intellect is underdeveloped, and the habit of relying on foreigners has become a disposition. When a blind person sings, all ignorantly respond to him like thunder—just like a moth flying into fire to throw away its life. Why is it that our innocent people have to be involved in these distressing circumstances?

Alas! Unless the time-honored disposition of relying on foreigners is broken down, how can one possibly save the lives of our ignorant twenty million people? Even at present, we still do not have a stratagem for both survival and advancement. I am afraid that in the next several decades there will be a patriot, molded by civil-service examinations (Viet. *bát cổ biến tướng*), using the excuse that our country has been under China's protection (Viet. *bảo hộ*) in the past as a precedent to appeal to the people. Because our people have not awakened from a confused dream, if they hear that proposition, they will risk their lives to restore that situation. Once both the losers have been wounded, the other side will have the chance to acquire the fisherman's profit.

The future outlook is precarious, and our country is facing a moment of life and death. Once the opportunity to save it is gone, it will never come back.

---

[17] It should be noted that Phan Châu Trinh was overcritical of the Lê and Nguyễn dynasties. These dynasties were not comparatively more reliant on, or subservient to, China than others had been, although the Vietnamese elite did become more Sinicized during this period. When Phan suggested that the Nguyễn dynasty "has entrusted its fate to China," he may have been referring to its request for help from China to fight against the French—assistance justified by their tributary relationship—prior to the French conquest of Vietnam in the mid-1880s.

[18] One of China's "five most famous mountains," located in Shandong province. A metaphor for the greatest power.

[19] Phan Châu Trinh seems to be alluding to Phan Bội Châu, who first went to Japan in 1905 to ask for its military assistance.

[20] The "Island Country" is a metaphor for Japan.

People of great France, a progressive people of Europe! In accord to your chivalrous and philanthropic spirit, would you care to provide our Vietnamese people a lifeline to survive in the twentieth century? Our people of Vietnam! We should rid ourselves of our disposition to rely on China!

Deeply mortified by this question, I have lost all my hair. Alas! I wish that I would say nothing, but how can I remain silent?

History of the Relationship between Vietnam and France

The more than sixty years that have passed since the relationship between France and Vietnam began can be divided into two periods: the period of power formation and the period of power consolidation. The French policy has thus varied according to the time: during the former, it was one of support and enlightenment; during the latter, it was one of control and autocracy.

At this point, it would be appropriate to add a discussion of the interpretations of these two policies, but I assume that many in our country are able to understand their gist, so I will not include it here.

Someone asked me: "What were the causes of the insurrection in 1908 in Trung Kỳ and the mutiny in Bắc Kỳ?"[21] The following is my answer:

It has been more than sixty years since the arrival of the French in Vietnam. When their power had not yet been consolidated, there were various attempts to resist them: by the imperial court from above and by the Loyalist (Viet. *Cần Vương*) Movement in various provinces. After the Loyalist Movement had been pacified, there were acts of resistance carried out by remnants of the Taiping Rebellion in Bắc Kỳ,[22] by Cử Phục in Quảng Ngãi, by the Liêm Rebellion in Bình Định, and by

---

[21] The insurrection in 1908 was the tax revolt that started in Đại Lộc prefecture, Quảng Nam province, and expanded to other provinces in central Vietnam. In this piece ("A New Vietnam"), Phan Châu Trinh gives his account of the incident as follows: "I heard that, at the time, public speeches were prohibited, short hair was banned, and those who kept their short hair were imprisoned. The prefect of Đại Lộc took advantage of the troubled situation to increase by five-fold the number of people recruited to do forced labor. When villagers came to his office to protest, the officials regarded them as bandits and reported them to the Résident-supérieur. The insurrection then started." Following the incident, Phan Châu Trinh was imprisoned on Poulo Condore Island.

The mutiny at Bắc Kỳ was an abortive uprising carried out by sympathetic army cooks and soldiers, who tried to poison the militia overseeing the Hanoi prison in 1908. The authorities executed thirteen rebels and made hundreds of arrests. It has been speculated that the renowned resistance leader Đề Thám was involved in the 1908 mutiny. Note that when reference is made to an "abortive uprising/insurrection" that took place during the 1910s, one tends to think of rebellions that are better known, such as Emperor Duy Tân's uprising in 1916, or the 1917 Thái Nguyên uprising. However, since we know that Phan Châu Trinh wrote this article in 1910–11, the year of the mutiny to which he refers in this case should be 1908.

[22] The most renowned member of the remnants of the Taiping (Viet. *Thái Bình Thiên Quốc*) Rebellions in Bắc Kỳ was Liu Yongfu (Viet. *Lưu Vĩnh Phúc*) of the Black Flags (Viet. *quân Cờ Đen*). Liu was the recipient of official Vietnamese court rank, and he led his followers to harass French ships, harassment that led to the dispatch of an expeditionary force under Commandant Henri Rivière in 1881 and precipitated the Sino-French War. Liu also besieged a battalion of French troops in Tuyên Quang province. Before returning to Guangdong in 1895, Liu crossed to Formosa to combat the Japanese. It is interesting to note that on his way to Japan in 1906, Phan Châu Trinh met with Phan Bội Châu and others at Liu's residence in Guangdong.

Nguyễn Trứ in Phú Yên.[23] These resistance movements did not have a sufficient impact on the entire situation to warrant an in-depth treatment here—though their causes may have been justified or unjustified, their undertakings may have been on a large or small scale, those who initiated them may have been well-learned or ignorant, or their results may have been extended or brief.

With respect to the matter of the present day, even though the ideas [of the leaders of the resistance] are most simplistic, their knowledge is most primitive, their action is most barbarous, and the situation is most deplorable and most detestable, the success or failure of the relationship between France and Vietnam in the future will depend entirely on them.

We must calmly reflect upon matters of the past and carefully consider those of the future. Concerning external matters, we must look at the trends in East Asia. Concerning internal matters, we must examine the prospects of our nation—keeping in mind that an ant hill could lead to the collapse of a dam, and that by gathering feathers one might break an axle. We must be able to envision a larger picture by observing minor things and see through the entire matter by holding one of its parts. This is a highly fascinating subject of importance that deserves to be studied. Don't think that it is trivial and overlook it. Don't consider that it is not worthwhile and ignore it. If you wish to listen to the story, please take a seat.

[When assessing the 1908 insurrection], one finds that at the outset there were remote causes and immediate causes, along with common causes and particular causes. Each cause was highly complicated, and their manifestations were difficult to define. Unless one is a curiosity seeker (Viet. *hiếu sự*) or has an adventurous temperament ready to risk one's life in order to see inner aspects, one is not aware of them. Unless one has piercing eyes and an impartial mind with which to contemplate our remote national history and observe recent conditions, one is not aware of them. If one looks only at a phenomenon without observing its contents, mistaking the immediate causes for remote causes and particular causes for common causes, picking up the small and throwing away the big, seeing the form without looking for its spirit, but still thinking that one understands the matter, then in the act of using this understanding as the basis to assess a changing situation, one would deceive not only others but also oneself. A course of action that stems from that understanding is not only useless but also extremely harmful.

A popular saying states, "Let him who tied the bell on the tiger loosen it." As one of those who were directly involved, I would like to tell the inside story.

Remote causes and common causes: The Vietnamese people have possessed throughout their history two diametrically opposed specific traits: one being an anti-foreign versus relying-on-foreigner trait, and the other being a self-aggrandizing versus self-abasing trait. These two specific traits exist in the nature of our people. In everyone's mind, these traits interact with one another as both cause and effect. At times, they have provided us with benefits. At times, they shielded our potential. Depending on the conditions and circumstances, one of these traits will appear. At the time of its appearance, it goes to extremes. Once these distinctive traits have gone

---

[23] Cử Phục, Liêm, and Nguyễn Trứ appear to have been participants in the 1908 tax revolt. "Cử Phục" means a certain man named Phục (only the personal name was given) who passed his examinations to be recognized as *cử nhân* (recommended man). His identity, as well as that of the other two men, is unknown.

to their extremes, each having its habitual reasons, interests are obscured and cannot be seen.

The history of the above is precisely the history of the danger and hardship of my entire life. The public will decide my merit or lack of merit, and the success or failure of my career. On many occasions, I deliberately touched upon the taboos and did not shun others' suspicion and jealousy. That is why I have been either warmly received, or spit on and reviled in the most extreme manner. My self-confidence is enormous, and my fighting spirit is immense; nonetheless, I have also often thrown myself into traps. With respect to the history of this story, I am indeed the most involved person. But those who love me or dislike me, those who trust me or suspect me, those who wish me to live or to perish—they all do not understand me. Alas! I wish not to say anything, but how is it possible for me not to say anything?

The investigation of the causes of the affair by high officials of two countries and the measure they adopted: In the midst of confusion following the tax revolt, the protectorate government, without thinking, used military forces to suppress the rebellion, while condemning to death or exiling those suspected of being involved, without missing a single person.[24] The measure was an unavoidable response, given that it was a time of emergency. After the affair was resolved, the high officials of the two countries met to investigate the causes of this revolt. They basically stated: "The Vietnamese are tame and submissive—the easiest people to rule. They also love France. The revolt was no more than a provocation carried out by a few frustrated literati." With respect to the response of the authorities, the measures have been discussed in the so-called "External arrangements" and "Domestic arrangements" in Minister Hoàng Cao Khải's[25] *Mirror of Vietnamese History* (Viet. *Việt sử kính*). An assessment of all methods of response is to be based on the observations in this document.

The external policy of the party: Phan Bội Châu was the overseas representative designated by the party. He was ignited by vengeful thoughts that led him to adopt an extremist position, vowing to confront the French in the future.

A COMPARISON OF THE STRENGTHS AND WEAKNESSES OF OUR PEOPLE AND THE CHINESE PEOPLE. THE SIMILARITIES AND DIFFERENCES, AND THE SUCCESS AND FAILURE, OF THE APPROACHES OF VIETNAM AND CHINA IN RESPONDING TO TROUBLES FROM WITHOUT (Viet. *ngoại hoạn*)

China is located at the center of East Asia. All countries bordering China to the south are small and do not threaten China. To China, troubles from without thus come from the north, such as the Xianyun (Viet. *Hiểm Doãn*) during the Zhou (Viet. *Chu*) dynasty; the Xiongnu (Viet. *Hung Nô*) during the Qin (Viet. *Tần*) and the Han

---

[24] The tax revolt erupted in 1908 in Quảng Nam and other cities in central Vietnam. Phan Châu Trinh was accused of having spurred the public to join in revolt and maintained surreptitious contacts with Phan Bội Châu. As punishment, Phan Châu Trinh and many of his associates were arrested and interned on Poulo Condore Island.

[25] Hoàng Cao Khải, 1850–1933. His pen name was Thái Xuyên, and he was a native of Hà Tĩnh. He was well known for his collaboration with the colonial authorities to put down the Loyalist Movement. Promoted to Minister of the Army in 1897, Hoàng was also the author of a number of historical and literary works, including the one noted above.

(Viet. *Hán*) dynasties; the Tujue (Viet. *Đột Quyết*) during the Tang (Viet. *Đường*) dynasty; the Qiedan (Viet. *Khiết Đan*) during the Five Dynasties (Viet. *Ngũ Quý*) period; the Liao (Viet. *Liêu*), the Jin (Viet. *Kim*), and the Yuan (Viet. *Nguyên*) during the Northern and Southern Song (Viet. *Lưỡng Tống*) dynasties; and the Mongols (Viet. *Mông Cổ*) during the Ming (Viet. *Minh*) dynasty. How to deal with the enemies from the North thus has been a vital issue to the Chinese people from ancient times to the present day.

Vietnam is located in the south of East Asia. Countries bordering the South of China are all of small size. Though there were uprisings in these countries, they did not pose any threat to China. External threats to China always occurred in the North. Similarly, our country, prior to the time of Đinh Tiên Hoàng, was conquered by China; then, during the Trần dynasty, [it was conquered by] by Omar (Viet. Ô Mã Nhi) of the Mongols; during the late Trần by Zhang Fu (Viet. Trương Phụ) and Mu Sheng (Viet. Mộc Thạnh) of the Ming; and during the late Lê dynasty by Sun Shiyi (Viet. Tôn Sĩ Nghị) of the Qing (Viet. *Thanh*). For that reason, our people have thus always considered dealing with the northern neighbor as their greatest concern.

With respect to China's response to the northern invaders, prior to the Tang dynasty, China frequently won and the North frequently lost. From the Five Dynasties period (Viet. *Ngũ Đại*; in the tenth century) onward, however, China frequently lost and the North frequently won. This is why it has been said that "Beijing was devastated for more than one thousand years." Previously, China was conquered and ruled by the Mongols for more than one hundred years; at present, it has been ruled by the Qing for more than two hundred years. These occurrences display China's weakness.

In contrast, prior to the Five Dynasties period of a thousand years ago, Vietnam frequently lost and China frequently won. From the Song dynasty [Northern Song, 960–1127; Southern Song, 1127–79] onward, however, China frequently lost and Vietnam frequently won. That is why Đinh Tiên Hoàng was able to raise the flag and achieve national independence, and Lý Thường Kiệt advanced as far as Qinzhou (Viet. *Khâm Châu*) and Lianzhou (Viet. *Liêm Châu*, Guangdong Province). Trần Quốc Tuấn then fought the Mongols on the Bạch Đằng River, Lê Thái Tổ commanded his army at Chi Lăng pass [against the Ming], and [Nguyễn] Quang Trung defeated the Qing at Cầu Giấy.[26] All these accomplishments show not only Vietnam's strength but also its difference from China. For approximately three thousand years, China has

---

[26] Lý Thường Kiệt (1019–1105) was a celebrated general during the Lý dynasty who staged a preemptive strike against an anticipated Song (Viet. *Tống*) invasion in 1075. Trần Hưng Đạo (his real name was Trần Quốc Tuấn, 1226–1300) was architect of the two victories against the invading Mongol armies in 1284–85 and in 1287–88. When the Mongols invaded Vietnam for the third time, Trần Hưng Đạo staged an ambush at the Bạch Đằng River, achieving an overwhelming victory. Lê Thái Tổ (his real name was Lê Lợi, 1385–1433) led the Vietnamese in a ten-year resistance against the invading Chinese (Ming) and became the first emperor of the Lê dynasty (r. 1428–33) following its final victory. Chi Lăng was the place where Lê Lợi obtained his biggest victory, killing the general of his enemy Liễu Thăng. Nguyễn Quang Trung (his real name was Nguyễn Huệ, 1753–92) was the youngest of the three Tây Sơn brothers who destroyed the invading Chinese (Qing) army in Đống Đa (Hanoi) in 1789. Though Emperor Quang Trung's reign was brief (1788–93), it was one of the most vigorous eras in Vietnamese history. It is interesting that Phan Châu Trinh named Cầu Giấy as the location of the decisive victory battle, rather than Đống Đa, which is more usual, though the two places are near to one another. It should be noted that French commander Francis Garnier was killed in Cầu Giấy. Thus, is it possible that Phan referred to Cầu Giấy in this case because the location would have resonated with readers as the site of a victory over the French?

considered the question of how to deal with the North of paramount importance. For this reason, ever since the Han and the Tang periods, China's policy has been one of using amity, gold and silk, as the principal means of diplomacy. China also employed military forces to quench rebellions—but, given the time and circumstances, this was nothing unusual. In this way, the Shi (Viet. *Thạch*) clan during the Jin (Viet. *Tấn*) dynasty [265–420] ceded its land and professed to be the descendants of the Northerners, and the Southern Song (Viet. *Nam Tống*) also ceded its land to show its respect for the Jin (Viet. *Kim*), and professed to be the latter's vassals and descendants. All these show China's weakness.

Our country has also attached great importance to the question of how to deal with the North. From the time of the Đinh and the Lê dynasties, therefore, Vietnam's principal approach to diplomacy has been paying tribute and receiving investitures from China. Our country also employed military forces to ward off China's invasions, but, given the time and circumstances, this was nothing unusual.

From the outset, China saw our country as its tributary state or an external vassalage. The kings of early dynasties did not take pride in being invested by China—only the later kings did so. This was Vietnam's strength.

When the traitor minister (Viet. *gian thần*) Hồ Hán Thương[27] ceded our land, and later the usurping Trịnh clan sought secretly to receive investiture from China, these events were of an abnormal nature (Viet. *biến*). These were the causes.

Although China is a large country, it has often suffered under pressure from the North. It does not know how to strengthen itself, entrusting itself to neighbors, and therefore it is not revitalized.[28] Its policy has been one of using amity, gold and silk, as the principal means of diplomacy. Despite its annual expenditure, amounting to several million taels of gold, China is still in big trouble. This is China's mistake.

By comparison, our country is a small country. It has also suffered under pressure from the North and does not know how to strengthen itself. Although it had to pay tributes to, and receive investiture from, China, it never professed itself to be the nephew, niece, or descendant of China. Its annual expenditure was no more than several dozen thousand taels. Though this is a small and negligible amount, Vietnam was able to adopt the strategy of "making friends with a country afar in order to attack a country nearby"[29] (Viet. *viễn giao cận công*)—exerting its full power to the South in order to reduce Champa to nothing, to overtake Chenla, to expand our territory several thousand *li*,[30] and, today, to establish itself firmly as a great country in the South. This is our success that also shows our difference from China.

---

[27] Hồ Hán Thương, son of Hồ Quý Ly (1336–1407), founder of the short-lived Hồ dynasty. Hồ Hán Thương succeeded his father and reigned from 1401 to 1407. To obtain an upper hand against his domestic rivals, Hồ Hán Thương sought to receive investiture from China. Notwithstanding, he was captured in 1407, together with other members of his family, by the Ming and was transported to China. He was killed with his father and his son in Jinling, Nanjing (Viet. *Kim Lăng*, Nam Kinh).

[28] Throughout history, China's borders were not well defined. Within the Chinese tributary system, the countries bordering China were seen as being within its sphere of influence, but were left to determine the defense of their own borders unless they specifically called upon China for assistance and China was willing and able to help.

[29] This strategy is believed to have been devised by Fan Shu (Viet. Phạm Tuy/Huy) of the Qin in the Warring Period in China. Fan Shu once said: "The best strategy is 'allying with a country afar in order to offend a country nearby.'" *Shih chi* (Viet. *Sử ký*), "Fan Shu zhuan." See *Kadokawa Daijiten*, p. 1500.

[30] A measure of length, equivalent to 1,890 feet (more than one-third of a mile).

Further observation reveals the many similarities between our country and China. Nevertheless, within similarities there are differences; and within dissimilarities there are similarities. Without looking into them carefully, one cannot see them.

For example, from ancient times to the present, in China, not one of those [men] who became emperor after unifying the country began his undertaking in the south. Although it was in Kuaiji (Viet. *Cối Kê*, in southeastern China) that Xiang Yu (Viet. Hạng Võ/Vũ) led three thousand followers to raise his flag and prevail in China, he was defeated before unifying the vassal states. The founder of the Ming dynasty, Ming Taizu (Viet. Minh Thái Tổ), also raised his flag in the South and unified China, but within two hundred years[31] his imperial dynasty was lost to the Manchu after all.

In our country, from ancient times to the present, efforts to unify the country all started in the north, not in the south. With respect to Emperor Quang Trung, with an empty hand he raised his flag in Quảng Ngãi[32] and unified our country. But the imperial dynasty he founded collapsed before the completion of a second generation. The founder of the current Nguyễn dynasty also started in the south, unified the country, and became its emperor; but his imperial dynasty did not go beyond one hundred years before we saw its conquest by France.

Above is just a sketch. Let's now consider our country. Because Vietnam received China's literary traditions, it regarded the latter with extraordinary respect and attempted to copy it so excessively that Vietnam lost its own essential character (Viet. *chân tướng*). For example, following the rise of the Qing, who came from the Northern barbarians, the Hans (Viet. *Hán*) and the Manchus have been treated differently. Similarly, because our current [Nguyễn] dynasty came from the South, the South and North have been treated differently. This is an evil that exceeds in evil those who tried to imitate Xi Zi (Viet. Tây Tử) in knitting their brows.[33]

The similarities and dissimilarities, and success and failure, of anti-foreignism versus reliance-on-foreigners in Vietnam and China: Consider China, a country of enormous size and with a population of a hundred million people. It suffered from

---

[31] Actually, the Ming dynasty, which lasted from 1368 to 1644, is considered to have been one of the great eras of orderly government and social stability in Chinese history as well as in human history.

[32] In the present day, it is more acceptable to say that Quang Trung was a native of Tây Sơn village in the mountain area of Bình Định province. Phan Châu Trinh's identification of Quang Trung's birthplace as Quảng Ngãi was not without reason: not long before Phan wrote this piece, the Nguyễn dynasty under Emperor Thành Thái created the mountain defense post (Viet. *sơn phòng*) Nghĩa Định to overlook the mountain region of Quảng Ngãi and Bình Định. See Đào Duy Anh, *Đất nước Việt Nam qua các đời* [Vietnam through Successive Dynasties] (Huế: Nxb Thuận Hoá, 1996), pp. 210–11.

[33] More commonly known as Xi Shi (Viet. Tây Thi), a famous beauty in China during the fifth century, BCE. An account of this episode may be found in *Zhuangzi*, "Tianyun." Burton Watson translated this passage as follows: Xi Shi, "troubled with heartburn, frowned at her neighbors. An ugly woman of the neighborhood, seeing that Xi Shi was beautiful, went home and likewise pounded her breast and frowned at her neighbors. But at the sight of her, the rich men of the neighborhood shut tight their gates and would not venture out, while the poor men grabbed their wives and children by the hand and scampered off." "The Turning of Heaven," in *The Complete Works of Chuang Tzu*, trans. Burton Watson (New York, NY: Columbia University Press, 1968), pp. 160–61. The episode is used to allude to those who slavishly try to imitate another person, including his or her bad habits, and therefore fail to accomplish the result expected.

[the aggressions of] the Northern barbarians. Having no choice, it even had to marry its princesses to them. In our country, the Trần dynasty also married one of its princesses to the king of Champa, but this was because it wanted to acquire the latter's land, and not because it had no choice.

In any case, every year China had to pay tribute, spending as much as several million taels on gold and silk. Nonetheless, China was still conquered by the Jin, the Mongols, and the Manchus. The Song (Viet. *Tống*) dynasty was also under great pressure from the Northern barbarians. Consider Kou Zhun's (Viet. Khấu Chuẩn) feat in Danyuan (Viet. *Đàn Uyên*),[34] and Yue Fei's (Viet. Nhạc Phi) drunken cup of victory in Huanglong (Viet. *Hoàng Long*).[35] Can they be compared with Trần Hưng Đạo's accomplishment on the Bạch Đằng River, or Emperor Lê Thái Tổ's exploit at Chi Lăng, or Emperor Quang Trung's daring battle at Cầu Giấy?[36] Fu Bi (Viet. Phú Bật)[37] was an envoy of a supreme state (Viet. *thượng quốc*), but was unable to take advantage of the influence of China's victory to subdue the enemy, and as a result he lost a thousand taels of gold and silk in order to acquire recognition of his tribute. Such stupidity in diplomacy was horrendous. Can all these be compared with Mạc Đĩnh Chi of our country, who dared to destroy the painting scroll to humiliate the Northerners?[38]

---

[34] Kou Zhun (Viet. Khấu Chuẩn; 961–1023) was high minister in the Northern Song (Viet. *Bắc Tống*). His pen name was Pingzhong (Viet. Bình Trọng) or Zhongmin (Viet. Trung Mẫn). Danyuan is a prefecture in Henan (Viet. *Hà Nam*). During the Zhenzong era (Viet. *Chân Tông*; 998–1022), he defeated the Qiedan (Viet. *Khiết Đan*), but jealous of Wang Qinruo (Viet. Vương Khâm Nhược), he quit his official position. Later on, he reentered public service and became a high minister. He was appointed Laiquogong (Viet. *Lai Quốc Công*). See *Song shi* (Viet. *Tống sử*), "Kou Zhun zhuan," *Kadokawa Daijiten*, p. 493.

[35] Yue Fei (Viet. Nhạc Phi; 1103–42) was a famous high minister of the Southern Song (Viet. *Nam Tống*). He was born in Tangyin (Viet. *Thang Âm*) county of Henan (Viet. *Hà Nam*) province, and his pen name was Pengju (Viet. Bằng Cử). For his loyalist service, he was given the flag displaying four large characters "*Jingzhong Yue Fei*" (Yue Fei—An Absolute Loyalist) by Emperor Gaozong (Viet. Cao Tông). From time to time, Yue Fei achieved victories against the Jin. His allegiances were thus opposed to Qin Hui (Viet. Tần Cối), and for this he was arrested and died in prison. His writings were edited and published in *Yuewu muji* (Viet. *Nhạc Vũ mục tập*; The Collected Works of Yue Fei). See *Song shi*, "Yue Fei zhuan," *Kadokawa Daijiten*, p. 529. Huanglong (Viet. *Hoàng Long*) was the name of a small country that belonged to the Tartars.

[36] See previous note in the same chapter.

[37] Fu Bi (1004–83) was a famed minister of the Northern Song. His pen name was Yanguo (Viet. Nhan Quốc). During the reign of Emperor Yingzong (Viet. Anh Tông), he did not get along well with Wang Anshi (Viet. Vương An Thạch), and he finished his life in obscurity. See *Song shi*, "Fu Bi zhuan," *Kadokawa Daijiten*, p. 495.

[38] Mạc Đĩnh Chi (1280–1350) was a renowned scholar who was the highest-scoring graduate (Viet. *trạng nguyên*) in the palace examinations when he was only twenty-four years old. He served three emperors—Anh Tông, Minh Tông, and Hiến Tông of the Trần dynasty—and was twice dispatched as envoy to the Chinese court. It is said that when he was sent to China as an envoy, one day he was invited to an official reception at the residence of the prime minister of the Yuan dynasty. On the wall of the hallway of the residence, there was an embroidered picture depicting a sparrow standing on a bamboo branch. Thinking that it was a real sparrow, Mạc came near the wall and was about to catch the bird. The prime minister and the rest of the company all burst into laughter. Not to be humiliated, Mạc quickly took down the embroidery from the wall. When asked why he dared to do so at such a formal reception, Mạc explained: "The bamboo tree is a symbol of a man of complete virtue [Viet. *quân tử*], and the sparrow is a symbol of a mean man [Viet. *tiểu nhân*]. How is it possible to see a work of art in Your Excellency's residence that has a mean man standing atop a man of complete virtue?

In light of the above, the answer must be clear concerning the question "Between our people or the Chinese people, who is fitter and more successful?" Nonetheless, following our country's absorption of Chinese civilization, we have tried to adopt everything Chinese. We were not selective in our adoption, making no distinction between the good and the evil. Even in examinations, which were designed to select the literati (Viet. *sĩ*), the questions for the major composition (Viet. *văn sách*) were mainly about historical events in China, with only very few questions touching on our national history—not to speak of the questions related to the classics and commentary (Viet. *kinh truyện*). For this reason, our students vied with one another to study Chinese history without paying attention to our national history. The impact of the legacy of this error is enormous, and the obsession is so deeply rooted that students in our country have copied and memorized exhaustively not only the names of the affairs and the people in China, but also its geographical names, names of mountains, rivers, villages, and streets, that are not worth knowing at all. In the meantime, when asked about the names of our country's national heroes, historical sites, high mountains, and big rivers, they simply open their eyes widely and cannot respond. They have thus lost their original traits. Occasionally, they see themselves as Chinese and boastfully consider themselves civilized.[39] But they are so insecure, just like a lamb hidden underneath the skin of a leopard, or a shrimp disguised as a crab.

* * *

More than sixty years have elapsed since the beginning of the interactions between Vietnam and France; during the process, Vietnam became a French protectorate (Viet. *bảo hộ*). Yet the learned world, above and below, has degenerated to the extremes, and the people's minds have been helplessly poisoned. For example, Nguyễn Trứ in Phú Yên and remnants of the Taiping Rebellion (Viet. *Thái Bình Thiên Quốc*) in Bắc Kỳ were able to employ amulets to deceive the people because they could take advantage of the people's weakness.

A critical situation was about to explode at any time. Those who aspired to save the country quickly became concerned about the precarious conditions. Confused by the current trends and handicapped by their lack of knowledge, they could not, however, find the way.

Ever since the translations of Western books were imported to our country, the elite people began to be aware of the dominant trends in the world and the critical future of our people. Covered over by the scholarship of the civil-service examinations (Viet. *khoa cử*), the time-honored great national traits and the shining spiritual qualities (Viet. *linh chất*) were hiding themselves inside and could not develop to endure independently. These traits and qualities bordered on the fringe of perishing, yet no one realized it. One day, all of a sudden, those who aspired to save the country were awakened from confusion and were able to see the blue sky beyond

---

That is why I took it down from the wall." The Chinese hosts had to agree that Mạc had made a good case.

[39] Apparently, Phan Châu Trinh is speaking in cultural terms. Although the Vietnamese did closely identify with the culture and civilization of China, they always distinguished themselves as a separate ethnic group.

the clouds and fogs—just like coming from a dark room and seeing the sun and the moon. What a delightful feeling!

Because the impact of the legacy of the error is enormous and the obsession is so deep-rooted, and because they had just escaped from the abyss, their souls were not settled. It is like a prisoner who has been chained down for a long time; upon coming out from prison, he has to lean on the people around him because his legs are still badly shaking. Or like a naïve farmer from a remote village who, upon entering a city, cannot tell what is real and what is unreal. He has to make sure about everything with the passers-by. Now he feels joyful, now he feels sad. He is incredulous and is plunged in deep reverie and silent meditation.

It is indeed impossible to describe and characterize the mental state of our people of the present day. Given the time and the circumstances, the questions of life-or-death and the success or failure of the nation are at a critical stage—like a heavy weight hanging by a hair. A few men of high purpose (Viet. *chí sĩ*) are being entrusted to envision the [country's] future direction and provide guidance for the people. But unlike the time of the changing of the guard, when the new age uneventfully replaced the old, at present those who are thoroughly versed in the affairs of the time are very few, but the stubborn are many.

In the eyes of the civil-service scholars (Viet. *bát cổ gia*), whose minds have not been rid of all contamination and deviation, the curious spectacle of the world appears and changes so quickly, like a kaleidoscope. These people are neither astute nor incompetent. Intoxicated, they have made nonsensical appeals—neither innovative nor old-fashioned.

All of a sudden, the shock wave from the news of the Russo-Japanese War shook the world like a bolt from the blue. It became a driving force behind China's modernization, the impact of which in turn shook our entire country; all movements and parties were thereby initiated.

At the outset, there was only one party. Phan Bội Châu at first advocated violence (Viet. *bạo động*). I rebutted that position when he and I met in the imperial city (Huế) in the Year of the Hare (1903). We worked together at first to rally the graduates who had succeeded at the preliminary examination (Viet. *cống sĩ*)[40] to petition for the abolition of the civil-service examinations and call for political reform. In support of this cause, Võ Phương Trứ[41] and I did our best for several days. The literati at the time, however, had not been awakened from the illusion of the examinations, and only a few responded to our call. Because Phan Bội Châu did not pass the metropolitan examinations, he did not wish to sign the petition, and the attempt finally came to an end. Phan Bội Châu soon left for Japan, and since that time the party has been divided into two. That was the first time that he and I came to know one another.

I realized at the first meeting with Phan Bội Châu that his knowledge is not sufficient, though he is courageous and has a strong will, along with a dogged and robust self-confidence. Because, at the time, writing in the civil-service examination

---

[40] Those who passed the provincial examinations and became *cử nhân* degree holders were called *cống sĩ*.

[41] According to Nguyễn Q. Thắng, Võ Phương Trứ (1870– ?) was a native of Mỹ Duệ, Cẩm Xuyên prefecture, Hà Tĩnh province. Võ was a *cử nhân* graduate, having passed the provincial examination (*thi hương*) in Nghệ An in 1897. He was not successful, however, in the metropolitan examination. See Nguyễn Q. Thắng, ed., *Phan Châu Trinh: Cuộc đời và tác phẩm* [Phan Châu Trinh: His Life and Works] (Hanoi: Nxb Văn Học, 2001), p. 388.

style was in vogue, he was most celebrated and was widely admired by the literati all over the country. Therefore, [I thought,] collaborating with him to appeal to the people inside the country must bring success. If he were allowed to go overseas [to gain support for revolution], he would destroy my vision [of democracy and self-reliance]. I therefore did my best to work with him. Phan Bội Châu also realized that I was able to destroy his vision, so he also tried his best to solicit me. The relationship between him and me thus began. Afterward, I paid no attention to suspicion and neglected danger. At times, I went as far as overseas. At times, I dissolved my party inside the country.[42] At first, the relationship was one of friendship. At the end, it was one of enmity. There was a time when I joined his party; there was also a time I left his party to stay outside. It was changeable and impossible to tell the difference. On those counts, I was ignorant and silly, and therein lay my agony. The cause that led to my failure and to my being buried alive without a chance for survival was also there.

In the next phase, the party was divided into two: one was the Revolutionary Party (Viet. *Cách mạng đảng*) and the other was the Self-rule Party (Viet. *Tự trị đảng*). Members of the two parties kept changing their affiliations; at first some might have been superior to others, but later the former might become junior to the latter. It was thus difficult to draw the dividing line between the two parties, and disputes between them were incessant. Every action must be well focused; every undertaking must be launched in advance. Related information must be analyzed carefully by clear-sighted persons, otherwise things cannot be understood. At present, because of the insurrection and the mutiny, many people have been murdered or sent to prisons.

With respect to my activities and my failure, it was hoped that the high ministers of the two countries would carry out a thorough investigation. I have requested various offices to do so, but none has done it. The suspicion about me thus has not been cleared. Not surprisingly, a big net was cast, and every single suspect was imprisoned. This unprecedented tragedy is still going on at present, involving many innocent people.

Now, the insurrection has been settled, and the cases in court have been made public. Remedial measures for reform have also been carried out. Questions related to the principles of the two parties have not been resolved. Take, for example: "Which party is right and which party is wrong?" "Who should be commended and who should be punished?" "Who has been punished appropriately and who has been punished on a false charge?" No distinction has been made between the innocent and the guilty. All have been treated indiscriminately as discontented (Viet. *bất đắc chí*) elements, or the whole event has been considered as a coordinated movement from both within and without the country. Men of high purpose are about to perish in remote mountains and on a distant island: if the charge is grave, they are executed, if the charge is light, they are imprisoned. The ignorant common people, in the meantime, must swallow their tears.

---

[42] When Phan Châu Trinh discusses parties, he is not referring to formalized bodies, but to groups of people who share the same views.

Although I was favored with release, I am placed in a corner under surveillance.[43] My activities are being watched, and I cannot speak from the bottom of my heart. I feel ashamed for having offended my late friend.

My late friend is Dr. Trần Quý Cáp, an erudite scholar and also a man of principle. He looked on the advocacy of violence with unconcealed aversion. He wrote an essay entitled "[A Scholar's] Argumentation for Self-rule" (Viet. [*Sĩ phu] tự trị luận*) to rebut Phan Bội Châu. For unknown reasons, he was murdered in Khánh Hòa.[44] Alas! How lamentable it is!

I have no means to justify myself to our people. I had advised people in my province to build many primary schools and agricultural societies (Viet. *Nông phố hội*). But I heard that, after the insurrection, wherever there were schools and agricultural societies, local soldiers came to occupy them and harassed people. Inside the country, I am suspected by officials of the two countries—the French and Vietnamese officials consider members of my party as rebels (Viet. *ngược tặc*). Outside the country, the opposite party is laughing at me. In Hong Kong, during my return to Vietnam from Japan, Phan Bội Châu said to me: "In the future, if the undertaking proves unsuccessful, please remember my words." Looking at heaven and earth, I cannot forgive myself. Left alone, I am alive but I am useless.

Alas! To whom can I reveal my agony? Between Hades and Heaven, is it true that the only people who understand me are progressive peoples in Europe? That is to say, those French people who treasure chivalry, justice, philanthropy, and equality? I wish to remain silent, but how is it possible to say nothing?

THE TRUE STATE OF THE TWO PARTIES

All discourses on political parties in Vietnam at present focus on the true state (Viet. *chân tướng*) of the movements inside and outside the country. Those who were involved in the movement have been indiscriminately treated as discontented elements: their daily activities are not worthwhile activities, and their personalities are not worthwhile personalities. For this reason, there has been no careful observation and objective analysis of these figures. Generalized and vague terms have been used to refer to them, such as "shameless" or "disreputable," etc. Thus, when grasses are cut or animals are hunted, none is left.

Nonetheless, an ant hill can lead to the collapse of a dam, and by gathering feathers one might break an axle. Thus, even though certain factors might be minor, they must not be overlooked because they might produce a crucial impact on the outcome of the Franco–Vietnamese alliance, on the life-or-death future of the Vietnamese people, or on the success or failure of the ongoing policy. If the regulations are made stricter, many things will be entrusted to deliberation by the officials, without paying attention to the animosity felt by the literati. The situation thus will be pressed to become extreme, and many will disperse and risk danger to go overseas. The root of the problem has not yet been eradicated, but in the meantime [the violent] party has a chance to kick up its heels. I heard that this time,

---

[43] This is one of the two clues that help to date this work: Phan Châu Trinh was kept in Mỹ Tho city, located in the Mekong delta, after his release from Poulo Condore Island in June 1910 and prior to his departure for France in March 1911.

[44] At this point, Phan Châu Trinh had not heard about the details of Trần Quý Cáp's murder. He soon learned them before he left for France.

to avoid imprisonment and execution, the number of people who have fled abroad is extremely high, though their names are not known yet. The cause of the problem is deep-rooted, but the consequence has been fully revealed. This time the insurrection occurred only on a small scale!

When a container is empty and water outside the container is full, the water will leak in wherever there is a hole. I heard that after the recent insurrection, the literati inside the country all kept their mouths bound and only the [Phan Bội Châu's] ex-patriot party was able to express its opposition thanks to the freedom of expression. Now that its members are returning to the country, they have an enormous advantage and an extremely lucid argument. When an opportunity arises, the leak might be dealt with, but when something is under pressure for a long time, it will necessarily erupt when given the opportunity. Today, half of our people have been silenced, but the field fire has not been extinguished; thus, when the spring breeze blows, it will revive. So no one knows for sure about the disastrous aftermath.

Quietly contemplating the past to envision the future, I see our country is facing a critical moment. I feel the danger [to myself], but I dare not remain silent. I will now therefore be dealing with the contents of the political positions (Viet. *chủ nghĩa*), the arrangements (Viet. *bố trí*), and the policies (Viet. *phương châm*) of the two parties. I will also be talking about the personality of the founders, the reasons for the division, and the history of the arrangements of the so-called two groups inside and outside of the country—thus providing the authorities with all information for their scrutiny.

Now, let us divide the national movement into two parties. At that point [early 1905], they were in practice not parties, to be precise, but rather were two competing positions. One was the Revolutionary Party, and the other was the Self-rule Party.

The Revolutionary Party was founded by Phan Bội Châu, and the Self-rule Party by me, Phan Châu Trinh. Because Phan Bội Châu first created the Revolutionary Party outside the country, it has two components, one inside and one outside of the country. The Self-rule Party does not have inside and outside components. I am a native of Quảng Nam province, and in the province I was its leader, and there is no one [in my party] who has gone overseas. I heard that when the insurrection broke out, because Trần Quý Cáp was murdered, some of his disciples went overseas.

The two parties were rooted in their different positions. As their branches, there were two [auxiliary] parties: The Revolution Support Party (Viet. *Cách mạng Phù hội đảng*) and the Self-rule Support Party (Viet. *Tự trị Phù hội đảng*). At the beginning, these two parties had no entrenched political doctrines and no arrangements. But the party that notoriously practiced deception on people to collect money, causing damage to them, was the Revolution Support Party. In contrast, members of the Self-rule Support Party did no more than debate with one another cheerfully, but, unfortunately, this party had to endure calamities. Nonetheless, in retrospect, the mutiny this time was carried out following the script found in Phan Bội Châu's books, which thoroughly manifests his political position. With respect to the induction of local soldiers (Viet. *lính tập*), see his *History of the Loss of Vietnam* (Viet. *Việt Nam vong quốc sử*), and with respect to the induction of the paramilitary (Viet. *dân binh*), see his *A Letter Written in Blood from Overseas* (Viet. *Hải ngoại huyết thư*). I was inside the country at the time and was considered one of its [the mutiny's] instigators.

The authorities of the two countries responded by arresting members of the party inside the country without missing a single person. It was impossible to do anything to those outside as they were beyond the reach of the law. In short, Phan Bội Châu was the driving force behind these events, and he is the key person. The handling of Phan Bội Châu is the most crucial question at present. Now, I would like to speak about Phan Bội Châu, along with his views and his tactics.

Phan Bội Châu is a person of unparalleled will, power, energy, patience, and audacity. Once he believes in something, he adheres to it and never abandons it. Even thunder cannot change his mind. He advocated a policy of violence, which was refuted by me several times, so he did not like to be in my company. In the Year of the Cat (1903), he came to look for me at my boarding house in Huế after we had met one another twice, but I was away. In Hong Kong, when he and I were engaged in a debate, he ran out of argument and just cried. I hold him dearly because of that. There is no scholar in our country with comparable qualities. Regrettably, besides having shallow knowledge, he is ignorant of world trends and is fond of using intrigues, fooling himself and the people. He is also stubborn and is not willing to alter his views. Being thoroughly conservative, he adamantly refuses to read New Books. The books he wrote, therefore, are not based on reasoning and pay no attention to world trends. In these books, at times he deliberately curses people, at times he weeps bitterly. His writings are, as a matter of fact, molded by the eight-legged compositions (Viet. *văn chương bát cổ biến tướng*), which are not worth a penny. Nonetheless, they fit well with the level and temperament of our people, and therefore mislead them. He talks big, incomparably. He entraps people into fatal actions, without realizing that he has become notorious. I heard that in the present insurrection and the mutiny, it was just as if he were the murderer. Not only does France consider him a rebel, but the civil law (Viet. *dân luật*) of Vietnam would also define him as a rebel on the basis of his crimes against the public (Viet. *công tội*). He would have no way to deny that charge. Nonetheless, he is still querulously saying that he is a patriot. What extreme stupidity! From now on, he will be saying that even louder. This time, I was suspected from the outset as well, because of my record of association with Phan Bội Châu.

Now, in the following lines, I would like to present his motives and his arrangements, along with the motives and the arrangements that I have made to oppose his policy.

The commitment to revenge advocated persistently by Phan Bội Châu is both erroneous and extreme. It only entraps our people. It goes against world trends and does not follow reason. However, without knowing his personality and the reasons behind his exploitation of the people, one cannot see clearly the path that led me to oppose him consistently.

Phan Bội Châu is the person who exemplifies our national traits (Viet. *tập quán dân tộc*), shaped throughout the history of the Vietnamese people over the last millennium. If one does not know the real nature of the Vietnamese, just look at him. Our people have abundant anti-foreignism, and in him, anti-foreignism reaches an extreme. Our people like to rely on foreigners, and in him, reliance on foreigners goes to extremes. Our people lack the spirit of independence, and in him, this lack is even more conspicuous. His dispositions and standards fit well to the dispositions and standards of our people. He thus makes use of the strengths and weaknesses of our people. This is the so-called "using a weakness to one's advantage" (Viet. *tắc nhân tắc dụng*) strategy.

What he is concerned about is that the resentment among our people against France is not deep enough. The books he wrote do not discuss world trends and do not deal with the merits and demerits of various matters. He makes up things out of nowhere to deceive himself and other people. For example, in *History of the Loss of Vietnam* he talks about "the sale of Heaven" (Viet. *mại thiên*);[45] and, by and large, the arguments in his book are written in that vein. In short, all he is calling for is malicious feelings among the people. Waiting until those feelings have been implanted in the people's minds and rebellions break out everywhere, he will eventually take advantage of the situation to satisfy his penchant for destruction.

It is not that he does not know it is impossible to carry out a revolution, but that he can't help but take advantage of our people's stupidity, i.e., their anti-foreignism. It is not that he is unaware that Japan cannot do much, but that he can't help but take advantage of our people's weakness, i.e., the penchant for relying on foreigners. That our people have followed him blindly, even to death, without realizing that they have been used, is because their deeply rooted penchant is similar to his. His inclination and tactics are as described.

Those who do not know Phan Bội Châu therefore would say that he is totally an ignorant person, without realizing that he is making use of the ignorance of the people to manifest his cleverness and that he is making use of the weakness of the people proudly to display his strength. Alas! If he did that without being aware of their ignorance and their weakness, it would be forgivable. But being aware of their ignorance and their weakness, and of the fact that they were outmatched by the colonial power, he still makes use of them to fulfill his ambitions! Where is his mind? Nonetheless, from his side, he would have different words to say.

Later generations should know the evil of the civil-service scholarship, an evil that is sufficient to ruin the family and the nation. He [Phan Bội Châu] has not detached himself from the impact of this scholarship, but has now molded himself into a new appearance, leading the nation to an unprecedented act of genocide. Otherwise, why is it that he professes himself to be a man of high purpose (Viet. *chí sĩ*), or a farsighted leader (Viet. *tiên giác*) of the people? In the meantime, while standing in an entirely safe place, he had dynamite and explosives thrown randomly at blind folks and children, separating people's necks and legs without showing a bit of sympathy.

Why is it that I was his friend? This is because during the time of the civil-service examinations, he was admired by most people in our country. I met him in 1903, at the Metropolitan Examinations (Viet. *thi hội*). He was also a proud and courageous man who dared to risk his life. I came into contact with him in order to talk over national affairs to see if things might work out between us. During the discussion, he advocated for his conviction. I rebutted him, exhaustively analyzing the merits and demerits, strengths and weaknesses, of both positions. At the time, he also considered my advocacy for reform and self-rule (Viet. *biến pháp tự trị*) to be sound.

---

[45] In *History of the Loss of Vietnam*, there is a section on taxes under French rule that tells a story as follows: People of a village asked the French for help with the "head tax," and they were told to sell their families and their properties to earn the money to pay these taxes. The villagers cried, saying: "We have sold wives and children, houses, and rice fields. There is only Heaven that we have not sold!" The French laughed and said: "Well, you have not sold Heaven, so you can write it on the paper and sell it to me." People wrote it on a piece of paper, and they were asked to sign underneath. They soon found that it was very dark if they stayed inside their houses, but they could not get out of their houses because they had sold Heaven. See Văn Tạo et al., ed., *Những tác phẩm của Phan Bội Châu*, tập 1: *Việt Nam vong quốc sử, Việt Nam quốc sử khảo* [Phan Bội Châu's Works, vol. 1: History of the Loss of Vietnam and Study in Vietnam's National History] (Hà Nội: Nxb Khoa học Xã hội, 1982), pp. 100–03.

Why is it that I was his friend? Because he is a proud and courageous man who dares to risk his life. His sense of self-confidence is most powerful. I have not seen another Vietnamese who could be compared with him. These are his strengths. Yet he is man of empty pride and obstinacy, who indiscreetly shows his self-satisfaction. Ignorant about world trends, he has the nerve to murder people (Viet. *cẩm ư sát nhân*), seeing all others as less valuable than he is (Viet. *thị nhân giai mạc kỷ*). These are his weaknesses. In addition, during the time of the civil-service examinations, he was most celebrated, while I was considered to be ignorant and a lunatic (Viet. *ngu cuồng*), and no one knew me. He advocates violence, but I believe in "holding on to France and looking for independence" (Viet. *trì Pháp tự lập*). When I discussed [these matters] with him, I analyzed exhaustively the merits and demerits, along with the strengths and weaknesses, of both positions, and he also saw that my position was sound. I met him for the first time at the Metropolitan Examinations in 1903. At first glance, I recognized that he is a vigorous (Viet. *hữu vi*) intellectual, but after debating with him, I found his defect. I then tried to work together with him to rally the literati in petitioning for the abolition of the civil-service examinations. He also agreed to it. When Võ Phương Trứ and I did our best for that cause for several days, and when we were about to achieve the objective, Phan Bội Châu failed the examination and was not willing to sign. Other literati also refused to sign, because at the time they trusted him. Võ Phương Trứ also failed the examination.

I therefore wished to make friends with Phan Bội Châu in order to make use of his name and his strengths, and to overcome his weaknesses, in the hope [that we would be able] to petition the French government for improvements to the people's conditions. Moreover, realizing that I was the only individual who could destroy his political position, he did his best to ally with me. I also realized that he was able to destroy my political position, so I did my best to ally with him. In this way, we started off as friends, but subsequently we have become enemies.

Why is it that Phan Bội Châu went overseas? According to what he said at the time, he did not have a political conviction yet. But he knew then that if he were to adhere to his conviction and fight against France, his forces would be outmatched by the French and he would surely perish. If he were to cling to France while looking for Vietnam's independence, the French would not tolerate him and he would surely perish. If he were to perish, he would like to perish according to the way that he believed. He therefore did his best to advocate violence without regret.

He then heard that the French authorities were about to arrest him as punishment [for his political actions]. In 1903, they wanted to arrest him twice. The first time, they arrested, questioned, and released him. The second time, they wanted to arrest him but could not catch him. These are true stories. He realized that, being a proud man, he could not put up with the humiliation and he would surely die. He thus wished to make a getaway, but at the beginning he did not know where to go. Upon hearing the news of the Russo–Japanese War, he was all of a sudden inspired with the penchant for anti-foreignism and for relying on foreigners. Precisely at that time, Tăng Bạt Hổ[46] returned from overseas. Tăng guided him [Phan Bội Châu] abroad. He then did his best to cause damage to the French, taking no heed of their

---

[46] Tăng Bạt Hổ, 1858–1906. A native of Bình Định province, Tăng Bạt Hổ participated in the Loyalist Movement in his home province. Working as a sailor on foreign merchant ships, he had been to China, Siam, Japan, and Russia before acting as a guide for Phan Bội Châu in the latter's first voyage to Japan in 1905.

power. He said that he, in fact, went abroad in the Fourth Month of the Year of the Dragon (1904).[47]

Why is it that I followed him to go abroad? At the beginning, when I heard that he had gone abroad, I thought that he had no choice but to go, as there was no place for him to hide inside the country, so he had to go abroad, and, such being the circumstances, everyone else thought so, too. Nonetheless, it is appropriate if one goes abroad to promote study overseas, or to promote the idea of "clinging to France and looking for Vietnam's independence." But why did he have to promote violence? When I read his book *History of the Loss of Vietnam*, I found that he is foolish and irrational, and I realized that his initial violent penchant had not died down. But I still thought that it was because he had been fooled by the influence of the civil-service examinations at home that he came to promote violence, and now that he had gone abroad, he would broaden his knowledge, deepen his scholarship, and he would change his illusions about anti-foreignism and relying on foreigners. When I read the misleading books that he sent back to the country from overseas, I realized that he still maintained his political resolution to carry out cruel activities and manifest his penchant [for violence]. The Vietnamese people are, however, not a single entity.

I am conscious of the fact that Phan Bội Châu's conviction is extremely weak in its rationales, but when it is applied to the Vietnamese people, it will unite them and become extremely powerful. His conviction will certainly triumph (Viet. *tất thắng*). In contrast, my conviction is extremely strong in its rationales, but when it is applied to the Vietnamese people, owing to their national traits and the current circumstances, it will become exceedingly weak. His conviction is especially suitable to the proclivities and the intellectual level of our people, making use of their strengths. Living abroad, he enjoys the freedom of speech, and it is easy for people to follow him. This is why his conviction will triumph. My conviction, on the other hand, is contradictory (Viet. *tương phản*) as it relates to the proclivities and the intellectual level of our people. I have tried to save our people from their weakness. In addition, at the time, I was inside the country, subject to the control of the authorities and the focus of suspicion. Since my activities and speech were not free, it was difficult for the people to follow me. My endeavors thus will certainly fail (Viet. *tất bại*). That I risked my life to go abroad secretly was because I wanted to take up a position against him [Phan Bội Châu] in order to refute his ignorance and to rebut his illusion. I hoped that he would feel sorry for the people so he might change his position. I thus told him about the sacrifice and suffering of the people. I hoped that he might be persuaded by our mutual friendly feelings in the past. I also hoped he might not oppose and destroy my endeavor because of the warm feelings he had had for me. Without saying anything, he was unyielding and obstinately adhered to his conviction—remaining unmoved by human sacrifice. I then bade farewell to him on foreign soil. I did not look back and returned to our homeland. He did what he believed in, and I did what I believed in. From then on, the party was divided into two, and the two opposing positions emerged.

---

[47] In *Ngục trung thư* (Prison Diaries), Phan Bội Châu indicated that, since he planned first to travel to Japan via China, he left Quảng Nam for Hải Phòng on the second day of the First Month of the Year of the Snake (February 7, 1905). He arrived in Kôbe, Japan, in the last decade of the Fourth Month of the same year, i.e., late May or early June, 1905. See *Overturned Chariot: The Autobiography of Phan Bội Châu*, trans. Vinh Sinh and Nicholas Wickenden (Honolulu, HI: SHAPS Library of Translation, University of Hawai'i Press), p. 84.

Why is it that I did not stay abroad to promote overseas study? My resolution was to ally with France. I encouraged the youth to go abroad to study, but the French did not employ them upon their return, therefore, although the students had completed their study, they were not allowed to help the country. That is the first reason. In addition, the Vietnamese had just awakened from their reverie, and their intellectual level was not developed. Those who were wealthy did not necessarily have conviction; those who had conviction were not necessarily wealthy. Even if one wished to rally those who had conviction and those who were wealthy to work together so that they might help the cause, in the first place, the accommodating wealthy would not dare to give their money—much less [could one expect assistance from] those unwilling to participate. Even if they gave money, should the undertaking fail one day, misfortune would come to the wealthy: not only would they lose their money, but also they would be implicated in misfortune. Even if it meant dying, I would never do anything that might implicate others. That is the second reason. Thus, it is not that I did not advocate overseas study, but my position was as described—that this should be done after the formation of a Franco-Vietnamese alliance.

Why is it that I did not stay abroad to promote a Franco-Vietnamese alliance? A man of high purpose should not fear death. I had a conviction, and I would put it into practice and risk my life for it. Now, if I escaped to go abroad in order to avoid death and chose to promote my conviction afterward, who would then trust me enough to follow me? That is the first reason. As a promoter of a Franco-Vietnamese alliance, if I escaped to go abroad to avoid death, then all men who saw themselves to be "men of high purpose" would follow in my steps to go abroad. Who would then remain in the country to plan for the alliance? That is the second reason. In addition, the French are highly skeptical; they would not have trusted and tolerated those who stayed outside of the country and called for such an alliance; they even wanted to murder those within the country. That is the third reason. That was why I returned to the country and did not stay abroad.

Again, there is another crucial question that must be clarified here. That is the question of whether or not I am contented with myself. With respect to Phan Bội Châu, people held that he ran away to Japan because he was discontented with his failure in the examinations. (That everyone said that Phan Bội Châu called for revolution because he was discontented with himself was wrong. Even if the French put him into an important position (Viet. *trọng dụng*), he would not necessarily accede to it. That is his temperament.)

As I resigned my official position in the imperial capital and promoted the New Books (Viet. *Tân thư*), I was also one of those who were discontented with themselves. From my childhood until my adulthood, from the time I attended school until the time I passed the examinations and became an official, there was no one who knew me. There was no single moment I was happy with myself. At home, I expressed my indignation with the world of that time, and my brother and sister thought that I was ignorant and idiotic. When I grew up and attended school, I wrote compositions in which I expressed my indignation. (Generally, when I wrote compositions, I paid no attention to the eight-legged format. My poetry and rhyming compositions all sprang up from my indignation.) My teachers also thought that I was ignorant and idiotic. From the time I passed the examinations and became an official, I was all the more indignant with the world. The Minister and my colleagues either assumed that I was ignorant and idiotic, or asked why I was so ignorant and idiotic. I did not care and only laughed and accepted it.

That was the reality, so far as I was concerned, at the time I was taking the civil-service examinations. Then came the time when I began to read the New Books, which were given to me by Đào Nguyên Phổ in the Year of the Tiger, i.e., 1902. So delighted, I said: "This is the time that the ignorant and the idiotic may be useful! If I were to put my ignorant and idiotic conviction into action, who can be certain that it will not be of some use to our people?"

In any case, at present what makes people successful is not their professional training or their talent in politics and law. I was working at the Ministry of Rites for two years, I was aware of the techniques, the capabilities, and the glory of other people. I know them all, and it was not that I could not copy them. But this was not what I aspired to achieve. Not only did I not gain or receive pleasure from joining officialdom, but also I took pleasure in being a prisoner. I would rather be tied up in restraint on an island on the high seas far away from the people of my village, flogged by a whip, and spit on and reviled. I did not wish to profess myself as being successful by riding on a chariot, keeping concubines, or proudly boasting to friends. For this reason, all the Vietnamese have considered me to be an ignorant and idiotic fellow, who tried to imitate the French and examined the French ideas of philanthropy and equality but could not put them into practice.

Nonetheless, at present, all judgments concerning merits and demerits are made on the basis of whether or not the person is successful or unsuccessful. No wonder the successful rose up to the highest Heavens (Viet. *Cửu thiên*), and the unsuccessful fell down to "the Abyss" (Viet. *Cửu uyên*) and until now have not received any helping hand. I have no choice but to say that!

What were the excuses that Phan Bội Châu used to promote revolution? He said: "At present, the French rule is so oppressive. They look down on us and humiliate us. They take advantage of the ignorance of our people to use us. The only recourse left for me is death. Now that I am in revolt against the French, they will not tolerate me. My power will stand no comparison to that of the French—such being the case, I will then perish. If I argue for 'working within the French system for self-rule,' they will not necessarily be pleased hearing that, but will suppress me. I will not submit myself to them, and I will also perish. Whatever I do I will perish, and I would rather follow my conviction to conduct violent action in order to appease my current indignation. If lucky, I may be successful. If I fail, it will not be too late for me to die then!"

Did he not realize the ignorance of the people and care about their deaths? He would certainly say: "The people from the outset are ignorant. The French took advantage of that and made them even more ignorant. In the world of the present day, to be ignorant is to perish. If we continue to be idle spectators, the French will take advantage of our ignorance in order to bring us misfortune. So why shouldn't we adopt that very strategy, taking advantage of the ignorance of our people to bring misfortune to the French?" His idea was that, rather than perishing because of the ignorance of the French, it would be better for the people to perish because of his ignorance and by his hand.

Alas! His aspiration and the means that he adopted are as [described] above. In these, there was no concern for a balance of strengths versus weaknesses, wisdom versus ignorance. Neither did he pay attention to the dominant trends in the world. He exhausted all possible means to provoke the French, such as throwing a countless number of sticks of dynamite on innocent crowds, causing bloodshed among children. The dead bodies were piling up, yet he still regretted that the deaths caused by the dynamite were not sufficient [to provoke the French]. In the time to come, the venomous seeds sown by him will [sprout and] reach an unprecedented level.

Did I not realize that by promoting "working within the French system for self-rule," I would be met with misfortune and perish? I am well aware of it, and I thought about it thoroughly. Why is it that I did not take the time to explain my position to the Vietnamese officials and to persuade the French officials before promoting my position? I have presented my position to the Vietnamese officials; they thought that I was ignorant. I have met the French officials; they shared the Vietnamese officials' view of me. During the past several decades, the French have not adopted an enlightened policy in Vietnam because they have believed that the Vietnamese are contented with their ignorance, feel at home with calamities, and profit from danger. The French did not have anything to do with those circumstances. What the French did was merely to accommodate the contentment, the tranquility, and the profit from the hardship of the Vietnamese; and they did not lead the Vietnamese to a place of death.

Now that I promote my conviction, hopefully if the French support it according to their spirit of philanthropy and equality, it will not cause any harm to the French but will bring about tremendous benefits to the Vietnamese, and restrict their calamities to a small scale. If the French are not willing to extend their hands, I will be the only one to perish, and no damage will be done to our people. It is not that I did not realize the French officials viewed me with suspicion. It is not that I did not realize the Vietnamese officials hate me. It is not that I did not realize that Phan Bội Châu bore a grudge against me. It is not that I did not realize our people are speaking ill of me. But I did not avoid suspicion. I did not flee abroad when seeing difficulties. I sang and cried together with our people. Being surrounded by foes, I relied on my own strength to fight in a desperate situation, using my life as a target for everyone's arrows. I looked for life in death, but even when on the verge of perishing I felt no regret.

I remember that when I talked about that aspiration to my late friend Trần Quý Cáp, he said to me: "At present, you and I do not measure well our own strength when we promote this wonderful idea. Should it succeed, fortunately, then our people will be able to rejoice in our success. Should it fail, unfortunately, we will be transported to the market to face execution, while looking at one another. What a delight that will be!" Now, unfortunately, what he said has come true, and he is smiling in the other world. I was unable both to join the dearest and most cherished friend of my life in going to the guillotine, and to bow in front of his grave to apologize for the shameful breaking of my promise to him. For I have to bear disgrace to clarify, in some way, my conviction, rather than hiding myself in a corner and doing nothing. That is why I have had no tasty meal and no peaceful sleep and have persistently been struck with an eternal sorrow.

Above is a straightforward account of the history of the relations that I had with Phan Bội Châu. Now I would like to talk about the arrangements that I have made to oppose his means.

- Sent a petition to the French government denouncing the Vietnamese officials;
- Created Commercial Societies;
- Established general primary schools in rural areas;

– Created the New Learning Society;
– Created the Public Speech Society;
– Created the Arbor Society;
– Created the Short-Hair and Short-Clothes Societies.

The above societies and schools have been created. The societies that had been planned but have not yet been created are as follows:

– Sericulture Reform Society;
– Domestic Cotton Reform Society.

Why is it that I wrote a petition to the French government? Phan Bội Châu's strategy was to take advantage of the people's resentment against France. That is why in the *History of the Loss of Vietnam*, he blames France exclusively for this resentment and encourages our people to appeal to and ask for help from other countries.

I also realize that popular resentment against France [in Vietnam] is deep-rooted. But I focused [popular] resentment against France on France's inappropriate use of [Vietnamese] officials and thus criticized the use of those officials and appealed to France. Generally speaking, when people nourish resentment in their hearts, they are apt to resort to violence and will not listen even to sound words. If there were someone speaking on their behalf about their suffering and their despair, though the act might not necessarily bring any benefit to them, it would nevertheless provide them some measure of comfort by easing their resentment. I then gradually indicated to the people the path for broadening popular intellectual understanding and for improving living conditions, and it was easier for them to listen to me. That is why, without paying attention to advantages and disadvantages, taboos, and gains and losses, I explained every point exhaustively for them, along with its pros and cons. If the affection that the French officials have for the Vietnamese people is stronger than their affection for the Vietnamese officials, they should investigate thoroughly their [the people's] suffering and keep the Vietnamese officials under control. The latest insurrection was also a result of oppression by the Vietnamese officials. (I heard that at the time, public speeches were prohibited, short hair was banned, and those who kept their short hair were imprisoned. The prefect of Đại Lộc took advantage of the troubled situation to increase by five-fold the number of the people recruited to do forced labor. When villagers came to his office to protest, the officials regarded them as bandits and reported them to the Résident-supérieur. The insurrection then started.)

Alas! In peaceful times, the high officials, listening to the lower officials, treated the people like dirt. In times of emergency, they forced the people to risk their lives working for them. In this way, Vietnam became a colony of France. At present, France has also employed this policy. I do not know how to explain why the French have adopted this approach.

Now I will be talking about the history of the relationship between Phan Bội Châu and I, the reasons for the similarities and differences between our opinions, and our respective arguments.

The history of Phan Bội Châu is a sorrowful and gloomy history. It is a history full of hardship and challenge. His history is also the history of my life. His temperament is identical to mine, his aspiration is identical to mine, and his circumstances are identical to mine. Only his opinion is not identical to mine, and his conviction is just as different. That is why at the outset we were fond of one another, but eventually we parted from one another. At the beginning, we were friends, but later we were enemies. It was because of him that I paid no attention to suspicion and obstacles, and went after him to meet him abroad. It was because of him that I risked my life and paid no regard to taboos in order to appeal to the people inside the country. It was because of him that I failed—being beaten to the ground. I had nothing left, my comrades and friends were murdered or imprisoned, and even now I am still under suspicion and cannot speak my mind.

[My explanation of] this matter is a prelude to [my discussion of] the successes and failures, and the merits and demerits, of my conviction and his conviction. Without knowing him, it is impossible to know me. I thus would like to speak about his history.

The similarities and dissimilarities between Phan Bội Châu and me in temperaments (Viet. *tính chất*), *aspirations* (Viet. *chí khí*), *and circumstances* (Viet. *cảnh ngộ*): Phan Bội Châu is a man of character. He has willpower and courage and dares to risk his life. His self-confidence is enormous. He does not change his conviction—whatever it is—once he believes it is the right one. I am also that type of person.

He has possessed a powerful will and a spirit of indomitability ever since his childhood. Everyone thought that he was ignorant and was a lunatic, rushing himself to a place of death. Formerly, he had been excluded for life from taking examinations because of a previous offense. Thanks to the intervention of the academic officials who were fond of his literary talent, he was granted a pardon and afterward passed a regional examination.[48] I was in the same boat. When I was young, the academic official of my province (Viet. *huấn đạo*) regarded me with disfavor. Collaborating with others, he came up with a scheme to bar me from taking the examinations. Thanks to the help of the Director of Academic Affairs (Viet. *đốc học*), Trần Đình Phong, I was able to escape from that attempt [to constrain me].

Phan Bội Châu took the metropolitan examination without expecting to pass it. He only wished to convey his eminent name to the Vietnamese officials and let them know his opinions. He once wrote an essay entitled "On the Governing of the Nation" (Viet. *Trị quốc luận*) and gave it to the Minister of War, Hồ Lệ. The arguments in this essay contain numerous errors and distortions and are detached from reality. He advocates violence, but dares not say that clearly, so he presents [his argument] as the words of a man of high purpose from Liu Qiu (Viet. *Lưu Cầu*).[49]

Later, Phan Bội Châu did not pass the metropolitan examination and was suspected [of subversion], so he escaped because he was afraid of being arrested. I also came to the imperial city without looking to join officialdom; I only hoped to be trusted by the high officials of both countries so that I could present my position. As I found no one who trusted me, I resigned from my official position. This is a

---

[48] In his autobiography, Phan Bội Châu mentions this incident without defending himself. It is commonly believed that when he prepared to sit for the regional examination in 1897, one of his friends, meaning to be helpful, without his knowledge placed in his bag some prohibited materials that were discovered by the porter at the gate of the examination site. Phan Bội Châu received a pardon three years later, when Khiếu Năng Tĩnh, principal of the Imperial Academy and the governor of Nghệ An, in Đào Tấn province, defended his honesty.

[49] Liu Qiu (J. *Ryûkyû*) is present-day Okinawa, Japan.

similarity between him [Phan Bội Châu] and myself, and I liked him also because of that. But he relied too much on his willpower to commit violent acts, including murdering people with an unfeeling heart. He obstinately held onto his own ideas and considered all others to be less valuable. Because his scholarship was different from mine, our visions were also different, and our convictions were all the more different.

Let us assume that we now divide the country into two parties: one argues for an anti-French position and independence, and the other advocates working within the French system for self-rule. But at that time, none of the parties had taken shape, as the two parties in practice were struggling against one another, and, prior to the insurrection, the latter party was about to defeat the former party. For that reason, people in the two parties kept changing their affiliations, and at first some were superior to others, but later their ranking order would be reversed. Every activity and the target of every attack was aimed against its counterpart. Every arrangement was made in order to outmaneuver the other party. Unless one were sensitive and clear-sighted, it would not have been easy indeed to distinguish among the information that came to one's ears in these parties.

The one who advocated an anti-French stand was Phan Bội Châu, and the one who advocated the position of working within the French system was me. We were indeed the two crucial figures in the rise of the two positions. In adopting an "independence" position, Phan Bội Châu must necessarily oppose the French. Having adopted an anti-French position, he must necessarily benefit from the people's anti-French sentiments. In his arguments, therefore, he blamed every defect on the French and considered France as the source of [all Vietnamese] resentments. He used all he had in his power to attack it. Opposing France was the means by which he gained his foothold. Once he adopted an anti-French stand, and because his forces were not comparable to theirs, he necessarily looked for foreign help. Once he wished to look for foreign help, he had no choice but to run to foreign countries and use them as footholds. These were the circumstances (Viet. *thế*) to which such a cause (Viet. *nhân*) would lead.

As for me, having adopted a self-rule position, I had no choice but to rely on France. Once I decided to rely on France, I had to face the [Vietnamese] people's anti-French sentiments. Knowing the profound resentments of the people, in my arguments, therefore, I blamed every defect on the Vietnamese officials and considered them as the source of resentments. I used all I had in my power to attack them, and I had to escape to France to use it as a foothold. Once I criticized the Vietnamese officials, I had to realize that they must necessarily want revenge. I thus had no choice but to associate myself with the French in order to have a foothold for the contacts between the two countries. These were the circumstances to which my cause led.

(At an early stage, by the way, when I had an audience with the French Minister in our province, I presented my aspirations to him, but it appeared that he did not agree with me. I thus went to Bắc Kỳ to meet and establish contacts with the Vietnamese officials and Frenchmen of high purpose there. That was my aspiration. There were many Vietnamese officials in Bắc Kỳ who were well-versed in current world trends and sensitive to the conditions of the people. They were several times better than the officials in Trung Kỳ. In Bắc Kỳ, many men of high purpose took up official positions, whereas in Trung Kỳ all men of high purpose hid themselves and did not become officials.)

When Phan Bội Châu advocated an anti-French stand, he made no observation of world trends and gave no heed to advantages and disadvantages. The means he adopted had to be none other than violence—violence doomed to result in failure and death. Had the people known that it [this agenda] doomed them to failure and death, they would not have followed. Therefore, he [Phan Bội Châu] was required to take advantage of the people's ignorance and their desperation. Once he took advantage of the people's ignorance and desperation, he would not say anything about their intellectual understanding and their resources. Neither would he say anything about the creation of academic societies, public speech societies, or commercial societies. He feared that if the people became wise and if they were not desperate, they would not necessarily listen to him. Once he advocated violence, he had to make use of underground (Viet. *ám*) activities. The activities of his party were therefore all conducted surreptitiously through the people, beguiling the ignorant to take their money. Yet the participants and their activities never came to the surface, and thus it has been very difficult to observe them. Because his party took advantage of the people's ignorance and conducted underground activities, many of its followers were vagrants and wanderers who would risk their lives if they saw a chance for profit. The number of those from the middle stream of society was no more than a few; the rest were all headstrong, uneducated, and ignorant of world conditions and, as such, were negligible. These were also the circumstances to which his cause would lead.

As for me, once I called for working within the French system, my means must necessarily not exceed the framework of self-rule. Self-rule is a big undertaking, and not an easy matter. Should the undertaking fail, one would perish. Unless one is a patriotic man of high purpose, who is prepared to risk his life and is well-versed in world affairs, one would not dare to call for self-rule. I must therefore rely on popular intellectual understanding and resources. If I were to rely on popular intellectual understanding and resources, I could not help but talk about the people's enlightenment and the improvement of their resources, also about the establishment of many academic societies, public speech societies, and commercial societies. Because I placed my hope on popular intellectual understanding and resources, even if I was the only person to speak, people still followed me.

Naturally, if the conviction [the agenda being advocated] is self-rule, our activities in practice must be unconcealed. For that reason, the activities of my party were always open and aboveboard. In public speeches, meetings of men of high purpose, and discussions in loud voice of politics and current affairs, the participants and their acts could be seen and observed easily by all. My philosophy was to make use of popular intellectual understanding. Because the means that I adopted to make use of popular intellectual understanding were clear, many of the participants were well-read persons and men of principle, ready to sacrifice their lives for the country. When the matter became clear, a few who at the outset had been confused by Phan Bội Châu left him and joined my party. This was also a circumstance to which my cause might lead.

But why is it that the insurrection occurred? The insurrection in Trung Kỳ was essentially set in motion by a fight between the "relying-on-the-French" and the "anti-French" parties, and afterward was a reaction to harsh suppression carried out by the French and by Vietnamese officials. I criticized the Vietnamese officials because I wanted to express the popular resentments and to win the trust of the French officials—the foothold for my "relying-on–the-French" stand. I also wished to win the people's confidence, then use it as a means to root out the advocacy for violence. This was why the Vietnamese officials had a deep-rooted rancor against my party, and the French officials, all the more, suspected my party and wanted to exterminate it.

On the other hand, the overseas anti-French party also wished to meddle with my stand in order to achieve their objectives. Opposing my position, its misleading literature of all types made every effort to call for violence. My position at the time was indeed surrounded by foes.

The anti-French party took advantage of the people's ignorance to promote itself; the French officials and Vietnamese officials were not interested in the question of the people's intellectual understanding. So far as my party's stand was concerned, apart from [fostering] the people's enlightenment and the improvement of their resources, there was no other way to attain self-rule. Public speeches and academic societies are good medicine for the development of popular intellectual understanding. The ban of society activities this time was, therefore, not different from snatching good medicine out of the hands of a man who has been long sick and throwing it away without letting him drink. His resentment must be deep.

At that juncture, all of a sudden the deceitful booklet (Viet. *Hải ngoại huyết thư*) written by Phan Bội Châu, which calls for boycotting taxes and forced labor, was surreptitiously brought into the country. In addition, the Vietnamese officials were looking for an excuse for provocation. As the Đại Lộc prefecture in Quảng Nam province increased by several times the number of people recruited to do forced labor, the insurrection naturally broke out. The insurrection this time was, in fact, the awful result of three positions (i.e., anti-French, working within the French system for self-rule, and despotism) that provoked (Viet. *tương kích*), collided, and clashed against one another (Viet. *tương xung tương đột*).

But why is it that the mutiny broke out? The mutiny was, in reality, brought about by the insurrection; without the insurrection there would not have been the mutiny. At the time, there were only two parties in the country; once one withdrew from one party, one would join the other. If the Self-rule Party had acquired a foothold as a result of working within the French system and had not been compelled to face extinction after a single failure, people would have hastened to join the Self-rule Party, and the Anti-French Party would have had no foothold. But once the Self-rule Party had been defeated by despotism, and imprisonment and murder occurred incessantly, people knew that the Self-rule Party was not in a position to be successful. They thus had no choice but to run away and rally under the flag of the Anti-French Party, and they therefore were convinced that violence must be the trend of the time and that it made sense to use violence.

In the present day, who is winning and who is losing? On the basis of what we can observe from the current state of affairs, the authorities are winning and the people are losing. The Anti-French Party is winning and the party advocating working within the French system is losing. France, on the other hand, is standing between victory and defeat.

LETTER TO EMPEROR KHẢI ĐỊNH

[Written in literary Chinese in Paris, July 15, 1922]

I, Trinh, was born at a time when my country was in a parlous condition, while every country in the outside world was vying with the others in making progress. I love democracy, abhor the tyranny of autocratic monarchy, and deplore the cold-heartedness and venality of self-serving government officials. Sympathizing with the tribulations of our people, I have risked my life to make strenuous efforts in the hope of helping to drive away the danger.

In 1907, I sent a petition to the Governor-General of the Protectorate Government, strongly urging reforms. The measures I proposed at that time all required immediate attention: the establishment of schools for instruction in French and *quốc ngữ* [the modern form of the Vietnamese language], the creation of agricultural and commercial societies for the betterment of the people's living conditions in order to restore our rightful economic status, the adoption of Western dress, etc. These proposals could be seen and heard openly by the public, so there was nothing reprehensible about them. Nevertheless, the Vietnamese authorities in our country, from top to bottom, continued to adhere steadfastly to autocracy to profit themselves and their families. They held reforms in contempt as if they were their enemy. They treated their people like grass or bits of straw. They looked for excuses and pretexts to cause trouble in every way and to murder men of conscience and wisdom.

In 1908, when the tax revolt erupted in twelve provinces in Trung Kỳ (Annam), the number of the literati and others who were murdered or imprisoned amounted to several thousands. How lamentable! Taking advantage of such a situation, government officials fabricated charges, one after another, to involve me in a criminal offense: first they imposed a death penalty on me, and then later changed my sentence to exile on Poulo Condore Island.[1]

Alas! Some thirty or forty years have elapsed since our country became a protectorate of France, but there has been no attempt to follow the latter's example or to initiate reform. The venom of autocracy remains. The civilization of the protecting country has not brought any benefits to the protectorate, neither has the protectorate received any enlightenment from the protecting country. Strange, indeed! This sort of story is rarely heard in the world.

I could not be here today without the help of the benevolent and high-spirited Frenchmen who managed to save my life in the name of philanthropy and equality. That I am still alive is all thanks to the civility of the French people.[2] In 1910 I was

---

[1] Now called Côn Đảo.

[2] In a collection of his manuscripts that contains the "Letter to Emperor Khải Định," Phan Châu Trinh added in parentheses "(thanks to the *Ligue des droits de l'homme*)." See "Thư thất điều gởi vua Khải Định," in Trần Gia Thoại, *Tâm sự nhà chí sĩ Phan Châu Trinh* [Phan Châu Trinh's Intimate Feelings as Reflected in his Poetry (and Prose)] (Đà Nẵng: Nhà sách Nguyễn

released from prison, and in the following year I was allowed to travel to France to observe European civilization. Over the past twelve years, I have lived in the land of democracy, breathed the air of liberty. Thanks to that, I became familiar with the principles of universal justice, recognized the duties of the citizens in a country, and understood the prevailing trends of progress and civilization in the modern world. I have come to believe that unless people in our country make a united and strenuous effort to fight against the despotic monarch and corrupt mandarins, unless we put an end to the evil influence of the several-thousand-year autocracy and extract its roots once and for all, it will be impossible for people in our country to see daylight again.

The gist of my conviction and my objectives are as above. Never since Your Majesty was enthroned seven years ago have I heard that you have practiced good government. I have heard of nothing but arrogance, lustful excesses, immoral conduct, breaches of regulated practices, reckless promotion of autocratic monarchy, unfair rewards and penalties, the trampling of the people under the heel of your tyranny, reckless extravagance, actions contrary to humanity and civilization, obstruction of the people's progress, and the list goes on.

In accordance with the constitutional law in civilized European and Asian countries, if the monarch acted against the constitution, the people would chastise him. It is only in our country that popular rights are still being suppressed, a constitution has not been adopted, the monarch is still allowed to make arbitrary decisions, and the people do not have the freedom of public expression. If one applied universal justice, it would be impossible for Your Majesty to escape punishment from our people. In the following, I have recapitulated the seven offenses that you have committed against our national destiny and the living conditions of the masses (Viet. *quốc kế dân sinh*). After the receipt of this letter, it is expected that Your Majesty will pass judgment on your case accordingly.

1. Reckless promotion of autocratic monarchy: Following your enthronement, you issued imperial edicts forcing people to respect the sovereignty of the monarchy. On what ground did Your Majesty base your arguments? Your Majesty has often stated that from the olden days our country held Confucianism in reverence.

In Confucianism, none was more eminent than Confucius and Mencius. Duke Ding (Viet. Định Công) once asked Confucius, "Is there a single saying that can lead a country to prosperity?" Confucius answered, "Yes. There is a saying amongst men: 'It is difficult to be a ruler, and it is not easy to be a subject either.'" Duke Ding then asked, "Is there a saying that can lead the state to ruin?" Confucius answered, "Yes. There is a saying amongst men: 'I do not at all enjoy being a ruler, except for the fact that no one goes against what I say.'"[3]

Hữu Uẩn, 1958), p. 73. The translation of "Letter to Emperor Khải Định" included in Trần Gia Thoại's book is excellent because Phan Châu Trinh did the translation himself for most parts of the letter. For that reason, although I used mainly Phan's original work in literary Chinese for my translation, footnotes will cite Trần Gia Thoại's book for the reader's convenience.

[3] The source for this quotation can be found in *The Confucian Analects*, Book XIII, 13.15. See *Han-Ying Sishu* [The Four Books in Chinese and in English], trans. James Legge, annot. Luo Zhiye (Hunan: Hunan Chubanshe, 1992), pp. 180–82. In the original text, this dialogue runs as follows: "Duke Ting [i.e., Ding] asked, 'Is there such a single saying that can lead a country to prosperity?' Confucius answered, 'A saying cannot quite do that. There is a saying amongst men: "It is difficult to be a ruler, and it is not easy to be a subject either." If the ruler understands the difficulty of being a ruler, then is it not almost a case of leading the state to prosperity?' 'Is there such a thing as a saying that can lead a state to ruin?' Confucius

Mencius said, "The people are the most important element [in a nation]; the spirits of the land and grain are the next; the ruler is of the least account,"[4] or "Whoever enjoys the trust of the people will be emperor,"[5] and there are numerous sayings to the same effect. If Your Majesty opened the *Five Classics* and the *Four Books*, could you find an indication that autocracy should be promoted? If your position is above everyone, you should place your heart below everyone—that is the spirit of Confucianism. If you arrogantly tell your people, "You must pay respect to me! You must pay respect to me!"—that is a self-destructive act.

In ancient times King Jie (Viet. Kiệt) [of the Xia (Viet. Hạ) dynasty] said, "I am to the world what the sun is to the sky. It is only when the sun disappears that I shall disappear." The people replied in return, "When the sun disappears, you and we shall disappear together." King Zhou (Viet. Trụ) [last ruler of the Yin (Viet. Ân) dynasty] once said, "That I was born, was this not the Mandate of Heaven?" The people replied to him, saying: "What Heaven sees is what we people see. What Heaven hears is what we people hear." These examples are a testimony to the self-promotion of autocratic monarchy. Eventually, King Jie was sent into exile in Nanzhao (Viet. *Nam Sào*), King Zhou had his head stuck on a flagpole. "Tang [Viet. Thang] chased out King Jie and King Wu [Viet. Võ] defeated King Zhou," Confucius remarked with approval, "each of these responding to the Mandate of Heaven and following the will of the people." Mencius also said, "I have heard of the beheading of that fellow Zhou, but I have not heard of the execution of a sovereign."[6] Is this not genuine Confucianism? The *Classics* and the *Books* are still available, all were compiled from the sayings of Confucius and Mencius—I did not fabricate them to deceive myself and then go on to deceive others. By issuing edicts for the promotion of autocracy, are you yourself not acting against Confucianism? Is there any king who, acting against the national religion (Viet. *quốc giáo*), can remain on the throne for long?

According to European political principles, a nation is made up of people and a government is delegated by its people to act in accord with their mandate in the nation's interest and for the people's well-being. A monarch or president is simply a representative of a country, like the head of a village. Whoever undertakes the responsibility of the position will be given the benefits, but he should also do his best to fulfill his duty; otherwise, just like anyone else, he will be punished by the people according to the law. This is what theories of liberty and equality call for, and it is also the reason why a cabinet headed by a prime minister is instituted to hold responsibility on behalf of a monarch or a president [in civilized nations]. If a monarch or president considered his nation as his private property, the offense would not be different from that committed by a thief or a robber. If he abused his

---

answered, 'A saying cannot quite do that. There is a saying amongst men: "I do not at all enjoy being a ruler, except for the fact that no one goes against what I say." If what he says is good and no one goes against him, good. But if what he says is not good and no one goes against him, then is this not almost a case of leading the state to ruin?"' The translation here is from *Confucius: The Analects (Lun yu)*, trans. D. C. Lau (Hong Kong: The Chinese University Press, 1983), pp. 126–27.

[4] The source for this quotation can be found in *Mencius*, Book VIII (Jin xin), Part II, 14.14. See *Han-Ying Sishu*, pp. 540–41.

[5] Ibid.

[6] The source for this quotation can be found in *Mencius*, Book II (King Hui of Liang), Part II.B, 8. See *Han-Ying Sishu*, pp. 540–41.

power recklessly to practice despotism against his people, his offense would be dealt with as treason by the law.

The above principles are most essential to the peoples in civilized countries, like water, fire, and grain. They worship them as unchangeable precepts. People who follow them will thrive, those who oppose them will perish. In any country that has a constitutional government, be it democratic or monarchical, these principles are observed. Louis XIV once said: "*L'État, c'est moi*" ["I am the state"]. The French people consider him unethical and a traitor; even now historians are still infuriated at him.[7]

The essence of these principles is compatible with the spirit of our country's Confucianism. Confucius said: "If a ruler dislikes the things that the people like, and wishes for the things that the people hate, then disaster will come upon him immediately." Again, he said: "Barbarian tribes with their rulers are inferior to civilized states without them."[8] Mencius likewise said: "This world belongs to the people of the world, it does not belong to the king" and "The people are of supreme importance, the altars to the gods of earth and grain come next, the ruler is of the least account."[9] Zhuangzi (Viet. Trang Tử) also said: "He who steals a belt buckle pays with his life; he who steals a state gets to be a feudal lord,"[10] and so forth. All of these remarks are in accord with the above principles.

Your Majesty was born in a Confucian country, and you are a twentieth-century sovereign of a country under the protection of France—a democratic country; nonetheless, you dare to promote yourself as being sacred, pompously placing yourself above the heads of the people.[11] It is clear that you are betraying the teachings of Confucius and Mencius, and surreptitiously defying the civilized world. For all this, you will be neither forgiven by our people nor tolerated by the French people.

Let us now look at the present situation in Asia and Europe. Japan is a country sharing the same culture with us. Forty years ago, a popularly elected assembly (Viet. *dân tuyển nghị viện*) was created, all matters were discussed publicly and decided according to public opinion, and the emperor was not allowed to be autocratic. It [Japan] has thus become powerful and thriving, leading other Asian countries. The people, nonetheless, still felt that the power of the emperor was too great, therefore toward the end of the Meiji era there was an assassination attempt

---

[7] Obviously Phan is generalizing in assessing the reputation of Louis XIV in France. Although Louis XIV may have been a tyrant, even Voltaire, in *Siècle de Louis XIV* (1751), declared: "It is impossible to mention his name without a sense of respect and without recalling an age which will be eternally unforgettable." Regarding the quote, "*Le roi, c'est moi*," some say the quote is actually, "*Je m'en vais, mais l'État demeurera toujours.*" (I depart, but the State shall always remain). See Marquis de Dangeau [Philippe de Courcillon de Dangeau], *Mémoire sur la mort de Louis XIV* (Paris: Didot frères, fils, 1858).

[8] The source for this quotation can be found in *The Confucian Analects*, Book III, 3.5. See *Han-Ying Sishu*, pp. 78–79.

[9] The source for this quotation can be found in *Mencius*, Book VIII (Jin Xin), Part II, 14.14. See *Han-Ying Sishu*, pp. 540–41.

[10] The source for this quotation can be found in *Zhuangzi*, Book X (Rifling Trunk). See Burton Watson, trans., *The Complete Works of Chuang Tzu* (New York, NY: Columbia University Press, 1968), p. 110.

[11] In this case, Phan Châu Trinh's criticism of the emperor is unfair. The French were not willing to allow more democracy in Vietnam, and it was the "sacred" image of the monarchy that they were most interested in preserving.

against the emperor;[12] and last year [1921] Prime Minister Hara Kei was assassinated for the same reason.[13]

With respect to Europe, autocratic monarchy was most pronounced in the cases of the Tsar of Russia, then the Kaiser of Germany and the Emperor of Austria. Following his defeat in the War, Nicholas II and his family were cruelly murdered. William II had to seek refuge in Holland and barely managed to save his life. Charles I twice surreptitiously returned to his country in an attempt to regain his throne, but was chased away by his people, like a hog, and eventually died in exile on a desolate island.

The Asian and European monarchs cited above were gallant and high-spirited in their disposition, and were versed in world affairs. Though they were somewhat autocratic toward their peoples, this does not necessarily imply that they did not contribute valuable things to their countries. If they were successful, their countries became prosperous and powerful; but even if their policies failed, it did not necessarily lead to the loss of the sovereignty of their countries. The people in these countries, however, were extremely harsh toward their monarchs; they hated them as if they were warts or lumps, they looked on them with aversion as if they were poisonous snakes. If they [the monarchs] were not careful in their conduct, their people caught them immediately; if they planned something unsuccessfully, it might cost them their lives. Judging from the above examples, one can see how well-developed is the intellectual level of [European] people!

Our country has been ruled by autocratic monarchy from ancient times to the present day. The emperor holds all political power at the court, and the people are not allowed to express their opinion (the law in our country forbids the literati and others to send memoranda addressing political matters to the emperor).

During the last eighty years, the emperors at the top have been despotic, the ministers below deceitful, the laws severe, the punishments ruthless, and the people thus have had no one to depend on. Owing to Emperor Gia Long's adoption of the law of Qianlong [Viet. *Càn Long*] of the Qing [Viet. *Thanh*] dynasty—the oldest autocratic monarchy in East Asia—there has been no freedom of discussion in our country. Soon after this law was adopted [in Vietnam], Nguyễn Văn Thành—a person who had rendered most distinguished services to the founding of the Nguyễn dynasty—was executed, together with his son, on the charge that the latter had composed a poem.[14] Through this, one can see the unjustness of this law and why after less than fifty years the country's fortunes came to an end.

---

[12] Phan must be referring to the case of Kôtoku Shûsui (1871–1911), who was suspected of involvement in the attempted assassination of Emperor Meiji. Kôtoku was executed in 1911.

[13] When translating into *quốc ngữ*, Phan added: "The Japanese prime minister was assassinated in a railway station for the same reason." See "Thư thất điều gởi vua Khải Định," in Trần Gia Thoại, *Tâm sự nhà chí sĩ Phan Châu Trinh*, p. 80. Unlike his predecessors, as prime minister, Hara Kei (also known as Hara Takashi, 1856–1921) came from a commoner class background; yet when he came to power, he was involved in repressing the movement that called for universal suffrage. Ironically, but not coincidentally, this prime minister was assassinated by a railway worker. Had Phan Châu Trinh used this incident as an exemplary case in his discussion of the Japanese movement demanding the expansion of popular rights (but not necessarily opposing the promotion of autocracy), it might have been more appropriate in this context.

[14] Phan provided an extended explanatory passage when he translated into *quốc ngữ*: "On the excuse of a poem composed by his son [Nguyễn Văn Thuyên], the motive of which was maliciously distorted afterward by deceitful ministers [in a manner suggesting that Nguyễn

As its education was corrupt and the students' level of knowledge was poor, our country's fortunes slid downhill, and we were considered second-rate. Even if Vietnam had not come under French protection, it might well have drifted into another country's hands. Who should take the blame for all this? Who else, if not the emperors? No matter how eloquent one might be, it would be impossible to defend them [the emperors]. Not only should the power of autocratic monarchy not be promoted, but the throne should be abolished altogether. Yet, because the monarchy still exists even now, the intellectual progress of our people is impeded. How pitiful it is! The public's loyalty and honesty, nonetheless, should be applauded. How noble they are![15]

Before you were enthroned, not a single good thing, only misdeeds, had been heard about Your Majesty. After using every possible means to win the throne, you have spoken as if you were a divine being, yet in practice you have acted like Satan. During the seven years since your enthronement, popular sentiments have been filled with resentment. Notwithstanding, you still attempt to rely on brute force to coerce our people to pay respect to you! In Europe and Asia, according to the laws of all ages dealing with monarchs, it would not be unjustified if you were sentenced to either execution or expulsion. The above is the first offense.

2. *Unfair rewards and punishments:* Rewards and punishments are a consequential matter in a country, affecting the life of its people and its national polity. Confucius said: "When the punishments do not fit the crimes, the common people will not know where to put their hand or foot."[16] Mencius also said: "A country will survive only by a fluke if those above have no principles to maintain, and those below have no laws to observe."[17]

In ancient times, rewards were conferred at the court in order to show that the entire country provided the reward; punishments were carried out in the marketplace to show that they were punishments [approved] by the entire country. But if the rewards and punishments have lost all their fairness, why must the people have a government?

I have heard from a reliable source that the so-and-so gang took Your Majesty to risqué quarters of ill-repute in the evenings. After your enthronement, you

---

Văn Thành was plotting a rebellion], Nguyễn Văn Thành's entire family was murdered [1817]. Through this, one can see how unsparingly this law was implemented. From that time on, the distance between the people and the emperor became increasingly greater, the government officials in between had their own way in everything, and the people had no means to make complaints. After the Minh Mạng era [1820–41], revolts occurred incessantly. Then, during the Tự Đức era [1847–83], the French came and we lost our national independence. Though the ancestors of the Nguyễn dynasty had developed the country and almost doubled its size, and their meritorious services to our country were so great, within less than fifty years, owing to the reasons noted above, their descendants failed to preserve her national independence. How deplorable!" See "Thư thất điều gởi vua Khải Định," in Trần Gia Thoại, *Tâm sự nhà chí sĩ Phan Châu Trinh*, p. 82.

[15] Phan Châu Trinh added a sentence in his translation of this work into modern Vietnamese: "In response to these popular sentiments, it is expected that the emperor should devote himself to working for the benefit of the people to make them happy." Ibid., p. 83.

[16] The source for this quotation can be found in *The Confucian Analects*, Book XIII, 13.3. See *Han-Ying Sishu*, pp. 176–77.

[17] The source for this quotation can be found in *Mencius*, Book VII (Li Lou), Part I, 7.1. See *Han-Ying Sishu*, pp. 390–91.

immediately gave some of them [members of this gang] important positions, placing them around you; others you appointed to junior and senior official positions.[18] I have also heard that on such-and-such board there was a vice-president (Viet. *Thị lang*) whose wife had previously incurred Your Majesty's displeasure. After your enthronement, he happened to make a slight mistake and was immediately removed from service. Then there was the president of such-and-such board, who often divulged your private affairs. Taking advantage of a time when he had no one to count on, and using fabricated evidence, Your Majesty passed a grave sentence on him: imprisonment with perpetual forced labor.[19] The sentence was pronounced. Later, when you heard that the man, being a wealthy fellow, would pay as much as 50,000 taels of gold [for his release], the sentence was diminished to demotion of rank and removal from active service. In this way, rewards and punishments have been determined by your personal opinions, without paying attention to the law of the nation, only encouraging corruption and bribery. Why is such a monarch needed?

I have also heard that Your Majesty keeps around you a platoon of secret police, more than forty, who go morning and evening to spy in towns and villages to see if there are any dissenters. If there are, Your Majesty will look for a way to incriminate them by law, or to harass them surreptitiously. Your private police are rascals, responsible for numerous outrageous acts. The people all suffer from them but can do nothing and are left helplessly looking at one another on the streets.

In ancient times, King Li (Viet. *Lệ*) of the Zhou (Viet. *Chu/Châu*) dynasty was immoral. Fearing people would gossip, he enacted an edict, just as Your Majesty did, banning people from gossiping. As he paid no attention to the advice of Prince Zhao (Viet. *Thiệu Công*), King Li was eventually killed by his people. Why does Your Majesty not take it as an example? The above is the second offense.

3. Reckless demand for kowtow: Kowtow (prostration) is, after all, no more than an expression of obedience. But in this ritual, one man is exalted on high, while many below, wearing court robes and hats, prostrate themselves. It is an ugly sight to observe; the practice takes no account of human dignity and serves to make the one above feel more arrogant and the ones below lose their self-esteem. This practice is extremely barbarous![20]

At present, this ritual can be found nowhere among civilized European and Asian countries, only in savage and undeveloped regions. It is a shame for our country indeed.

---

[18] In his translation into modern Vietnamese, Phan Châu Trinh reworded this part as follows: "I have heard from an accurate source that the So-and-so gangs were previously your companions when Your Majesty frequented disreputable districts. After your enthronement, one of them was appointed by you as Marshal to serve in your entourage, some were appointed governors or prefects, provincial officials or metropolitan officials, etc." See "Thư thất điều gởi vua Khải Định," in Trần Gia Thoại, *Tâm sự nhà chí sĩ Phan Châu Trinh*, p. 84.

[19] In French legal terminology, "*travaux forcés à perpétué.*" Phan Châu Trinh was more specific in modern Vietnamese: "he was given a grave sentence, i.e., eight years of imprisonment." Ibid., p. 85.

[20] In his translation of this work into modern Vietnamese, Phan Châu Trinh added an observation in brackets: "In ancient practice, when a person bowed to another person, the latter also bowed to the former in return; this practice was kept in Japan, but now is also abolished there, as it is too troublesome." Ibid., p. 86. The assertion that bowing was not practiced in contemporary Japan is, of course, not an accurate statement. Probably Phan was unaware of the difference between kowtow and bowing in Japanese social etiquette.

In 1906, Governor-General Beau issued instructions to abolish this practice, but the ranking government officials of our country were stubborn and shameless; they surreptitiously upheld the practice and gave orders to neglect those instructions. The people all regretted the lost opportunity.

Soon after M. Sarraut was appointed Governor-General, the abolition of this practice was strictly implemented for the first time, and the people under his jurisdiction were delighted by the decision.[21] Even now, Your Majesty alone persistently clings to this barbaric practice. Not only have you not abolished it, being as fond of it as of fine food and drink, but you have even promoted it as a grand ritual. Every time there is a kowtow session at the court, you bring in people to take photographs to sell all over the country. By now, these photographs are in circulation in Europe and America.

I have heard that when Your Majesty departed for France, an elaborate kowtow session took place at the Đà Nẵng railway station where the court officials saw you off. This protocol was repeated when your boat arrived at the old port of Marseille. Kowtow is not a civilized practice, a monarch is not someone who should be respected as Heaven, and court officials and the people are not slaves. A railway station is not an imperial ancestral temple, and a seaport is not a place for imperial celebration. Why is it that you forced your entourage to prostrate themselves in their full formal dress amid mire and coals, treating people as if they were cows and horses, making foreigners look down on us and damaging our national honor? A single act has caused ten injuries and losses; our people are ashamed of it. Notwithstanding, Your Majesty took pleasure in doing it. How could this be possible unless you were most foolish?

Even worse, you specifically ordered wax statues of yourself and of the court officials posed in kowtow and placed them at the Marseille Exposition to present yourself to the international community. In your statue, Your Majesty holds a jade scepter in your hand while sitting on an elevated golden throne. Meanwhile, aged senior and junior officials with grey moustaches and gray hair, in full formal dress, close their eyes while prostrating themselves, bending their arms in front of their heads, like a band of otters offering sacrifices to a fish,[22] or a troop of monkeys entertaining their spectators. You have no understanding of what human beings call shame. When learned Europeans see these casts, they cannot help but laugh—a disgrace to our national polity, is it not? It has been said that "The king whose temperament goes against the people will necessarily come to a bad end."[23] Mencius said: "If a king treats his officials as dogs and horses, they will treat him as a stranger. If he treats them as mud and grass, they will treat him as an enemy."[24] If this is true for your officials, it goes without saying for the people. Your Majesty is therefore either "a stranger" or "an enemy" to our people. How can you escape from being cast down by our people? The above is the third offense.

---

[21] When translating into *quốc ngữ*, Phan made this point clearer: "In Nam Kỳ (Cochinchina) and Bắc Kỳ (Tongkin) this practice has been abolished." Ibid., p. 87.

[22] This idiom, in Sino-Vietnamese *thát tế ngư* (or *rái tế cá* in modern Vietnamese), means "otter sacrifices to fish."

[23] The source for this quotation can be found in *The Great Learning*, Chapter 10. See *Kadokawa Daijiten* [Kadokawa Great Dictionary of Etymology] ed. Ozaki Yujirô et al. (Tokyo: Kadokawa Shoten, 1992, p. 139.

[24] The source for this quotation can be found in *Mencius*, Book VIII (Li Lou), Part II, 8.3. See *Han-Ying Sishu*, pp. 410-11.

4. *Reckless extravagance:* To build a grand palace in An Cựu village, Your Majesty purchased ancient porcelains from China; the cost of each amounted to several thousand piastres. You then ordered them broken into pieces, using only those with colorful flower motifs to compose the dragon and phoenix mosaics that decorate the palace. People in our country know that before you were enthroned, you did not possess even a penny. This money is therefore not from your private savings, but must have been taken from the public treasury.

I have also heard that during your voyage to France, every day, whenever you met passengers on board, you treated them to the most exquisite champagne; the tips you gave to the waiters alone amounted to no less than twenty-five thousand francs. People have been going around gossiping about this—do you have a means to counter this rumor?

Alas! In the Trung Kỳ region of our country, the peasants have been living in extreme poverty. Its land is barren. It has been struck by natural calamities of all sorts, one after another. The government officials are greedy and corrupt. To make matters even worse, during the war,[25] prices soared. The situation of the displaced thus far has not been tackled. The burden of taxes is too heavy for the peasants to shoulder. It goes without saying that the question of raising their intellectual level and improving their living conditions is still a long way off. As compared to the other two regions, i.e. Nam Kỳ and Bắc Kỳ, the difference is perfectly clear: they are thriving, and Trung Kỳ is destitute. As a means to address the budget deficit, the people were forced to purchase opium and alcohol to enrich the public treasury, in spite of the fact that they were already so poor that they did not have any money to spend. There is no need to say anything further.

Then again, during the years 1916, 1917, and 1918, i.e., the three years following your enthronement, it was reported in the newspapers that in the provinces of Thanh Hoá, Nghệ An, Hà Tĩnh, Thừa Thiên, Quảng Nam, and Quảng Ngãi, people suffered incessantly from typhoons, floods, drought, starvation, and plague. The pitiful circumstances were simply unprecedented! Nonetheless, I have not heard that Your Majesty has engaged in any charitable act to help those who survived or has given even a piastre to help the starving people!

You have thus for a long time severed your feelings from our people and even now dare to steal our national treasury to make it your private property, use it for reckless extravagance, or throw it out the window. Judging from this, what personal value and credentials [can you claim that would justify your decision] to place yourself above our country's people? Had you used the money you spent on renovating your palace to build a university in Huế, the capital city, or the money you spent on Chinese porcelains to purchase scientific equipment for that university, or the money you wasted on the boat to support some dozens of students studying in France for a year, the benefit that this money generated would have been entirely different.

How pitiful it is! Our people work hard for the entire year, but the money earned by the sweat of their brows is used only to pay public taxes to the government, while their wives have not enough food to eat, their children suffer from the cold, and they themselves have neither sufficient clothing nor food, and hope only that the tax they pay will be used in their common interest. When your government collects money, it collects even trifling amounts, but when you spend it, you scatter it like dirt. Why is

---

[25] The First World War.

it that our people endure suffering and hardship, and sacrifice their blood so a despot can waste it?

At the time when Your Majesty was spending so lavishly, did you not hear of the deed of the current President Li Yuanhong (Viet. Lê Nguyên Hồng) of the Chinese Republic? Seeing that the national treasury suffered from a deficit, he voluntarily donated his annual stipend, equivalent to more than 3,500,000 francs, to public charity, an act that the French press has not stopped praising. Alas! China is a country with vast territory, extensive resources, and the largest population in the world. In addition, it is an independent country. Though it is poor, it is not without recourse. Nonetheless, the president of such a great and dignified country, out of patriotism and concern for his people, has refused to accept his legitimate annual stipend in order to lighten the burden on his people.

As a monarch of a protectorate, the position of Your Majesty is below that of the Governor-General, your jurisdiction is confined to only twelve central provinces, and your achievements have not been apparent to even a single citizen. Why is it that you dare to liken yourself to the Son of Heaven, while you act like a robber? Apart from your annual stipend, you have wasted public money on palace renovation and on all sorts of extravagance. In your letter to the Governor-General, you called yourself "the parent of the people." Parents have been respected in the family ethics of our country from the olden days; how is it possible to have a parent who is so cruel and wicked? It is much closer to reality to call you the public enemy (Viet. *dân tặc*). The above is the fourth offense.

5. Improper dressing: Your Majesty has designed for yourself a new style of formal dress and worn it when appearing at court. To the former embroidered long robe, the new design adds two Western-style epaulettes and a lot of showy gold and precious stones around the collar and on the sleeves. It looks neither European nor Asiatic. Furthermore, dragon-and-phoenix design embroidery was added to the former imperial hat. I have heard that when Marshal Joffre visited our country, Your Majesty wore that newly designed dress at the reception. When you went to pay tribute at the Tomb of the Unknown Soldier during your tour of France, you also wore it. Fortunately, the French did not pay much attention to our country's formal dress, therefore they did not notice; otherwise, if there had been anyone somewhat familiar with Vietnamese decorum (Viet. *hội điển*), he might have pressed you with the question: "Was your dress a formal military uniform of Vietnam?" What would you have said in reply?

In every civilized country in the world, formal court dress is fixed for different occasions, e.g. receiving guests, reviewing troops, appearing at court, or having an audience. Formal dress is related to the national polity (Viet. *quốc thể*), and no public person is exempted from it. Internationally, carelessness regarding formal dress may bring shame because it would constitute a breach of etiquette; domestically, carelessness may be an offense because it violates the code of conduct. In our country in the olden days, this code of conduct was strictly observed by everyone, from the emperor at the top to the general populace at the bottom. Each [stratum of the populace] had its own set of rules, prescribed in the book of decorum and treated as public ordinances; whoever violated them would be punished accordingly.

If the old formal dress is outdated, it is appropriate to augment and renovate it to suit the time. China and Japan have both adopted Western costume for their formal dress. But there should be fixed codes applied uniformly from top to bottom. These codes can be modified to reflect a new era and should be made public. Why is it not possible to do so?

At present, Your Majesty has designed your formal dress by yourself, without consultation, and it is worn by you alone; you are looking only for self-aggrandizement. People in our country do not see it as appropriate, and the way that foreigners view our country will also be distorted. This will be detrimental to our country's external relations and a disgrace to our national polity. According to the law of our nation, you should be subject to a penalty (Viet. *điển hình*). The above is the fifth offense.

6. *Excessive pleasure outings:* Following Your Majesty's enthronement, you have increased enormously the pomp and ceremony of your imperial regime and have multiplied the frequency of outings that are simply for pleasure. There are elephants, palanquins, carriages, and horses. Your attendants number at least thirty or forty and as many as one hundred. Day and night, you and your entourage, dressed in brightly colored costumes, ride through the roads in the city. Your guards bully, and your attendants are arrogant. In the previous forty years there has been nothing like this in our country. The passers-by are annoyed since they have to run away; the residents are disturbed by this nuisance. Your Majesty, nonetheless, is full of conceit as if your wish were to make a statement to the populace: "Now you realize for the first time how esteemed is the Emperor!"

According to the laws in the civilized nations, there is no right that is not accompanied by duty. At present, however, Your Majesty is recklessly promoting autocratic monarchy, giving yourself omnipotent power, while political affairs are at a standstill, as you pay absolutely no attention to them. People are suffering from hunger and cold, yet you do not bother to inquire into the situation; instead, day after day you conduct pleasure outings, displaying your haughty and overbearing manner to the populace. How could you shift the blame onto your officials? Your Majesty is highly esteemed indeed, but why is it that the people are suffering under your rule? This is because you know only how to enjoy your rights and are not aware of your duties.

Judging from the fact that you have not fulfilled your duties, you must bear responsibility in accordance with the law with respect to the offense of deceiving the country and betraying the people. Your Majesty will be at the top of the list of the accused. The above is the sixth offense.

7. *Shady deals behind the present visit to France:* Many of those who pay attention to national affairs in our country have suspiciously followed news of Your Majesty's present visit to France: at the beginning with apprehension, then with concern, and finally with mockery, while regarding one another. You have stated that the purpose of the visit is to bring the Crown Prince to France to study, to pay your respects at the monument of the war dead[26] from our country, and to visit the cities devastated by the war. These are all [matters related to] your personal business and not the public affairs of our country. Neither are they urgent matters.

You have stated that the purpose of the visit to France is to study its civilization in order to carry out political reform in our country. But Your Majesty is not a person who could do that. France is a democratic country, but you are a king who promotes

---

[26] From the First World War.

autocratic monarchy. It is like trying to force a square bar through a circular hole, only causing damage to the bar. In addition, you do not know the French language, and the ministers accompanying you, like M. So-and-so, are from the vulgar class in our country, and their knowledge is below that of a ten-year-old French boy. I have heard that while Your Majesty has been in France, you have gone to watch a horse race, placed a bet, and won 200 francs. You have not stepped into a museum, a university, a chamber of commerce, a manufacturing plant, a monument of French civilization, or the like. How can you say that you came here to study, not having been to these places?

You have stated that you came here to attend the Inter-colonial Exposition in Marseille. That is to say, to exhibit the products of our country. But these are the works of the inhabitants either of Bắc Kỳ or of Nam Kỳ, i.e., the works of people living in the regions under the direct rule of French authorities (the only item from Trung Kỳ sent to this Exposition are bamboo blinds, which have not improved much in the last fifty years). In the twelve provinces of Trung Kỳ under Your Majesty's autocratic rule, the literati are ignorant—being completely shut out in the dark—and the peasants are skinny, like pieces of wood; what sort of skills could one expect from them? Your ministers and your court officials only possess skills in kowtow, in bribery, and in misappropriation of public funds to enrich themselves. Regrettably, scoundrels and devils like that in France have been either drowned or thrown into the flames like wolves some sixty or seventy years ago; therefore, those who are accompanying Your Majesty have no one to compete with at the Exposition! Thus it is not difficult to discover those who are pulling the wires behind your present visit, as well as their machinations.

I have heard that several years ago Your Majesty, relying on autocratic power, illicitly sold off the property of the people and used the money to purchase the most luxurious goods from our country and every other East Asian country. In addition, you amassed the treasures from preceding reigns. Altogether, they amounted to more than one hundred chests.[27] You brought all of them with you on this trip and have used them as gifts to certain men to persuade them to campaign, through the French Monarchist Party, for the consolidation of the throne for yourself and your son. With their support, you hope to fulfill your dream of promoting autocratic monarchy. Once this plan has been achieved, you will return to our country, recklessly flaunt your excessive authority, and silence the voice of the people. Afterward, you will conclude certain treaties as a favor in return. Although this scheme is supposedly a secret, it has been the talk of the town, and this rumor is not groundless. Everyone believes it—as a French saying goes: "There is no smoke without fire."

Nonetheless, if Your Majesty is thinking of such a plan, it is a useless one. You wish to consolidate a regime of autocratic monarchy, on the one hand, but you are soliciting the people of a democratic country, on the other. From the outset, I have known that this business stands absolutely no chance of success. Your Majesty is handicapped by stupidity and ignorance—not having read anything on the history of the Revolution of the French people. Once you become aware of this, you will hang your head in chagrin and return home ashamed.

---

[27] The French translation gives an exact number: 104 chests. See No. 2431/S.G., SPCE 371, CAOM, p. 26 (SPCA: Service de Protection du Corps Expéditionnaire; CAOM: Archives à Centre des Archives d'Outre-Mer, Aix-en-Provence).

In Europe, at the end of the eighteenth century, the power of autocratic monarchy reached its peak. Rewards and punishments were decided arbitrarily. *"L'État c'est moi."* The emperors saw the people as their slaves and spent money as if throwing away dust. Their palaces were imposing, and their pleasure outings were extravagant. Their costumes were luxurious, and the etiquette for kneeling in homage was strictly observed. These were things that surpassed the imaginings of a monarch of a nominally semi-independent nation in the present day, like Your Majesty. When things go to the extreme, they provoke a reaction. That is the natural way.

In France at that time, distinguished philosophers such as J. J. Rousseau, Montesquieu, Voltaire, and others, one after another, rose up to expound their views of popular rights (Viet. *dân quyền*). Within a few decades, the influence of their ideas was felt throughout Europe. When the French people, the pioneers, waved their arms, the response resounded everywhere. Some were executed. Others failed and rose up again. The more they fought, the more passionate they became. Eventually, their ideas triumphed. The head of the French king, Louis XVI, was thus set on top of the guillotine.

Your Majesty has been to Paris; along its long boulevards and in the large public squares, you must have seen the bronze statues commemorating the philosophers and the heroes who risked their lives in defense of freedom. You must have seen the pillar that reaches up into the clouds; atop it stands a Goddess who holds in her hand the flame of Liberty radiating in four directions. That is the Goddess of Liberty, who illuminates the whole world and has no mercy for any tyrant monarch on earth. If you use your spare time to visit the Place de la Concorde and Versailles, it was at Versailles that Louis XVI was captured and at the Place de la Concorde that he was executed. After you have seen these reminders of the final moments of a tyrant monarch, you may reflect upon yourself.

From that time on, France adopted a republican system, with a parliament with legislative power and a governing cabinet responsible to the parliament. At present, the fact that autocratic monarchy is vanishing in the world, and that mankind thus can enjoy liberty, is all thanks to the sanguinary struggle of the French people. Why doesn't Your Majesty make arrangements with the minister of colonial affairs to take a tour of the Palais Bourbon, where you may obtain some notion of the spirit of Liberty, Equality, and Fraternity of the people of the Republic? If you will compare it with the gloomy, thousand-year tyranny in our country, you will see that the sacred and inviolable ideals of popular rights are like the sun at noon, shining all over the world and leaving no room for autocratic monarchy to survive, let alone a barbaric tyranny!

Was not all this done by human power? An evolutionary process (Viet. *thiên diễn*) like this was inevitable. At present, the people in the world consider France "the founding country of popular rights." Is it not most appropriate? Is it not most appropriate?

To such an honorable nation and to such an honorable people, the more than one hundred chests of treasure Your Majesty has brought are worth nothing. Notwithstanding, you have tried to use white jade and gold to lure and bribe people, going against the dominant trends of the world and betraying human justice. You have sullied the honor of our people to secure the survival of autocratic monarchy, which is already as fragile as the morning dew. The anger of the twenty million people of our country is a small thing compared to the disgrace that our country must suffer vis-à-vis the other countries in the world!

Your present visit, therefore, will end in failure. There is absolutely no doubt about this. Regrettably, the wealth of our people, worth six or seven million piastres, along with priceless national treasures accumulated by our country over the past several hundred years, have been thrown away into the waves of the Atlantic Ocean by your single act of carelessness! The above is the seventh offense.

These seven offenses all relate to our national destiny and the living conditions of the masses, therefore they have been listed and discussed. There are numerous other grievances that have not been listed because they do not directly relate to national affairs, or are simply of a personal nature.

Behold! In the world [outside Vietnam] of the present day, the intellectual level of the people is advancing one thousand miles every day. Several decades ago, the constitutional monarchs in Europe and Asia entrusted, unconditionally, all political matters in their countries to their people and dared not look back. Day and night, they hoped only to retain the nominal fame of being above their people. They would consider it a blessing from heaven if they could preserve the succession of their dynasty and avoid bringing shame to their ancestral temple. Nonetheless, even now, their people are still annoyed by their extravagance and have devised all sorts of schemes to remove them from the throne so that the genuine ideals of populism (Viet. *bình dân*) might be realized. From now on, the day is certainly not far away when monarchy will be washed away in the deluge, and one does not have to be an intelligent person to realize this. As a matter of fact, during the Great World War, thirty-eight kings, including three great emperors,[28] were murdered by their people.

From the olden days, as already mentioned, our country has adopted autocratic monarchy as her political system. Our people have not been allowed to question the advantages and disadvantages of a policy or to ask whether a government official is wise or ignorant. During our times, the fortune of our country has gone from bad to worse; it has even ceased to exist as a sovereign nation in the world. Look around East Asia: with respect to China and Japan, it goes without saying that they are sovereign nations. Even the Siamese—formerly less advanced than we were—at present squarely stand as equal to other nations in the world.

Within our country, the two regions of Nam Kỳ and Bắc Kỳ, which were placed under French administration several decades ago, soon escaped from the yoke of autocracy; thus, the injurious effect of the government officials' corruption was mitigated to a certain extent.[29] The development of industry and commerce, and the

---

[28] Phan Châu Trinh exaggerated when he referred to "thirty-eight kings" being "murdered." As for the "three great emperors," the list should include the heir of Emperor Franz Joseph of Austria-Hungary, archduke Franz Ferdinand (1863–1914), who was assassinated on June 28, 1914, in Sarajevo—his death triggered the First World War—and Tsar Nicholas II (1868–1918), the last Emperor of Russia, King of Poland, and Grand Duke of Finland, who was killed on the night of July 16–17, 1918, by a squad of Bolshevik secret police. As for the third emperor, it is not clear whom Phan Châu Trinh had in mind. Emperor Franz Josef (1830–1916), father of Franz Ferdinand, is the most likely candidate: he died during the war, his reign lasted sixty-six years, and he was the last significant Habsburg monarch. But Emperor Franz Josef was not "murdered" by his people.

[29] As a person who was born in Quảng Nam, Annam, Phan Châu Trinh focused on the problems in that area and tended to overlook the issues in Bắc Kỳ (Tongkin) and Nam Kỳ

renovation of the water supply system, also have helped to improve the people's "living conditions" somewhat. The twelve provinces of Trung Kỳ were, however, left outside of the protectorate, and even now are still groaning under an irresponsible autocratic government, finding no protection even at their last gasp.[30] Whose crime is it? Whose crime is it? It can be said that no one else but the incumbent monarch of the present day should take the blame and be dethroned. But if one looks into the origins of the problem, then one sees that the monarchs of past generations also cannot escape open condemnation by the people.

In view of such dominant trends in the outside world and such conditions inside our country, your throne is indeed as fragile as a pile of eggs. Your present position is exactly like that of Emperor Xiandi (Viet. Hiến Đế) of the Han (Viet. Hán) dynasty[31] when he said: "I do not know how long my life will last!" But out of ignorance, Your Majesty is unaware of this. You compare yourself to a divine being, yet you direct a band of base fellows who under your shelter practice open bribery. You ignore what the people say to you. You are unconcerned about what the people resent. You go against the trend of the time (Viet. *thời thế*) and against the popular sentiment (Viet. *nhân tâm*). You try to rekindle the fire of autocratic monarchy from its ashes. You try to choke off the people's spirit (Viet. *dân khí*), which has already been enfeebled for a long time. You empty the national treasury and exhaust the wealth of the people. You care only for your own interest and ignore the resentment of ten thousand souls.

Is the land of Vietnam your personal property? Are the more than twenty million inhabitants of our country your private slaves? Are you afraid that the corruption of the officials in our country has not gone far enough so that Your Majesty must incite their greed? Are you so afraid that the blood and the fat of our people have not been exhausted yet that Your Majesty still needs to squander them? Are you afraid that Vietnam, the name of our country, has not been sullied enough that Your Majesty has to bring an even worse odor upon it, making other people ridicule it, not counting it as a part of mankind? What evil deed has our country committed that it has to put up with this retribution? What offense have our people perpetrated that we are forced to contend with this demon as our ruler? If, together with the mass of the people, we do not oust him, we shall certainly have to drown with him in the future.

Now that I have written this much, my brush is worn down, my arm is sore, my paper has run out, yet the things that I wish to say have still not been exhausted. These thousand words that I have written without stopping are not to attack Your Majesty personally but to attack a tyrant. It is not for self-interest that I have done this but for the overthrow of tyranny and the promotion of liberty on behalf of more than twenty million of my compatriots. Mencius said, "Indeed, I am not fond of disputing, but I am compelled to do it."[32] My inmost feelings are just the same.

(Cochinchina). The imperial mandarins in Bắc Kỳ and the Vietnamese officials in Nam Kỳ were not paragons of virtuous government.

[30] The twelve provinces of Trung Kỳ (Annam) were not "left outside the protectorate." Instead, they should be considered the core of the protectorate, even though the emperor remained in power there.

[31] Also known as Xiao Xiandi (Viet. Hiếu Hiến Đế; 180–234 CE, r. 189–220 CE). He was put on the throne by Dong Zhuo (Viet. Đổng Trác) and supported by Cao Cao (Viet. Tào Tháo), but was removed by Cao Pi (Viet. Tào Phi).

[32] The source for this quotation can be found in *Mencius*, "Teng Wen Gong," Part II, pp. 378–79. See *Han-Ying Sishu*, pp. 378–79. In the original text, the cited statement was Mencius's

If Your Majesty still possesses natural goodness (Viet. *thiên lương*) and some sense of compunction, and realizes that autocratic monarchy is not to be relied on and people's resentment cannot be ignored, you should first abdicate, then return the power of governance to our people so they can collaborate directly with the French people for their mutual benefit.[33] If you do so, our people will bear the circumstances in mind and will not treat you badly. For Your Majesty, there is no better course of action.

If you make use of this visit, in defiance of popular sentiments, to further your ambition, hold onto the throne, and employ your autocratic power recklessly, causing serious damage to our national living conditions, in the face of this danger I must certainly declare an unrelenting war against you. I must domestically make a proclamation to our people and externally appeal to France. For the sake of twenty million Vietnamese compatriots, I vow that, if necessary, my head will fall, but only together with Your Majesty's barbaric autocratic monarchy. I am determined not to leave our country—its thousands of miles of mountains and rivers, its twenty million and more parents and children—in the hands of a tyrant forever!

[Notes:]

a) The original version of this letter in Chinese characters is sent to Your Majesty. Its French translation is dispatched to the French press and is also circulated as a flyer to solicit judgment from the French people.

b) Because the relationship between Your Majesty and me has already been severed, I have been speaking to you on equal terms. I have, therefore, not used the term "respectfully addressed to" (Viet. *thượng*) but simply "addressed to" (Viet. *ký*). I have employed the two-character term "Your Majesty" (Viet. *bệ hạ*) because it is a convenient form of address in Chinese and not because of any respect for you.

c) As I am a follower of Confucianism (Viet. *phục tùng Nho giáo*), I have not observed the autocratic etiquette that was instituted at the time of the First Emperor of Qin (who burned books and buried scholars, putting an end to [genuine] Confucianism): i.e., the avoidance of the use of the personal names of the sovereign. Japan abolished this practice a long time ago, and in the present-day world, it exists only in our country. In this letter I have therefore used the banned words deliberately in order to register my protest.

d) I have added end-of-sentence punctuation for sentences in this letter, fearing lest it might take you too much time to read.

Marseille, July 15, 1922
Phan Châu Trinh

---

reply to Gungduzi, one of his disciples, when the latter said to him: "Master, the people outside our school all speak of you as being fond of disputing. I venture to ask whether it be so."

[33] In this case, Phan Châu Trinh's assumption that, if the emperor stepped down, the Vietnamese people would be given "the power of governance," or that they would be able to "collaborate directly with the French people," is rather optimistic. There is no indication that the French would have agreed to this arrangement or, even if they did, that the French and Vietnamese would have been able to work together.

MORALITY AND ETHICS IN THE ORIENT AND THE OCCIDENT

[Lecture delivered at the Vietnam Society House, Saigon, in the evening of November 19, 1925. The original text was in modern Vietnamese (Viet. *quốc ngữ*)]

Dear Compatriots,

Seeing that I am an elder, who just returned from France after a long sojourn there, you are so kind to give me the opportunity of being the first person to stand before the podium in this Vietnam Society House to express the opinions and aspirations that I have been nurturing for Vietnam. For all this, I am very grateful, indeed.

You are certainly aware, I suppose, that it was in the interests of the Vietnamese people that I have exerted myself during the last eighteen years or so. During those eighteen years (four years in Poulo Condore Island and fourteen years in France), I longed to meet compatriots from our homeland to share the ideas that I had heard and seen implemented during my eventful sojourn in a foreign land. My dream has come true, unexpectedly, as finally I was able to step again on native soil and to meet so many brothers and sisters tonight. I am so gratified, indeed.

Compatriots! Now that I have the opportunity to meet all of you, allow me to present a few ideas on "Morality and Ethics in the Orient and the Occident," and I hope that you will see the reasons for my talk.

If one follows the fashion of the present day, there are many world-shaking and challenging issues that I could share with you. Notwithstanding, I have not selected one of these issues in vogue, but have deliberately chosen to speak on "Morality and Ethics," a subject that appears so commonplace and utterly outdated.

I have chosen this subject because I believe that, from ancient times to the present day, regardless of the people, regardless of the country, regardless of the race, and regardless of national power, once a nation is standing in the world to compete against other nations, it cannot count only on its material strength but must also rely on morality as its foundation. For a nation that has fallen down, in order to rise up and avoid being trampled over by others, it is all the more necessary to have a moral foundation even firmer than that of wealthier and stronger nations.

The kind of morality that I am going to expound on is by no means especially profound, but it is not the same kind of morality to which conservatives have often referred. Morality in this case is defined as follows: "Once a nation exists in the world and possesses a legitimate history, it must preserve the shining aspects of that history."[1] This is to say, the people must preserve the fine values and superior qualities that their ancestors, over thousands of years, have left, so that they will earn respect from other nations. In short, these characteristics have been crystallized over

---

[1] Source unidentifiable.

an extended period of time; like jade, they will not wear off when polished, and like tempered iron, they will not break into pieces when struck.

* * *

Compatriots! After living abroad for a long time, upon coming home and glancing at the current state of our country, I feel very sad, indeed. Alas! The old morality has, without notice, disappeared, but the new morality has not yet taken shape. Look, the scholars of the old school[2] unyieldingly state that the liberal-minded youth should be forced to observe the old morality. What an absurdity! While these gentlemen make such a statement, in practice they have lost not only qualities such as propriety, righteousness, modesty, and a sense of shame (Viet. *lễ, nghĩa, liêm, sỉ*), but also have allowed the morality that had been left by our ancient ancestors to drain away downstream. My point here is simply to say that they were unable to preserve it. Even if one compares our antiquated and time-honored ethics of several thousand years ago with the ethics in the Western world today, there are sharp contrasts. When the youth look at the obstinate old scholars, they become all the more arrogant; although they have not learned much, they think that they are already superior to the old men. They do not behave themselves, and as a result their conduct is halfway, neither French nor Vietnamese. With respect to this point, numerous French people who lived long in the colony have written books criticizing [the behavior of Vietnamese youth].

You have seen our people gathering in small groups to tell one another that the French are arrogant and look down on the Vietnamese. But we should ask ourselves whether or not we live and behave in a manner that deserves their respect. With regard to this state of affairs, there are so many examples that can be cited. In the past several decades, owing to the impact of world trends, in our country one saw the rise of the conservative party, the reformist party, the pacifist party, and the extremist party. These parties fought against one another vociferously, but at the conclusion there was no impact. When the situation went out of control, one found that they were all ruffians—those who blemish our national integrity, causing foreigners to look down upon our people and to trample us.

Confucius said, "Heaven helps those who are good and knocks down those who are degenerate." Mencius, on the other hand, stated, "A man must first despise himself, and then others will despise him."[3] In other words, we should blame ourselves and not somebody else. Today it is with that thought in mind that I have selected this topic.

From the ancient times to the present, when we learn anything, we only learn through our mouths, rarely do we try to analyze the meaning of each word, and therefore we often make a misinterpretation. For example, we often consider that morality (Viet. *đạo đức*) and ethics (Viet. *luân lý*) have the same connotation, but in fact morality is morality and ethics is ethics. Morality encompasses ethics, and ethics is no more than a part of morality.

---

[2] Scholars of Chinese studies (Viet. *Hán học*).

[3] The source for this quotation can be found in *Mencius*, Book 7 (Li Lou), Part I. See *Han-Ying Sishu* [The Four Books in Chinese and in English], trans. James Legge, annot. Luo Zhiye (Hunan: Hunan Chubanshe, 1992), pp. 396–97.

To be a human being, one is expected to have *nhân* (benevolence), *nghĩa* (righteousness), *lễ* (propriety), *trí* (wisdom), *tín* (trustworthiness), *cần* (diligence), and *kiệm* (frugality). *Nhân* is to have compassion for others; *nghĩa* is to do the righteous thing; *lễ* is to conduct life in accordance with proprieties; *trí* is to act correctly; *tín* is to keep promises made to others, to be trusted; *cần* is to be diligent in working; and *kiệm* is to be thrifty and sparing, saving for a rainy day. The person with morality is the one who behaves according to the way of human beings (Viet. *đạo làm người*). As such, morality remains the same, old or new, Oriental or Occidental. In other words, regardless of the time and the place, everyone must preserve morality in order to be a complete person. Even though new doctrines might be expounded by scholars, even though political systems might be different—be it democratic, monarchic, or communist—the truth of morality cannot be ignored, i.e., morality can never be changed.

Ethics are, however, different. Ethics are often variable. Depending on the time and the place, ethics may change. For example, in our country, under the Đinh dynasty,[4] it was possible to install five empresses at one time, but in later dynasties, i.e., Lê, Lý, Trần, Lê, Tây Sơn, and Nguyễn, only one empress was installed. During the Trần dynasty,[5] those who belonged to the same family clan could marry one another, but in later dynasties this practice was prohibited. As well, when the country was faced with an external invasion, the kings invited elders from across the country to the imperial palace to learn their opinions, but in later dynasties, everything was decided autocratically by the kings and their cohorts. When parents pass away, in one country it [the family's act of mourning] would be seen as filial only if their children eat their flesh or burn their bodies; but in another country grand funerals, with trumpets and drums, are an expression of filial piety. Seen from the above examples, ethics are changeable and, as a matter of fact, are variable according to the time. It is possible to change ethics, but it is impossible to change morality. That is the difference between ethics and morality. To illustrate, ethics are like a robe that can be changed according to the size of the person, but morality is like rice, water, and nutrition—all are needed for everyone, one cannot change [one's morality] even if one wishes to, and if it is changeable, it is false morality.

I have tried to explain clearly that morality and ethics are quite different from one another so I can discuss the need for a change of ethics in our country, and so you will not be stunned when you hear me say that "ethics must be changed." If I did not explain clearly the difference between morality and ethics, when I say "at present, in order to meet the trends of the time, we should replace autocratic monarchism with democracy," those of you who took morality and ethics to be identical would rise up and scream "if autocratic monarchism is abolished, then the old morality of our country will collapse!" But now I hope that this misunderstanding has been averted.

Now I would like to look briefly into Oriental and Occidental ethics. Western ethics teach children even more effectively than do our ethics that they must respect their parents; their [Vietnamese children's] first primers are the *Trimetrical Classic* (Viet. *Tam tự kinh*) and the *Three-thousand Characters* (Viet. *Tam thiên tự*). Western ethics are not different from ours, except that, according to the law, at age twenty-one, when boys and girls become adults, they can leave their parents and live on

---

[4] Đinh dynasty, 968–980 CE.
[5] Trần dynasty, 1225–1400 CE.

their own, assuming duties and responsibilities according to national ethics (Viet. *luân lý quốc gia*), and the burden for the family thus becomes lighter. Seeing that Western ethics are somewhat different and perhaps more simple than ours, our people thought that Westerners were barbaric. Our people do not realize that, in the olden days, their [Westerners'] ethics were similar to ours, but as their national ethics developed, their family ethics (Viet. *luân lý gia đình*) came to be less emphasized—this change is a natural evolution. Much in the same manner, as social movements in Europe have become powerful, numerous thinkers have begun contemplating means to break the stuffy family bondage so that everyone in the same country would be equal, i.e., both the rich and the poor are to be educated and to live in the same way, putting an end to the enormous gap that exists between them today. The purpose of breaking the wall that divides social classes is to maintain social order and to ensure that everyone is equal.

ON NATIONAL ETHICS IN EUROPE

In Europe, national ethics have been developing since the sixteenth century, when monarchism was still in vogue. Europe's monarchs at the time were like ours, that is, recklessly autocratic—they considered themselves as saints or gods. Owing to this, numerous philosophers clarified the distinction between the nature of a monarch and of a nation. As a result, people came to understand the importance of a nation and to place less emphasis on their family.

The second factor was that, during this time, the martial spirit among the European peoples was strong; they fought against one another and often took pride in victories and felt humiliated in defeats. Owing to that spirit of chivalry and their sense of self-esteem, European countries even so long ago acquired very solid national ethics. In short, their national ethics were created for these two reasons. Yet by now, the situation is in decline; after four years of the Great War, not only have people had to suffer within the defeated countries, but even within the victorious countries people have been afflicted with many problems. Everything was destroyed—a bad situation for everyone! The great politicians, great philosophers, and great educators all came to realize that the age of nationalism has passed and cannot be maintained, giving way to the age of social ethics (Viet. *luân lý xã hội*). Although in every country there is a conservative party that vehemently opposes this trend, the social movement is like a torrent, and how can it be halted? It is only natural that social ethics triumphed afterward.

We have seen how family ethics were replaced by national ethics, and national ethics have given way to social ethics.

* * *

Social ethics are not brute ethics imposed by a government on its people, or by a country on another country; they are, domestically, concerned with how an individual should treat another individual in the same country and, broadly speaking, concerned with how human beings should treat each other in the world.

At the time when national ethics were still popular in Europe, there was this saying: "There is justice between one individual and another individual, but there is no justice between one nation and another nation." At present, as human sentiment has moved toward social ethics, there is the following saying, diametrically opposed to the previous one: "There is even justice between one individual and another individual, so when hundred of thousands, millions and billions of people gather together to become a nation, how is it possible that there will be no justice?"

I have shown how widespread the principle of social ethics is in Europe. The implication of the question, "How should an individual interact with another individual in the same country?" can be illustrated in this way: Do the people help one another? Do the wealthy help the poor, that is, do the wealthy donate their money to build hospitals or schools for the poor? Or do the passers-by extend their help upon seeing someone badly treated on the streets? In short, social ethics are based on a sense of public justice (Viet. *công đức*), and public justice is in turn based on a sense of personal justice (Viet. *tư đức*).

To gain their livings and further their interests, the people in Europe compete against one another fiercely, but they compete only within the law. They help one another with respect to public justice and maintain a sense of respect for each other's interest. You might think I praise the Europeans because I was in France so long. I will say that in Europe there are also bad people; their public standards of moral goodness (Viet. *dân đức*) are not perfect. But even if 50 percent, or even only 30 percent, of the populace observes their ethics, it is possible to say they have them. In spite of the fact that their customs still have defects, there are those in the upper and middle classes who have social concerns, and great politicians, philosophers, writers, and educators make appeals, write books and plays, publish newspapers, and deliver speeches to denounce social evils. The social and democratic youth will support and unite with them [socially concerned, influential individuals] to tackle corrupt customs and evil practices. They have concerns not only for their own country, but also for the entire world.

In contrast, it is a shame that our people, though having to work throughout their lives, cannot look after their basic personal needs and prepare for their old age, let alone think of society or humanity! How could we not respect the Europeans if they are so superior to us?

* * *

Now let me compare our ethics to European ethics. Of the five human relationships[6] in our ethics, three are concerned with family ethics: i.e., *cha con* (father and son), *anh em* (brothers), and *vợ chồng* (husband and wife). If the ethical ideas of the ancient times were put into practice properly, there would be no room for criticism. According to Confucius, these ethical ideas included "affection between father and son, distinction between husband and wife, and orderly sequence between old and young."[7] Had we followed and elaborated on these principles, even if our family ethics were narrow-minded, it would have been much better than the lamentable ethics that we have today! The ethics in East Asia, especially in our country, have disintegrated so badly only because the autocratic monarchs have practiced incorrectly the teachings of Confucius and Mencius.

---

[6] In Sino-Vietnamese, "*luân thường*," "*ngũ luân*," or "*thiên luân*." The five human relationships are more commonly referred to by the following Sino-Vietnamese terms: *quân thần* (sovereign and subject), *phụ tử* (father and son), *phu phụ* (husband and wife), *huynh đệ* (brothers), and *bằng hữu* (friends).

[7] The source for this citation can be found in *Mencius*, Book 5 (Duke Wen of Teng,) Part I. See *Han-Ying Sishu*, pp. 358–59.

Not only were the kings autocratic; to maintain their tyranny, they also set up devices to pull those who were fathers and husbands into their trap. The ostentatious scholars (Viet. *hủ nho*) also got trapped—adding legs to a snake—and put forth shallow-brained ideas to restrain the people's freedom, such as: "Once we are born in this country, we must hold the king in high respect."[8] They [the scholars] paid no attention to the king's qualities and his policy. As long as the person was nominally a king, they revered him. As they revered the king, they necessarily had to treat the father with veneration, saying: "In the world there are no bad parents." Alas! Ostentatious scholars! It is only because of your heretical ideas that the family ethics of our country have become so degenerate!

Let me give you a commonplace example, which we often see but to which very few of us pay attention. The example is the poem and the drawings in loud colors that accompany "The Twenty-Four Examples of Filial Piety" (Viet. *Nhị thập tứ hiếu*),[9] often found hanging on the walls of Vietnamese houses. These drawings are in poor taste, and the poem, which one is sick of listening to, is merely harmful evidence of heretical Confucian morality. It is nonsensical that the good are presented as too good, the evil as too evil, and the things described are superstition, not the actual state of human behaviors. Consider! How is it possible that from a bamboo grove in the winter, when all the leaves have fallen, there would suddenly spring out bamboo shoots owing to the cries [of the young man, Meng Zong (Viet. Mạnh Tông)]?[10] How

---

[8] In Sino-Vietnamese, "*Quân thần chi nghĩa bất khả đào ư thiên địa chi gian*," which literally means, "The righteousness between the sovereign and subject cannot forsake in this life."

[9] The author was Guo Jujing (Viet. Quách Cư Kính) of the Yuan dynasty. Many different versions of *The Twenty-Four Examples of Filial Piety* can be found in China, with varied titles and story sequences. These versions all included folktales featuring iconic figures who exemplified traditional Confucian values having to do with filial piety. These stories were extremely popular in Vietnam because of the Vietnamese cultural emphasis on filial piety rather than on loyalty. In Vietnam, Lý Văn Phức (1785–1849) translated the book into Vietnamese 7-7-6-8 meter poetry (Viet. *song thất lục bát*) under the title *Nhị thập tứ hiếu diễn âm* (The Twenty-Four Examples of Filial Piety, in National [Vietnamese] Sounds).

Lý Văn Phức was born in Hà Nội; his pseudonyms were Lân Chi and Khắc Trai. As a high official, he experienced many ups and downs in his career. He served three emperors—Minh Mạng, Thiệu Trị, and Tự Đức. During his years of service, Lý Văn Phức traveled, as an envoy, to Bengal, Singapore, Canton, Fujian, and Macao. In addition to translating *The Twenty-Four Examples of Filial Piety*, he authored numerous other works, including: *Tây hành thi ký* (Collection of Poems While Traveling in the West; 1830), *Tây hành kiến văn lục* (Record of Observations in the West; 1834), *Việt hạnh ngâm* (Poems in Canton; 1834); *Việt hạnh tục ngâm* (Poems in Canton, Continued); *Mân hành thi thảo* (Poems in Fujian); *Kính hải tục ngâm* (Poems in Macao, Continued); and *Sứ trình chí thảo lược* (Abbreviated Record of Travels). Note that "the West" in "Traveling in the West" does not mean the West in the modern sense, but implies the region to the southwest of Vietnam, which included Bengal and Singapore. Part of the reason for referring to these regions as "*Tây*" may also be that they were under Western rule. See Trịnh Văn Thanh, *Thành ngữ điển tích, Danh nhân từ điển* [Dictionary of Phrases, Classical Allusions, and Historical Notables] (Soạn giả giữ bản quyền), vol. I, "Lý Văn Phức" (Sài Gòn: Hôn Thiêng, 1965–66), pp. 701–04.

[10] From Lý Văn Phức's *The Twenty-Four Examples of Filial Piety, in National Sounds*, Twentieth Story, Meng Zong (Viet. Mạnh Tông). Meng Zong, the protagonist, was believed to have been born in the epoch of the Three Kingdoms. Since his father died when he was young, in the story Meng Zong lives alone with his mother. One day, his mother becomes ill and tells him she longs for bamboo-shoot soup. Since it is winter, there are no young plants growing, but as Meng Zong searches in the cold, suddenly a shoot appears from the soil, and he cuts it gladly and brings it home to his mother, who makes a soup and drinks it and is cured. People believed that because of Meng Zong's filial piety, the bamboo shoot appeared magically.

is it possible that a fish could jump up from the icy water [so that Wang Xiang (Viet. Vương Tường) could make a fish dish for his step-mother]?[11] These absurd stories were created by Guo Jujing (Viet. Quách Cư Kính) of the Yuan (Viet. *Nguyên*) dynasty,[12] and not a long time ago. Many were caught in Guo's trap and hung these drawings on the walls of their houses as symbols of Confucianism. No one would dare to condemn the practice. If this is all family ethics are, how could they avoid being made more degenerate day by day? Consider the current state of the family in our country. Parents consider their children to be their fortunes, saying that since they give birth to their children, it is up to them [the parents] to decide their children's future. For example, if the parents do not wish to be engaged in social activities, they will not allow their children to engage in social activities. If the parents do not wish to travel far, they will not let their children travel far. If the parents wish to bend their heads under the gates of the powerful so their children may gain employment by securing some famous public office, they will force their children to act in the same way, giving their children absolutely no freedom. Such is the situation in wealthy families. In poor families, children are slapped, called names, and beaten, as the parents think that whipping is the best way to train their children and do not realize that by doing so they implant a submissive and servile mentality in them. When the children are at home, they have to breathe the authoritative atmosphere in their family; and when they go to school, they have to breathe the authoritative atmosphere of their school (our people like to send their children to strict and harsh teachers). When these children grow up and enter society, how can they possibly escape that submissive and servile mentality? The servile spirit of our people today comes precisely from the authoritarian atmosphere of our families.

The law of our country gives much power to the parents and to the husband. The bond between father and son now can only be observed among the peasants who work hard to support their parents; among those in the middle and upper classes, there is no such thing as filial piety. The majority [of children in more wealthy families] borrow only the appearance of absurd decorum from heretical Confucianism to block the public eye, but in practice they have neither filial piety nor a sense of duty to their parents. When their parents die, these children lie on the street, walk with a stick, cry at their parents' graves, and refrain from washing [for a

---

Owing to this popular story, in China there was a variety of bamboo shoot called "Meng Zong." See Trịnh Văn Thanh, *Thành ngữ điển tích, Danh nhân từ điển*, vol. II, "Nhị thập tứ hiếu," p. 914.

[11] From Lý Văn Phức's *The Twenty Four Examples of Filial Piety, in National Sounds*, Eighteenth Story, Wang Xiang (Viet. Vương Tường): Wang Xiang, the protagonist, was believed to have lived during the Jin (Viet. *Tấn*) dynasty. In the tale, his own mother dies and his father remarries. Wang Xiang's stepmother tells false stories about Wang Xiang, hoping to turn his father against him, and yet Wang Xiang treats her with respect and without resentment. It is wintertime, the water is frozen, and yet the stepmother yearns to eat fresh fish. Wang Xiang takes off his shirt and steps on the ice to look for fish. Suddenly the ice splits, and two carp jump out, which Wang Xiang carries home for his stepmother's soup. Impressed by this evidence of their son's sincerity, his father and stepmother regret their unjust treatment of Wang Xiang and from then on treat him kindly. See Trịnh Văn Thanh, *Thành ngữ điển tích, Danh nhân từ điển*, vol. II, "Nhị thập tứ hiếu," p. 913.

[12] The actual compiler of this work was Guo Jujing (Viet. Quách Cư Kính), of the Yuan (Viet. *Nguyên*) dynasty. Phan Châu Trinh mistakenly gives the author's name as Quách Thủ Chính (C. Guo Shoucheng) of the Ming (Viet. *Minh*) dynasty.

certain period of time],[13] but the truth is that they do not feel anguish or faint at their parent's death. This is simply a deceitful public display. Not only do they behave hypocritically when their parents die, they also deal with their parents insincerely when they are still alive.

With respect to the bond between husband and wife, there are sayings, such as "the wife follows what the husband says" (Viet. *phu xướng phụ tùng*), "the concubine and wife consider it appropriate to follow one's husband" (Viet. *thiếp phụ dĩ thuận vi chính*), or "the wife follows her husband after marriage" (Viet. *xuất giá tùng phu*); however, we all know that harmonious families are those in which both husband and wife demonstrate proper conduct and have equal footing. In cases where the wife is wiser than her husband, she will be in charge of that family. Seen in this light, every practice that is created against human nature cannot be forced upon the people, no matter how powerful a tyrannical power might be.

* * *

So far as national ethics are concerned, I can assert that they indubitably do not exist in our country. For the moment, let me say that our national ethics from the ancient times to the present day have been confined, parochially, to the two words "king" and "subjects" (Viet. *vua tôi*). There has been nothing about "people" and "country" (Viet. *dân và nước*), because the people have not been allowed to discuss national affairs!

Who was the king (Viet. *vua*)? The king was the one who held the governing power (Viet. *quyền chính*) in a country or was the head of a tribe. He might have been a hero who fought on behalf of his people against a brute force to restore their ancestral land and who had positioned himself to be their leader. He might have been a crafty person who took advantage of troubled times and used trickery to overthrow a dynasty to create his own. He might have fought his own compatriots to acquire autocratic power, or he might have been a foreigner who came with his forces and fought for his own interest. In short, the king was the one who considered public rights as his, and the land of others as his own.

Who were the subjects (Viet. *tôi*)? The subjects were those who submitted themselves to the king (i.e., the king's vassals), the slaves of the king, or those who worked for the king. They were those who risked their lives on the battlefields in exchange for a golden or red-stamped certificate of achievement; they were those who exposed themselves in torrential rains or under scorching sun in exchange for an insipid glass of wine or a word of congratulation. In short, the subjects were slaves who sold their spirits as well as their bodies to the king for a low price.

Because national ethics in our country from the ancient times to the present day have been so simplistic, the people in the country do not realize what popular rights are: What is love for their country and what are their duties? The kings in our country in the past have been like this, the subjects in the past have been like this, historical texts have described a country like this! The people are therefore not aware of the distinctions between the king and the country. They know only the duty of

---

[13] In the old days, some children demonstrated their filial piety by organizing elaborate funerals for their parents and hiring people to cry at the grave. They would also show their respect by lying on the street, overcome with grief, and using a stick for support when they walked, and they would not shave and clean their bodies for three years. Aspects of these rituals can still be found in Vietnam today.

revering the king and do not know the duty of loving their country. In those cases when there has been a decent king, who practiced fair government, the people loved him and risked their lives to fight against their enemies. In those cases when there has been a tyrannical King, who conducted various evil deeds, the people hated him, wanted revenge, and opened the citadel gates for the enemy to enter. For instance, when France launched an attack against Tongkin, it had only ninety soldiers, and these soldiers were able to capture four citadels in twenty-four hours, and the Vietnamese soldiers did not return a single shot. When Nguyễn Huệ took his troops from Huế to Hanoi, Nguyễn [Hữu] Chinh was stationed there, but even before the battle took place, his forces had already collapsed; as a result, the emperor was forced to flee and was robbed.[14] Mencius said, "If the king treats people as grass and garbage, they will treat him as a stranger."[15] Once the people had come to consider Emperor Chiêu Thống a stranger, it was no wonder they robbed him.

Thus, since ancient times our country has not had national ethics; there have been only laws that the king and his court vassals have forced their people to obey. There has been no ethical bond tying the king to his people, and the king has simply worked with his court vassals to gain the power necessary to repress the people.

An exception occurred during the Trần dynasty, during which the kings were very attached to the people. The kings' children played with the children of common people, and the elders were allowed to discuss national affairs. After the kings would abdicate the throne in favor of their crown princes, they frequently traveled around the country to study [unfamiliar] customs and politics so that they could make reforms according to the people's wishes. The people therefore loved their high-mindedness and risked their lives to cooperate with the kings on a number of occasions to fight against the Mongols. It was thanks to the people's cooperation that the kings were able to achieve such brilliant victories.

Today, when we read the glorious chapter of the Trần dynasty, we feel joyful, and when we come across the tragic history of the Lê and the Nguyễn dynasties, we are struck by a sense of sadness, but we have never thought about the roots of the rise and fall of a dynasty.

Anyone who has learned some French knows that its texts for kindergarten and elementary schools all teach that one must love one's family and love humankind. Notwithstanding, at present, I am amazed to see that no one [in our country] dares to open his [or her] mouth saying "I love my country!" Over the last sixty years, as our

---

[14] Nguyễn Hữu Chỉnh (?–1787) was a former follower of Nguyễn Huệ of the Tây Sơn. After successfully subduing the rival forces in Hanoi, Nguyễn Huệ withdrew his army from this ancient imperial city and appointed Nguyễn Hữu Chỉnh to be the caretaker there. The ambitious Nguyễn Hữu Chỉnh, however, quickly switched allegiance and declared his support for Emperor Lê Chiêu Thống (r. 1787–88), supporting him against the Tây Sơn. To counter Nguyễn Hữu Chỉnh's act of betrayal, in 1787 Nguyễn Huệ dispatched his generals, including Ngô Văn Sở, Phan Văn Lân, and Vũ Văn Nhậm, to Hanoi. Nguyễn Hữu Chỉnh was arrested and executed. Emperor Lê Chiêu Thống escaped from Hanoi and fled to China to ask for help from the Qing dynasty. That dynasty responded by dispatching a huge army in his support, but it was routed by the gifted Nguyễn Huệ in early 1789. Before he marched north to attack these invaders, Nguyễn Huệ was proclaimed the Quang Trung Emperor in late 1788. He reigned vigorously until his premature death in 1792.

[15] The full version in the original text for this quotation reads: "If a king treats his officials as his dogs and horses, they will treat him as a stranger. If he treats them as mud and grass, they will treat him as an enemy." The source for this quotation can be found in *Mencius*, Book 8 (Li Lou) Part II. See *Han-Ying Sishu*, pp. 410–11.

country has been under the protection of a country that is highly civilized and liberal, why is it that the seed of liberty has not sprouted?

Is it not because the root of autocratic evil was planted deeply in our minds from ancient times? The law under Emperor Gia Long banned the use of the term "patriotism" (Viet. *thương nước*). Students and the common populace were not allowed to talk or to be concerned about national affairs. Anyone who loved the country was imprisoned. In order to protect themselves, the hereditary families trained their children, casting them in a mold so they would be frightened of feeling concerned about the affairs of the world and of loving their country. What a fear! They are so frightened, as if they fear they would be despised and humiliated—be seen as thieves or robbers—if they talked about those matters. It is amazing that no one among the people in our country, living under the politics of the French, who consider love for one's country as a natural human disposition, dares to talk about this subject. It appears the people now are even more frightened than they were during the time of autocratic rule. There are those who believe that what I am saying is idealistic, arguing that "in France the French want to teach patriotism, but in this part of the world they do not teach such. Those who talk about patriotism will immediately have their names entered into the black list of the French *Sûreté* [and be marked] as subversives, so how could they not be frightened?"

I am more than aware of the above matter, but I wish to say that our ancestors have left that legacy. That "chain" was produced by our ancestors to restrain us. Other people have simply taken advantage of it to chain us down, but the chain was not brought over from France! The French use it because they know that we cannot respond. How can they stop us, however, if we reply, "A people who come from the same stock and share the same language, and who have lived on the land that over the past four thousand years their ancestors have shed sweat and blood to develop, how can they be stopped from enjoying their rights on that land, the right to live and to die on it, and to rely on it in good times as well as in bad times? How could they ever forget the graces of the land that they have come to call their 'motherland'? To such a people, if they do not love their motherland, whom should they love then?" If we respond to them properly in this way, no matter how cruel they might be, it will not be easy for them to neglect us. If that is the case, why do we not dare to say that we love our country?

The patriotism that I am referring to is not the one that instigates people to stage insurrection with "empty hands" or to go to other countries to beg for help and then come back to foment riots![16] Let me tell you, our country was weak; therefore, it fell into the hands of the French. Now, with patriotic love we must defend one another, to help one another, so in the future we can restore our integrity and rights. If the French prove unfair, we must work together to oppose them. If the French do something right, we must give credit to them. Do not act as if, since we have lost our sovereignty, we do not care to acknowledge the positive things that the French have done. If we love our country in the manner I propose, would our patriotism go

---

[16] Though he is not explicit, Phan Châu Trinh seems to have Phan Bội Châu in mind at this point. Phan Châu Trinh returned to Vietnam from France in 1925. Phan Bội Châu also arrived in Vietnam from Shanghai in 1925, having been arrested by the French authorities. At this time, Phan Bội Châu was living in Huế under house arrest. Since Phan Châu Trinh died shortly after presenting the above speeches, he and Phan Bội Châu met with each other for the last time in 1906.

against French interests? My answer is "No." It is only natural that the Vietnamese people hate whoever cripples their country.

In my opinion, it is only because our people are cowardly that foreigners can repress us. If the Vietnamese people would come to know how to love their country, come to know how to acquire wisdom that could benefit Vietnam, then the foreigners will have to look for a way to encourage our patriotism, because it is patriotism that will allow us to select the appropriate way to deal with them. If we love our country in an intelligent way, then we have true patriotism; if we love our country in a wrong way, not only will we not bring any benefit to our country, but also the lives of the people will be sacrificed. If we say that we love our country, but only in words and do not do anything and ask for people from another country to come, this is not different from a servant who switches from one master to another. I dare say that if the French do not allow us to love our country and just leave us aimless, it will provide no benefit to them, and it will dispirit us as well. Our patriotism will also benefit the French, as no Vietnamese would be willing to collaborate with the French without purpose.

I have not presented all my ideas, but as I have been long-winded, allow me to summarize my argument in this section. From now on, our Vietnamese people should love their country, this being a natural disposition, and hold no grudges against the French. Unless national ethics are implanted in our minds, our national independence cannot be achieved. You may be surprised to hear this statement from me, a person who has just returned from France. In Europe, people have already buried nationalism, yet I am now declaring publicly that we need it. Am I going against the movement in Europe? No, it is not so. We have to realize that people in a country are similar to students in a school: they have to make gradual progress, from lower class to higher class, without taking shortcuts. That is to say, we should move from family ethics to national ethics and from national ethics to social ethics. In other words, it will take us about twenty or thirty years to go through national ethics, and only then can we move on to social ethics.

* * *

"Social ethics" is not known at all in our country. Our people are much more ignorant about social ethics than about national ethics. It goes without saying that friendship alone cannot replace social ethics.

In the Confucian text, there is a saying: "regulate one's family, govern one's country, and pacify the whole empire [Viet. *thiên hạ*]."[17] The term "*thiên hạ*" here implies society. At present, those who study to become government officials also pretentiously refer to this term, but only to make informed people laugh. The real meaning of "*bình thiên hạ*" (pacify the whole empire) has long been lost.

Although socialism[18] (Viet. *xã hội chủ nghĩa*) is so popular in Europe and has been widely expanded, people in our country are completely unaware of it, as if sleeping.

---

[17] This saying is taken from *The Great Learning*, "The Text of Confucius." See *Han-Ying Sishu*, pp. 4-5.

[18] Used as a noun. The modern Vietnamese-language term for "socialism" (approximately post-1945) is *chủ nghĩa xã hội*, and the phrase *xã hội chủ nghĩa* is now used only as an adjective. But Phan Châu Trinh was writing this article in late 1925, following his repatriation from France, and at that time *xã hội chủ nghĩa* was still used as a noun—meaning "socialism." Đào Duy Anh's *Hán Việt từ điển* (Chinese–Vietnamese Dictionary) was published by Trường Thi

How pitiful! Not only do our people not understand the duties that humankind has toward humankind, but also they do not understand the duties that each person in a country should have. In France, if a person of power or the government uses authority to repress an individual or an association, people make an appeal, resist, or stage a demonstration until a fair solution is reached.

Why are people in France able to do so? It is because they have associations and a public awareness that promote their common interest. They believe if they allow a powerful person to abuse his power, then that person will necessarily intimidate them. Therefore, they work together in advance to prevent that from happening. They are all educated and able to consider things carefully and over the long term. What about our people? So far as our people are concerned, whoever meets with a misfortune is left alone, and no one cares! Whenever someone has an accident or whenever a weaker person is bullied by a stronger person on the street, people simply act as if they have nothing to do with the person in trouble.

Our ancestors understood that we have to help one another. For this reason, there are sayings, such as "It is impossible to break the chopsticks when they are in a bunch," or "Many people clapping their hands at the same time will produce a big sound." In other words, the Vietnamese people from the earliest times were aware of the strength of solidarity, of public interests, of the fact that "numerous winds put together will produce a typhoon," and that "a forest is made of individual trees." They were not segregated, opportunistic, or timid, as they are today.

Our people lost their sense of solidarity and public interest because, in the past three or four hundred years, the students in our country craved power and official position. Thirsty for glory bestowed by imperial dynasties, they became deceivers and cajolers, knew only the kings, and neglected the people. In order to protect their position and wealth, they created laws that broke down the solidarity among the people.

In spite of the sufferings and the hardships of the people, the kings, as long as they were on the throne and still had officials kowtowing to them from below, did not care if that situation would last for one hundred or one thousand years. To the kings, it did not matter if the people were wise or ignorant! They did not care if conditions were good for the people or bad for them! If the people possessed a servile spirit, this was considered entirely good because the king would be on the throne for a long time and the court officials would become even wealthier! Moreover, as indicated by the saying "if one person in the family becomes a court official, the entire family will receive benefits," no matter how greedy, how

---

(Saigon) in 1931. It is interesting to note that the person who revised (reviser, Viet. *hiệu đính*) Đào Duy Anh's dictionary was Phan Bội Châu, using his pseudonym Hãn Mạn Tử. Đào Duy Anh's original definition of *xã hội chủ nghĩa*, used as a noun, may be close to what Phan Châu Trinh had in mind when he talked about "socialism": "An economic and political movement that advocates collaborative rather than individual actions, intending to ameliorate inequities in society. This doctrine attacks the present-day capitalistic system, holding that all capital, lands, and possessions/wealth should be publicly owned. It can be divided into these schools: socialism (Viet. *xã hội chủ nghĩa*), which argues that progress must be made gradually; *syndicalism*, or trade unionism; and communism, which calls for revolution. Apart from these, socialism also includes corporate socialism, labor unions, and anarchism." Đào Duy Anh, *Hán Việt từ điển*, p. 572. This lecture, "Morality and Ethics in the Orient and the Occident," was the only work in which Phan Châu Trinh mentioned the term "socialism." He died roughly four months after he delivered this lecture. It would be of great interest to know exactly what Phan Châu Trinh had in mind when he talked about socialism and "socialist ideas."

corrupted, how covetous, how avaricious an official might be, no one would criticize him. Even if an official stripped the peasants of the rice they produced to purchase land and rice fields, or to build his residence, no one would denounce him. Those outside of these officials' families congratulated them on their luck, and those within their families relied on their authority. How could the greedy students not compete against one another to enter officialdom? The officials in the past and at present in our country are like this! The ethics of the higher classes (Viet. *thượng lưu*) are like this! I myself do not call them higher classes; I only use the term so that the audience can follow my points without difficulty.

In the past, these people were Confucian scholars who earned the bachelor (Viet. *cử nhân*) or doctorate (Viet. *tiến sĩ*) degrees; in the present day, they are those who have followed Western studies and worked as clerks and interpreters, or occasionally they have been cooks, but became government officials through the power of their masters. These government officials may be appropriately called "licensed robbers."

The wealth and power generated by officialdom also tempted those who had previously stayed outside of the government to enter it. They bribed the mandarins and employed every possible means, including renting out their rice fields or selling their buffaloes, in order to become village heads or heads of public services in a canton so that they could be sitting above others or could cast an imperious look at other people. It is amazing that no one criticizes or despises these people! Alas! What a deplorable situation! The population in a village is not big, but there is no moral or ethical tie among the villagers, as they just follow the motto, "Yield to the powerful!" That is the situation among the villagers, and toward residents coming from outside it is even worse. Alas! With such a people, how is it possible for revolutionary ideas to be born in their minds? It is also for this reason that there is no socialism (Viet. *xã hội chủ nghĩa*) in our country, Vietnam.

In order for Vietnam to have freedom and independence, in the first place the Vietnamese must have solidarity. In order to have solidarity, what can be better than circulating socialist ideas among the Vietnamese?

ON EUROPEAN MORALITY AND EAST ASIAN MORALITY

The Europeans are seen by us, on the surface, as aggressive, ferocious, and cruel. But this is not true: we are mistaken. Living with them for a long time, we will recognize that they have a morality of a much higher standard than ours. Their morality and ethics are high because they have been influenced by liberal ideas ever since the Greco-Roman age. They have also gone through a period of autocracy, but their public spirit (Viet. *dân khí*) is different from ours. Their public sentiment is very enthusiastic (Viet. *phấn phát*), and their character is highly dignified (Viet. *anh hùng*). The more autocratic the rulers became, the more undaunted were the philosophers who came forth to write books and songs to promote popular rights. No matter how distressing the path might be, they were fearless; this is why their bronze statues and their names carved on stone monuments still remain today. Those of you who have been in Paris must have seen the bronze statues of the philosophers who fought against Christian theocracy.

In the seventeenth and eighteenth centuries, Jean Jacques Rousseau wrote *Du contrat social* (1762), La Fontaine wrote *Fables*, Montesquieu wrote *De l'Esprit des Lois*

(1748), and Pascal,[19] Voltaire,[20] and others all contributed to unshackling their compatriots from autocratic rule. I have cited a few names to show that even under tyrannical rule, still there were people who took an interest in national affairs. Currently, the freedom of expression, publication, and speech is guaranteed, and those who are engaged in political and social affairs are indeed numberless. Only Confucius, Mencius, Mozi (Viet. Mặc Tử), Laozi (Viet. Lão Tử), or Zhuangzi (Viet. Trang Tử) of the Spring and Autumn (Viet. *Xuân Thu*) period [722–429 BCE] and the Warring (Viet. *Chiến Quốc*) period in ancient China might be compared to the men cited above. From the Qin (Viet. *Tần*) dynasty [221–206 BCE] on, not only in Vietnam, but in all East Asia, there has been no person of such caliber.

In our country at present, is there a person who may be called a moralist (Viet. *nhà đạo đức*)? Even since the time of the Lê dynasty,[21] is there anyone who may be called a moralist like those I mentioned? Nevertheless, in every dynasty there were always those who were commended by the king and worshipped in shrines built in their honor!

In short, no one dares to challenge those who have been revered by the king, and no one dares to revere those who have been destroyed by the king. Such being the case, how could a moralist in our country exist? People who advocate liberal ideas therefore are seen as eccentric, and the king sees them as subversive to his autocracy and moves to destroy them. In such a country, how is it possible to stop the flatterers from growing in number?

Montesquieu said, "The people who live under an autocratic monarch have no ideas about morality and see their social status as their chief source of pride. It is only under democracy that there is genuine morality."[22] For this reason, in order to have genuine democracy in our country, we should take this opportunity to break the tyrannical chain and bring in liberal ideas from Europe as a medicine for our people. Only when that has been done will new moralists appear in our country.

Let me tell you the story of Trần Quý Cáp in 1908,[23] which will illustrate how the autocratic regime has damaged morality and ethics in our country. Mr. Trần was an upright, honest, and erudite person, who taught in Nha Trang. As a teacher, he took it as his responsibility to encourage local people to build more schools. Simply

---

[19] Blaise Pascal (1623–62), French mathematician, physician, and philosopher. Author of *Pensées*.

[20] François-Marie Voltaire, 1694–1778. French writer and enlightenment thinker.

[21] Lê dynasty: 1428–1527; 1583–1788.

[22] Source unidentifiable. The difficulty in locating the source here stems partly from the fact that Phan Châu Trinh had read Montesquieu in a Chinese translation, rather than in the original French. Nonetheless, these ideas can be found in Montesquieu's discussion of forms of government in *De l'Esprit des Lois*. In this work, Montesquieu maintained that "honor" stands opposed to the principle of monarchical government, and the laws of a monarchy therefore are designed to preserve the power of the king and his allies. Montesquieu asserts that the core principle of democracy is political virtue, by which he means "the love of the laws and of our country."

[23] Trần Quý Cáp, 1870–1908. Trần Quý Cáp, a native of Quảng Nam, whose pen name was Thai Xuyên, passed the *tiến sĩ* examinations in 1904 and worked as a teacher in Khánh Hòa province. Like Phan Châu Trinh, Trần was an important voice in the modernization movement. When the tax revolts erupted in Trung Kỳ, Trần was arrested and executed in Khánh Hòa by its provincial judge (Viet. *án sát*), Phạm Ngọc Quát. It appears that Phan felt very bitter about Trần's death.

because of that, he was arrested by the prefect, Phạm Ngọc Quát,[24] when a riot broke out, and Trần was executed within twenty-four hours. Was it not because of autocratic rule that such a tragedy occurred?

Granted that we do not have public morality, now let me ask you, does each of us have personal justice? My answer is: We do not! In a country under autocratic rule, nothing related to morality can be born.

I often see that, among our compatriots, those who are a bit knowledgeable lie to the more ignorant people. So, not only are the "licensed robbers" pompous, but those who have not yet obtained their "license" are, too. I am aware that there are many of those whose social position is not as glorious as others, whose intellectual capacity is not superior to that of others, and whose qualifications are just good enough to fit them to be "servants for foreigners," yet when dealing with their compatriots they are so arrogant, claiming they are teachers, or that they are big bosses. It never crosses their minds to question themselves when they are claiming to be teachers and big bosses and ask whether or not they have done anything for "the Vietnamese," the voiceless suffering majority. I am also aware that there are those who have written articles in newspapers and magazines to point out that morality and ethics in our country are corrupted, but what they said has not brought about any effect, just like casting pearls before swine. Why is this? These writers did not put into practice what they wrote, so it only makes sense that people dare not follow them; what's more, the ethics advocated in their writings were based on the corrupt customs (Viet. *tệ tục*) of autocratic regimes. That the people do not pay attention to our national ethics should be of no surprise as they are inappropriate and unsuitable for modern times.

If we now introduce European morality and ethics, would there be any aspect opposed to the teachings of Confucius and Mencius? I have thus far criticized our ethics and praised Western ethics; probably the audience is astonished, thinking that I am betraying the teachings of Confucius and Mencius. I would like to tell you that ever since I came to understand Confucian morality to a certain extent, I have adored it. Even though Confucianism is outstanding, how can one find it today? Should one go to China to look for it? Should one look into Vietnamese history books? I suspect that even if one lights a torch to search for it, it will still be impossible to find, as Vietnam and China abandoned it long ago.

Contrary to what you might think, Confucianism is not an ideology that serves the autocratic monarchs. Confucianism is very fair (Viet. *bình đẳng*), teaching that the monarch and the people are both equally important (Viet. *quân dân tịnh trọng*). The monarch and the people both need to be equipped with morality and ethics; in other words, the people must respect the monarch as if he were their parent, and the monarch should understand the need to love and watch over the people as if they were his infants.

In *The Great Learning*, Master Zeng (Viet. Tăng [Sâm]) quoted Confucius, saying: "From the emperor down to the mass of the people, all must consider the cultivation of the person the root of everything."[25] Self-cultivation is such a crucial aspect, one

---

[24] When he wrote "A New Vietnam Following the Franco-Vietnamese Alliance," in 1910–11, Phan Châu Trinh still did not know under whose order his friend Trần Quý Cáp was killed. By the time Phan Châu Trinh composed this piece, however, he had learned details of his friend's death.

[25] The source for this citation can be found in *The Great Learning*, "The Text of Confucius." See *Han-Ying Sishu*, pp. 4–5.

which Confucius insisted the people and the monarch must practice. Was he not fair? This form of government (Viet. *chính thể*) has been practiced in Europe for a long time, i.e., the form of government in which power is divided between the monarch and the people (Viet. *quân dân cộng trị*),[26] which has been rendered into Chinese as *junzhu lixian* (constitutional monarchy; Viet. *quân chủ lập hiến*). At present, Britain, Belgium, and Japan practice this form of government. Because the intellectual level of the people in the first two countries is very advanced, the rights of the monarch have diminished; nonetheless, the people still have affection for their monarch and the monarch loves the people. The situation in Japan is not as good, but as it has adopted a constitutional monarchic system, it will attain its goals.

At the time of Mencius, because the kings of the vassal states had become so autocratic, he advocated democracy (Viet. *chủ nghĩa dân chủ*). As he said: "The people are the most important element [in a nation]; the spirits of the land and grain are the next; the ruler is insignificant."[27] At present, in spite of the fact that the forms of government in Germany, France, and Russia are somewhat different, these countries all practice democracy. Seen in this light, there is nothing in the present civilization of Europe that goes against the teachings of Confucius and Mencius. Confucius said that the monarch must love the people and the people must love the monarch, but it is regrettable that he did not say what the people should do if the monarch does not love the people. Mencius also said that the people are of the first importance and the monarch is of the least importance, but he does not mention what the people should do if they question the monarch and he answers that "the monarch is of the first importance and the people are of the least importance."

For this reason, since the time of Confucius and Mencius, in China as well as in Vietnam, the strongest clan has always become the ruling clan, and when they have grown weak, they have lost the throne; if the monarch was fair, the people followed him, and if the monarch was brutal, the people killed him. For this reason, the longest dynasty did not last more than several decades. When dynasties shifted, it caused chaos that led to internal fighting and slaughter: father killing son, son killing father, elder brother killing younger brother, younger brother killing elder brother, monarch killing his subjects, or subjects killing their monarch. There were no moral principles and standards.

Because the teachings of Confucius and Mencius are no longer properly understood, what would be better than introducing European democracy to our country in order to establish a solid morality and ethics? Democracy is a wonderfully efficacious remedy against the autocratic disease of our country. To bring in European civilization is to bring back the teachings of Confucius and Mencius. The teachings of Confucius and Mencius are the reasonable way (Viet. *đạo trung dung*) to meet regular daily [ethical] needs, such as respect for parents or love for humanity, and are not fanatical like some religions. In other words, the introduction of European civilization would not cause any harm, but it will help to enhance the teachings of Confucius and Mencius.

I would like to reiterate that the kind of civilization that should be introduced is the genuine Western civilization, which is harmonious with Confucianism in East Asia, and not the empty liberty and independence of the perplexed students of

---

[26] Can also be translated as "limited monarchy."

[27] The source for this citation can be found in *Mencius*, Book 8 ("Jin xin," Part II). See *Han-Ying Sishu*, pp. 540–41.

Western studies (Viet. *Tây học*) or the empty national spirit or national essence (Viet. *quốc hồn quốc tuý*) of the outdated scholars of Chinese studies (Viet. *Hán học*).

I suppose you understand, from what has been stated thus far, the point I would like to make is that because the teachings of Confucius and Mencius have been carried out in a mistaken manner, the countries that have practiced this heretical form of Confucianism (Viet. *tà nho*) for more than one thousand years are all weak and underdeveloped and have disgracefully lost their national independence. For example, in the case of Korea, when the Manchus invaded, it followed the Manchus; when the Mongols invaded, it followed the Mongols; and now Japan has come and annexed it. In the case of China, the Song (Viet. *Tống*) dynasty was replaced by the Yuan (Viet. *Thanh*) dynasty (of the Mongols), the Ming (Viet. *Minh*) dynasty was replaced by the Qing (Viet. *Thanh*) dynasty (of the Manchus). Alas! China was taken by the Mongols and the Manchus, and Korea was taken by Japan. Was it not because of corrupt, heretical Confucianism in China and Korea?

Is it not silly to entrust a monarch with the governing power over a country of millions of people? Even in the case of an intelligent monarch, it would be difficult for him to accomplish every responsibility, and things would be even worse under an ignorant monarch who committed cruelties and prohibited the learned people from participating in national affairs. Who would then dare to shoulder the burden? If a family has no one to take care of it, or if a country is not tended, how can that family and that country not collapse and disappear?

It is only natural, therefore, that China and Korea lost their independence. It is all the more painful to talk about our country. Less than fifty years after Emperor Lê Thánh Tông's adoption of the legal system of the Ming dynasty, the Lê dynasty was overthrown by the Mạc. The Trịnh rose under the excuse of restoring the Lê dynasty, but this justification was merely nominal, as the emperors of the Lê dynasty were still murdered one after another. There was no righteousness among the monarch and his ministers (Viet. *quân thần*), there were no ethics. When Emperor Gia Long adopted the Qianlong (Viet. *Càn Long*) code of laws, [the government] became all the more autocratic. In less than eighty years, the country was lost in a most humiliating manner. Was not it because of the monarchs and the court officials of the Lê and the Nguyễn dynasties?

Thanks to Korea's adoption of Western civilization in recent years, an independence movement took place in 1919. Similarly, in China, it is owing to the movement to boycott foreign goods that both Britain and France have tempered their arrogance. It is possible to say that nationalist sentiments have already sprung up in the minds of the Chinese and Korean peoples.

What about our country? People in our country remain in a perpetual sound sleep. As yet there has not been any sign that they are awaking. The older are finding the way to become government officials to feed their wives and children, the younger are anxious to become teachers to feed themselves. Apart from caring for their bodies, they think of nothing else. In addition, there is also a group of people who profess with elation that they love their country and love their race (Viet. *ái quốc ái chủng*), but when they are asked about how to expand our strength and reduce our weakness, or how to strengthen and rely on ourselves, they mumble as if they had been plunged into a deep reverie and are only awaiting another country to come in.

Is it because the Japanese people have adopted the tangible form of European civilization that they have become so wealthy and powerful, or because they have modified their ethics? Our people often claim that we are of the same race, same religion, and same culture (Viet. *đồng loại, đồng đạo, đồng văn*)[28] as the Japanese people. We sing their praises because they have made great progress, but we have never tried to consider the reasons for their progress. Is it because they have built ships and manufactured guns that they have become as powerful as they are today, or is it because they have also enriched their morality and modified their ethics? Those who have read Japanese history will know that the Japanese have worked hard for the enrichment of their morality. From the Meiji Restoration until the promulgation of the constitution some twenty-two years later, many people dedicated themselves to the overthrow of the Shogunate government and to drafting the constitution, and many sacrificed their blood to build an advanced, wealthy, and strong nation like the Japan of today.

I am curious about the [Vietnamese] returnees from Japan! I do not know what they did when they were there! There is a saying, "Near the ink you are black, near the light you will shine." Why was it that those who went to Japan did not bring back good things so that the Vietnamese people could benefit, but instead only contributed to the entrenchment of [the people's] slavery? Even despicable things that an average person would not do, these people would do without the slightest compunction! Is it because morality and ethics no longer exist in the conscience of our people that we cannot absorb the morality and ethics of other nations? Or is it because our people are like those whose lungs are not functional, so they cannot breathe, even when they are in a country that has pure air (Viet. *thanh khí*), such as Japan? Viewed from a historical perspective, the Vietnamese people are neither indecent nor unintelligent, so why is it that under the protectorate government in the past sixty years they have remained ignorant and stubborn, unable to learn the strengths and excellence of other people?

There are those who say that we are ignorant because the French have held us back from learning how to manufacture guns, airplanes, submarines, and the like. The people who make such statements do so because they have not learned French history and they love themselves too much—only blaming others and unable to blame themselves. Why do they forget that when the French arrived, the French feared that we might follow China, so they allowed us to go to France to study, but our people obstinately resisted the idea? Did not the French provide us with two thousand guns and five warships? But our people did not dare to hire even a single Frenchman to guide them [in the use of these weapons]. Our soldiers did not handle them [the guns] properly, and as a result they were all ruined. I do not intend to praise all the French as having good hearts, but only hope to point out to you that their diplomacy was so masterful and we were so clumsy. If we had made use of the opportunity to travel to their country to learn their skills, then now, even though we might still be inferior to Japan, compared to the Philippines and Siam we would not be that far behind.

In the olden days, when our eyes were closed, we knew of Chinese civilization but nothing else; it is therefore not difficult to understand that our wisdom was hindered by the Chinese-style civil-service examination system (Viet. *khoa cử*). Nowadays, though our eyes have been opened, we remain totally unaware of and unresponsive to the fact that China has undertaken important moves, such as sending students to the West or replacing monarchism with democracy. Moreover, the Vietnamese who have returned from China are talking nonsense, criticizing this

---

[28] The term more commonly used was "*đồng văn đồng chủng*" (same culture and same race).

person and denouncing that person, while they themselves possess no ability that deserves to be respected. One man even dares to criticize Sun Yat-sen (Viet. Tôn Dật Tiên), the representative of the present Chinese civilization, without realizing that his own achievement and ability are not worth even a tiny fraction when compared to those of Sun.[29] They have not learned about the qualities of the Chinese people; all they have learned are craftiness and greed. When things are seen in this light, it is possible to say that our people's spirit of morality and ethics has been poisoned to death by the civil-service examination system, and the only thing left is servility. The saying, "Once morality perishes, the nation will vanish," is true indeed.

There are a few heroic personalities who have not considered the matter carefully; they blindly believed ancient history, placed too much emphasis on imperial loyalty (Viet. *chủ nghĩa trung quân*) and revenge (Viet. *chủ nghĩa phục thù*), and employed plots, one after another, to deceive the people to rise up. Alas! What could one do with a knife or with a bamboo stick? It is pitiful for those who were executed by guns and guillotines. Unfortunately, the efforts of those who design these plots have brought no benefit and have only degraded our public morale (Viet. *dân đức*) and led servile and shameless groups to intimidate and bully the peaceable citizens.

Is it possible to adopt European ethics in lieu of the ethics we have lost? There are those who ask if it is possible to adopt European ethics in lieu of the ethics we have lost. My answer is no. In a country where the old ethics have been lost, the foundation is gone. Where would one graft the new ethics when adopted?

Take it for granted that the Western grafting techniques are marvelous. But [if there were an attempt] to graft a plant as healthy as Occidental ethics to a plant as withered as our Vietnamese ethics, one imagines that it would be impossible for the grafted plant to produce vibrant flowers and healthy fruits. In order to achieve a good result, prior to grafting, both plants should be nurtured so that from the outset they will have equal strength. The objective of my speech today is to express my hope that you will revitalize the old Vietnamese-ethics plant so that it may be grafted to the European-ethics plant.

* * *

Are European ethics perfect? What should we do to adopt them? European ethics are much superior to ours. But it would be impossible to say that European ethics are perfect. In the first place, as with any people, it is easy for Europeans to explain things in terms of morality and ethics, but it is difficult to act perfectly in accord with morality and ethics. In European society there are drawbacks, such as excessive freedom between men and women, high rates of divorce, enormous gaps between the rich and the poor, and people who are unemployed or overworked. Therefore, there is constant unrest brought about by the workers and capitalists. In addition, since fanatical nationalism was in vogue in the Middle Ages, love for one's country and antipathy toward foreign countries were excessive; as a result, wars have been incessant. Furthermore, because intellectual education takes precedence over moral

---

[29] Phan Châu Trinh does not identify this Vietnamese expatriate from China. It is worth noting, nonetheless, that by the time Phan Châu Trinh delivered this lecture in late November 1925, Phan Bội Châu had been arrested in Shanghai, China, and brought back to Vietnam.

education and diplomacy over honesty, social disputes have also been frequent. Those are just a summary; the list goes on.

Even though there are problems with European morality and ethics, the Europeans have remedies to deal with them. That is to say, there are philosophers and educators who devote themselves to remedying the evil effects, so that their morality and ethics will be uplifted day by day. In contrast, in our country only the good is shown and the bad is hidden, and thus the situation increasingly grows worse. For this reason, in assimilating Occidental ethics we must be purposeful and selective—only adopting that which is worthy of adoption.

*   *   *

My fellow compatriots,

I have spoken for a long time. Allow me to sum up by saying: We realize we have lost our national independence because of our ethics, and because of our loss of morality and ethics our people have become low-spirited and are looked down upon and trampled by foreigners. We must modify our ethics and nurture our morality. You have to try to do that.

[The audience applauded. Phan finished drinking a glass of water, then added a few sentences.]

My compatriots,

I realize that to restore the morality of a country in which things are in a big mess is not an easy task. But if we do not—on the grounds that it is too difficult to revive the old morality—then when will our country be able to join ranks with other nations? When I speak of the "old morality," I do not mean the morality in which children are the slaves of their fathers, wives are the slaves of their husbands, or the subjects are the slaves of their monarchs; but I rather wish to refer to the reasonable morality (Viet. *đạo đức trung dung*) of Confucianism, which can be applied any time and in any country. As I have mentioned before, it is neither old nor new and neither Oriental nor Occidental. This morality can be found in sayings such as "it is possible to murder a man but impossible to insult him,"[30] or "he cannot be led into dissipation by wealth and rank, nor deflected from his aim by poverty and obscurity, nor made to bend by power and force—all this is characteristic of a great man,"[31] and so forth.

---

[30] In Sino-Vietnamese: "*khả sát nhi bất khả nhục dã.*" The source for this quotation can be found in *Liji* (The Book of Rites; Viet. *Lễ ký*), Ruxing (The Conduct of the Scholar). See *Kadokawa Daijiten* [Kakokawa Great Dictionary of Etymology], ed., Ozaki Yujirô et al. (Tokyo: Kadokawa Shoten, 1992), p. 1734.

[31] The source for this quotation can be found in *Mencius*, Book VI (Teng Wen Gong, Part II). See *Han-Ying Sishu*, pp. 368–69. In these quotations, Phan Châu Trinh illustrates the nature of the morality he believed was necessary for the people of Vietnam to adopt as they confronted modern times and conditions. He emphasized that, regardless of the benefits or suffering associated with a situation, what mattered was one's core beliefs. At the national level, according to Phan Châu Trinh, strong morality and a strong will would provide Vietnam with the ability to chart its own course.

If we could preserve some aspects of our morality, adopt some aspects of European morality, and harmonize them, then if we could expand our ethics to include national ethics (for example, make all Vietnamese aware of their duty toward Vietnam), not only will the Vietnamese nation be wealthy and strong in the future, but no matter who will come to live with us on this land, they will no longer look down on us.

MONARCHY AND DEMOCRACY

[Lecture delivered at the Vietnam Society House, Saigon, on the evening of November 26, 1925. The original text was in modern Vietnamese (Viet. *quốc ngữ*).]

My fellow compatriots!

Ever since my exposure to New Learning (Viet. *tân học*), I have been agonized by a puzzle: Why is it that, in spite of the fact that all four East Asian countries belong to the same culture, practice monarchy, and venerate Confucianism, in the face of the expansion of European civilization to East Asia, it is only Japan that was able to abandon the Old Learning and adopt the New Learning, and within a mere forty years it was able join the ranks of the world powers? Furthermore, why is it that Siam, our neighbor that practices Buddhism and does not possess a Confucian tradition, is now able to join, on equal terms, the ranks of other countries in the world?

There is nothing extraordinary about this: if the English came, the Japanese and the Siamese let them come; if the French came, they let them come; they also treated the Americans and the Germans generously in order to learn things from these countries. In the remaining three countries—i.e., China, Korea, and our country—people are poor, the country is weak, and the illiteracy rate is 80 percent. Those who passed the "eight-legged" (Viet. *bát cổ*) essays [i.e., the civil-service examinations] alone occupy two-thirds of the so-called upper and middle classes. They have no understanding of true Confucianism, yet they have closed their eyes to condemn the new civilization as barbaric. This is the situation in China and Korea, and I will deal with Vietnam later.

The world trends, however, are unrelenting. Those who go with them are sailing with the wind, and those who go against them are pushed away and trampled on like grass. For this reason, the youth in Korea stood up to initiate a movement in 1919 that forced Japan to abandon its ambition and return to them their independence.[1] In China, there is a youth movement [1925],[2] which, if successful, will leave the world powers with no choice but to treat them [the Chinese] with fairness.

---

[1] It appears that Phan Châu Trinh mistakenly thought Korea won its independence in 1919. In fact, Korea gained its national independence on August 15, 1945—the day Japan declared its unconditional surrender. In January 1919, when the "Fourteen Points" outlining the right of national "self-determination" was proclaimed by US President Woodrow Wilson at the Paris Peace Conference, Korean students studying in Tokyo decided that the time to act had arrived. So on March 1, 1919, the thirty-three nationalists who constituted the core of the Samil (March First) Movement participated in the Manse (Long Live) Demonstrations and read the Korean Declaration of Independence to crowds gathered in Seoul, Korea. Newspapers estimated the size of the crowd at two million people. Japanese authorities were repressive but could not quell the public demonstrations that occurred thereafter throughout Korea.

[2] There were demonstrations throughout China after British troops killed twelve Chinese demonstrators in Shanghai on May 30, 1925. Soon after, unrest spread when fifty Whampoa (Viet. *Hoàng Phố*) Military Academy cadets were killed in an armed engagement with British

How deplorable is the situation of the Vietnamese people! Even at this moment, the so-called Confucian scholars (i.e., those who have studied Chinese characters and, in particular, those who have passed the degrees of *cử nhân* [bachelor] or *tiến sĩ* [doctorate]) do not know anything, I am sure, about Confucianism. Yet every time they open their mouths they use Confucianism to attack modern civilization—a civilization that they do not comprehend even a tiny bit.

With respect to the youth who pursue the New Learning, with the exception of a few who, thanks to their intelligence, are able more or less to discover something, the majority simply follow the old approach and hope only to acquire an official position or title, or to show off their erudite knowledge through their writings. There is no one who cares to compare the Western learning with our "Old Learning" and to single out what is good and what is bad so that our people may be able to judge and select the path for their future.

• • •

[Before we go into details] I must tell you that, owing to the huge topic of my lecture today, I will not be able to make everything crystal clear. Monarchy (Viet. *quân trị chủ nghĩa*) is government by men (Viet. *nhân trị*), and democracy is government by laws (Viet. *pháp trị*). To present a lucid explanation of this subject [how monarchies compare to democracies], one has to go back to the history of political science and political philosophy in Europe and Asia. So far as I am concerned, you know well that, with respect to the history of Chinese politics, I know something; but about Western things, I am highly ignorant. Nonetheless, I will do my best to tell you what I know; I will leave the explanation of profound aspects to those who know more than I do.

ON THE HISTORY OF MONARCHY

The state of monarchy in today's world is like a withered flower being blown by the wind. Look at East Asia: excluding the countries that have lost their independence, among the countries that are still going strong the monarchs are being kept as mere figureheads—only the Siamese king and the Japanese emperor are worth being called monarchs. In Europe, fourteen countries are democracies and only twelve countries still have a monarch. In the Americas, there is no country that maintains a monarchy. It is possible to say that among the eight billion people in the world, less than one-tenth still live under a monarchy.

What a glory was the authority of monarchy! How deplorable was the avarice of monarchy! During ancient times and the Middle Ages, the people were weak and ignorant; regardless of the country, they needed monarchical power to defend and protect them. Monarchy was a good remedy for mankind at the time.

Alas, human nature is such that one becomes more arrogant when one sees people showing their respect, and the more people there are who show their respect, the more one deifies oneself. Seeing that people act in accordance with one's wish, one wants to sit on people's heads! Moreover, one wants to have the power to be succeeded by one's descendants, generation after generation, as if one's country were

---

and French forces on June 23. Phan Châu Trinh may have read accounts of these events while traveling to Vietnam from France, as he arrived in Vietnam in June 1925.

one's private possession. Lands are given out at one's wish—as if selling a private rice field—and one treats people as slaves.

Look at history from the olden days until now: any given monarch who gained power did his best to hand down the throne to his descendants for generations. In the end, however, the longest dynasties lasted about one hundred years, and the short ones lasted less than ten years. This state of affairs happened in both Asia and Europe. But around the seventeenth and eighteenth centuries, in Europe the philosophers called for popular rights (Viet. *dân quyền*). The tyrannical monarchs who opposed the popular-rights movement were all overthrown; the monarchs who tried to be reconciled with their people managed to survive until now. With respect to this point, I wish to make it clear that monarchy in East Asia did not originate in Confucianism. I will show you clearly how this point has been misunderstood to the present day.

In their discussion of human history, European philosophers tend to start from the origin of mankind and progress to the creation of family heads, chieftains, lords, and kings. There is no time to talk about all this, and it would not bring much benefit to you today, anyway. For this reason, I will use Chinese history to explain so it might be easier for you to understand.

I will begin with Emperor Huangdi (i.e., the Yellow Emperor, Viet. Hoàng Đế). Emperor Huangdi was a powerful emperor in China. From the Kunlun (Viet. Côn Lôn) mountain region (western part of China), he moved down to northern China, fought against the Youmiao (Viet. *Hữu Miêu*), the local people along the Yangzi (Viet. *Dương Tử*) River, and killed their general, Chuiyou (Viet. Xuy Vưu). Huangdi was a prominent emperor of China, indeed. Yet, when Confucius composed his writings, he adopted Huangdi as the primal ancestor [rather than the first emperor] because of his bellicose inclination (Viet. *thượng binh thượng võ*); thus, Confucius began with Emperor Yao (Viet. Nghiêu) and Emperor Shun (Viet. Thuấn). Though they did not wish to become emperors, they had no choice because they were chosen and persuaded by the kings of vassal states (Viet. *chư hầu*). Succeeding Huangdi, Emperor Yao and Emperor Shun also had to dispatch an army against the Youmiao, but as [these emperors] achieved no success, within a month they withdrew their troops so they could devote their time to the improvement of their people's education and training.

It was during the time of Yao and Shun that the Chinese began teaching the five relationships (*ngũ luân*) to the people. They adopted a calendar with hours, days, and months, which was convenient for the farmers. They decided on weights and measures that the merchants could use in their balances. They laid down the standards for clothes and formal dresses, etc. ... so many other things that it is impossible for me to state all now. I wish to make this point clear: it was owing to Yao and Shun that Confucianism took form in East Asia. For this reason, Confucius spoke of Yao and Shun as the founding ancestors of Confucianism (Viet. *tổ thuật Nho giáo*). Mencius also commended only Yao and Shun. In Vietnam, those who have studied a few Chinese characters bring out Confucianism every time they open their mouths, without realizing this history whatsoever.

I would like now to give an account of China during the times of Yao and Shun. Yao and Shun were merely leaders of chieftains. On the basis of historical evidence, it can be estimated that there were at least fifteen thousand vassal states, and two hundred years later, when Emperor Wu (Viet. Võ/Vũ Vương) gathered the kings of the vassal states at Tushan (Viet. Đồ Sơn), this number had been reduced to approximately ten thousand. What were the protocols and what rights existed for the emperor at that time? The emperor resided in a small state, like those of the feudal princes, but there was a court etiquette stipulating that the feudal princes were to pay tribute to the emperor. The supreme right that the emperor (Viet. *thiên tử*; literally, "the Son of Heaven") possessed was to worship Heaven, and the feudal princes were allowed only to worship the mountains and rivers within their states. When the emperor visited the states, the feudal princes were obligated to welcome him. The emperor also had the right to appoint court officials, punish those who were guilty of offenses, and promote those who were meritorious to become feudal princes.

The brief summary that I have thus presented should be sufficient to give the idea that the emperor at the time was like a Secretary-General of the present-day League of Nations. The only differences are that the emperor received tributes from the feudal princes and, with the support of a majority of the princes, he had the right to reward or to mount a punitive expedition against a prince.

Pity those who pursued Chinese studies in Vietnam! When hearing the names of Yao and Shun, they would assume that these two emperors lived in a Five-Phoenix Tower (Viet. *Ngũ Phụng Lâu*), rode on a Six-Dragon Chariot (Viet. *Lục Long Xa*), and screamed at people at will, like our kings. But those who have studied geography or visited Pingyang (Viet. *Bình Dương*) and Puban (Viet. *Bồ Bản*) know that their capitals were very modest, equivalent only to two small citadels nowadays, i.e., not larger than two or three square miles.

After Yu (Viet. *Võ*) succeeded Shun, the emperors began to punish the prominent and stubborn feudal princes, i.e., those who had attempted to take over the imperial throne. For example, Yu killed Fangfeng (Viet. *Phòng Phong*), Kai (Viet. *Khải*) killed Youhu (Viet. *Hữu Hộ*), and Shaokang (Viet. *Thiếu Khang*) killed Houyi (Viet. *Hậu Nghệ*) of Youqiong (Viet. *Hữu Cùng*). I would call this the second stage in the evolution of the emperor's power. [The dynasty beginning with Yu's reign (2205–2198 BCE) is called Xia (Viet. *Hạ*).]

Four hundred years later, the throne came to [a tyrant called] Jie (Viet. *Kiệt*). There is no need to explain about Jie. Because the feudal princes did not have respect for Jie, they supported Tang (Viet. *Thang*), the prince of a small state, to be their leader and to drive Jie away; subsequently, Tang became emperor. As these things happened a thousand years ago, I am not certain as to their authenticity, and I only tell you what I know. When Tang was chosen by the feudal princes to be emperor, he told them and the people: "I am ashamed that I exiled Jie, but in order to save the people I had to do so." Even though he admitted this, the feudal princes nevertheless made Tang emperor [and thus began the Shang dynasty]. This was the third stage in the evolution of the emperor's power.

The descendants of Tang succeeded to the throne for six hundred years, and finally the throne passed to [a tyrant called] Zhou (Viet. *Trụ*). People did not have respect for Zhou, and the dynasty came to an end. At the time, two-thirds of the people under Zhou supported King Wen (Viet. *Văn Vương*), but King Wen did not wish to overthrow Zhou. It was Wen's son, King Wu (Viet. *Võ Vương*), who overturned Zhou [and began the Zhou (Viet. *Chu/Châu*) dynasty in 1122 BCE]. It can be inferred from the military campaigns that the soldiers' training by this time had become enormously thorough, orders were strict, arsenals and armor were formidable, honor was measured by the amount of bloodshed inflicted on the enemy, and the head of the captured enemy's commander was put on display—

similar to present-day barbarism. For this reason, Confucius commented that King Wen's virtue reached the highest point (Viet. *chí đức*), but he ridiculed King Wu as not being perfectly good (Viet. *vị tận thiện*).

From the time Yu created the Xia dynasty until the time of King Wu of the Zhou dynasty, there was a lapse of more than one thousand years. During Yu's time, there were more than ten thousand states. History books, by the way, do not mention the number of vassal states in existence when King Tang of the Shang dynasty drove away Jie. By the time King Wu of the Zhou dynasty overturned Zhou, there were eight hundred vassal states gathered to support him, though they were not solicited. Therefore, within one thousand years, more than nine thousand states disappeared. Under King Wu, the emperor's authority had become enormous; it is therefore possible to say that, by this time, the evolution of the emperor's power reached the fourth stage.

Let me sum up: Confucius, Mencius, Yao, Shun, Yu, Tang, Wen, and Wu were those who set the examples that kings of later generations could call Confucianism. We now have to consider whether or not the state of affairs and the practices of the later kings could be called Confucian.

During the Zhou dynasty, the people and the kings of the vassal states showed their respect for King Wen and King Wu, who destroyed King Zhou, King Cheng (Viet. Thành), and King Qing (Viet. Khang). But when the throne passed to King Li (Viet. Lệ) and King You (Viet. U), people rose up and murdered them, bringing an end to the [western] Zhou dynasty. This great period of history from Yao and Shun to King Wen and King Wu was like serene spring air and tender sunlight. Who would not praise it? Who would not long for it? Therefore it is appropriate that Confucius and Mencius relied on it to formulate their teachings.

It is strange indeed! With the coming of the Spring and Autumn period [722–429 BCE], i.e., the latter half of the Zhou dynasty, a new concept called hegemony emerged in the Five States (Viet. *Ngū Bá*), which paid no attention to benevolence and justice. Deception became a reciprocal affair [in the imperial court], and "emperor" became a nominal title. At this point, there were about three hundred states, which in a span of more than one hundred years were reduced to Seven Powers (Viet. *Thất Hùng*), which in turn were unified in less than a hundred years by [Shi Huangdi (Viet. Thủy/Thỉ Hoàng Đế), the First Emperor of] the Qin (Viet. *Tần*).

MONARCHY BECAME GOVERNMENT BY MAN

When Shi Huangdi (Viet. *Thủy/Thỉ Hoàng Đế*) took power, what did he do first? He laid the foundation for repressive monarchical autocracy. Fearing that the people might become wise, he ordered the burning of books. Fearing that scholars might challenge him, he ordered the burying alive of scholars. Fearing that leaving swords at large would allow people to use them to rise up against him, swords were confiscated, melted down, and recast into monumental statues. Local walls were destroyed and moats were filled, so people could not use them to resist his state. He took the popular saying "The nomadic barbarians will exterminate the Qin" (Viet. *Vong Tần dã Hồ*) as prophecy, and he conscripted people—including the old and the young—to construct the Great Wall, the construction of which was a source of great misery, and as a result the people resented his rule.

Shi Huangdi thought that by doing [those things] he would fear nothing. He built the Afeng (Viet. *A Phòng*) palace to accommodate thousands of imperial concubines. He constructed the Lishan (Viet. *Li Sơn*) tomb, which was three or four miles in length and had underground tunnels and citadels. He restricted the term "*Zhen*" (I/We; Viet. *Trẫm*) to use by the emperor only. As well, the emperor became known as "*Huangdi*" (Heavenly Emperor; Viet. *Hoàng đế*). Prior to that, "*huang*" (Heaven; Viet. *hoàng*) was "*huang*" and "*di*" (deity; Viet. *đế*) was "*di*" [they were not used together, nor used to describe the emperor]. The title of "*Wang*" (King; Viet. *Vương*) had been highly respected by Confucianism, but was used by Shi Huangdi to give to his followers.[3] Within fifteen years, the Chinese world fell into the hands of the Han when the second emperor was murdered by Zhao Gao (Viet. Triệu Cao); thus the tyranny was passed to another tyrant.

Here is my point. Please listen to it carefully! The Confucians in our country contradicted themselves. They loved Confucianism and hated the Qin because Shi Huangdi had betrayed Confucianism, yet in practice, no matter how evil their king was, they nonetheless compared him with Yao, Shun, Yu, Tang, Wen, and Wu, but never would they compare him with the Qin emperor. But would you, ladies and gentlemen, please consider the following? The king who addresses himself as "*Trẫm*" (I/We)—is he a Confucian or a follower of the Qin? The king who calls himself "*Hoàng đế*" (literally "Heavenly Emperor")—which side is he on? Isn't the king who practices the "*tru di tam tộc*" law (the execution of "three families/generations," i.e., the person, his sons, and his father) a follower of the Qin? The king who indulges in lust, living in his palace with hundreds of concubines—is he not emulating the Qin? Notwithstanding, the king says that he is a follower of Confucianism. That he would say so is understandable and that the mandarins who fawn upon the king would say so also makes sense. I do not understand, however, why on earth the venerable Confucian scholars argue themselves hoarse, claiming that:

> Our king follows Confucianism!
> Our court holds Confucianism in reverence!
> Our country practices Confucianism!
> Our people practice Confucianism!
> Where, then, is Confucianism?

During the 2,200 years from the Han dynasty to the Tang (Viet. *Đường*) dynasty, from the Tang to the Song (Viet. *Tống*) dynasty, from the Song to the Yuan (Viet. *Nguyên*) dynasty, from the Yuan to the Ming (Viet. *Minh*) dynasty, then from the Ming to the Qing (Viet. *Thanh*) dynasty, there has been a decline in the practice of Confucianism. Though the policy of the Han dynasty did not have any aspect that could be called generous or fair, the Han was still better than the Tang, the Tang was still better than the Song, the Song was still better than the Yuan, the Yuan was still better than the Ming, and the Ming was still better than the Qing.

When one looks into the history of monarchy in East Asia, one finds that, since the Qin dynasty [221–206 BCE], though the East Asian countries would consider they were practicing Confucianism, in actuality there was nothing Confucian in the policy practiced, only one or two things remained in the family traditions, and, apart from that, the absolute monarchs relied on Confucianism only to exert pressure upon their peoples.

---

[3] Shi Huangdi established *huangdi* as a new hierarchical system in which there was only one emperor but many *wang* (kings).

In what Manner Was Monarchical Autocracy in East Asia Craftier than It was in Europe?

With their tradition of chivalry, European monarchs tended to be aggressive in doing things, but honest-minded, even in their cruelty. In the old days, in order to suppress the people, [monarchs] entered into collusion with the church, saying that the king was God, acting on behalf of God, or as God-in-disguise—i.e., that the king was not of the same human race as the people, and therefore the people must respect him. When it was no longer possible to mislead the people with this deception, popular rights became stronger and the monarch's power was diminished.

The monarchs in East Asia took a different approach. To restrict and control the people, they selected from among the sayings of Confucius and Mencius, or from other classics, passages that would carry ambiguous meanings that they could take advantage of in making laws. For instance, they called themselves "Son of Heaven" (C: *tianzi*; Viet. *thiên tử, con Trời*), but at the same time regarded themselves as human beings. Furthermore, they deliberately presented themselves as participating in an intimate relationship with the people; as the saying goes, "sovereign, teacher, father" (C: *jun, shi, fu*; Viet. *quân, sư, phụ*), or more frequently, "sovereign, father, husband" (Viet. *vua, cha, chồng*). In the villages, though people are ignorant and do not know much about the king, when they hear that the king is related to them as their father, teacher, and husband, they think of him as someone within their intimate circle, without realizing that if he is infuriated he might have their "three families/generations" murdered. Father, teacher, and husband, in contrast, do benefit us and would not do such evil things. When we were born, our well-being was entirely in the hands of our parents; the king did not know anything about it. Notwithstanding, when we become adults, suddenly we are taught that "we are the subjects of the emperor who is the Son of Heaven." Our life and death are decided unilaterally by the king, and we have no rights to defend ourselves. We should ask ourselves why this is so!

Since Europe had the tradition of chivalry, a person had to render distinguished military services to be promoted to the rank of prince in the aristocracy, and once he had been promoted, it would be difficult to deprive him of this title. In contrast, in East Asia, the aristocrats were fond of literary endeavor, and it was in this art that they had to pass examinations to become officials. With respect to military officials, when there were invaders from outside or at the time a dynasty was founded, there were men of extraordinary talent; but in ordinary times, military official titles were used only to dispense as rewards to ignorant folk. For example, a man who joined the military service when he was twenty, regardless of his ignorance, by age fifty would be promoted to commander (Viet. *lãnh binh*), viceroy (Viet. *đề đốc*), or the like, enjoying riches and honor for a few years, although he had to behave in a way that would not make his superiors dislike him. This was a scheme purposely adopted by the monarchical autocrats in East Asia as a part of their obscurant policy.

Look at this example: our country lost its independence several decades ago, but when the civil-service examinations are held, all try their best to pass the examinations. If they pass the examinations, they consider that the graves of their ancestors have brought them good fortune.[4] Those who have connections or money will use them for bribery to become officials, obtaining merely empty rank (Viet. *hư hàm*). If we go to Hanoi, or to Huế, we shall see those who wear ivory mandarin badges jostling one another, and those who carry money looking for places where they can use it for bribery. We might think that they are foolish or ignorant and we just cannot understand their mentality, but the seed was sown by the kings a thousand years ago.

In sum, absolute monarchy in East Asia has been maintained by extolling heretical precepts (Viet. *tà thuyết*), such as "from the moment one comes into the world, one must perform one's duty as a subject toward the king" (Viet. *lọt lòng mẹ ra đã phải chịu nghĩa vua tôi*). But many have been unaware of the fact that the relationship between the king and his subjects (Viet. *quân thần*) should be a mutual one, as indicated by the saying "in the relationship between the king and his subject, duty [Viet. *nghĩa*] must be foremost." To punish those who wished to retire out of frustration with officialdom, the autocratic court made laws against "having talents but not allowing the king to use them" (Viet. *hữu tài bất di quân dụng*), or against "wheedling the king" or having talents but forcing the king to beg for one's services (C: *yaojun*; Viet. *nũng vua*) [as explained below]. Since the leaders feared that the people might stage a revolution if they were well-versed in politics, talking about political matters was prohibited. These autocratic measures were adopted by monarchs to ensure that the throne was kept for their descendants, regardless of the cost. They did not realize that, while they might protect their throne so well that none of their people would ever be able to take it away from their descendants, when foreigners came, the throne would be lost to them—this was because the people were so ignorant and had no idea about their country! For example, the Song (Viet. *Tống*) first lost to the Qietan (Viet. *Khiết Đan*), then to the Jin (Viet. *Kim*), then eventually to the Mongols; and the Ming lost to the Manchus. Korea was lost to Japan, and Vietnam to France.

What a pity that throughout two thousand years the kings paid no attention whatsoever to their national interests, only thinking about how to suppress the people's intellect so that the kings could keep the key to the throne in a steel cabinet exclusively for their descendants. They never realized that if the people were ignorant, the country remained weak. In addition, since the kings and their officials were corrupt, rebellion was unavoidable; and when rebellion occurred, the throne would be lost. If the people were so ignorant and weak that they could not rise in rebellion, it is understandable that foreigners would encroach upon their countries. In such a situation, who would save their countries? This was the reason why the imperial throne constantly changed hands, just like first-row seats in a theater.

Advantages and Disadvantages of Monarchy

Now, we may briefly survey the advantages and disadvantages of monarchy. Whether in Asia or Europe, the foundation of any country has been entirely due to the heroes of its earliest times, who led their people in dealings with other countries and put things in order within their own country. It goes without saying that the contribution of these heroes should be applauded and remembered. There were

---

[4] In Vietnam, some people believe that providing a suitable location for one's ancestors' graves brings good fortune to the descendants.

countries that were able to stand on their own at the beginning, but afterwards, as there were no heroes to lead them, they were annexed by others. Seen in this light, the merit of monarchy was enormous in ancient times. Although these heroes had their personal interests, such a thing is forgivable. In addition, [in modern times] there were countries that made good use of monarchy, e.g., Japan and Siam. When Westerners first arrived, the peoples of these two countries were naïve and unperceptive, but thanks to the heroic sovereigns at the apex and resourceful government officials below, these peoples were guided to make great progress. Apart from these cases, which brought about benefits to the people, [modern] monarchy is useless.

Look at China! Although thirty years ago Emperor Guangzu (Viet. Quang Tự) issued a decree for modernization, the Empress Dowager, infatuated with men and fortune, refused to carry out political reforms. As a result, the Qing dynasty was brought to an end, and China is still facing difficulties. With respect to the king of Korea, his wife's side supported modernization, his father was conservative; they fought against one another, on and on. In the end, his parents were imprisoned, his wife was murdered, the king himself had to carry his country in his hands to give it to Japan, and eventually he was removed from office.[5]

So far as our country was concerned, let me mention Mr. Tự Đức [r. 1848–83],[6] the king whom even at present the old mandarins and venerable Confucian scholars still glorify as "the sage king" (Viet. *thánh quân*). When the French first came, military officials such as Nguyễn Tri Phương[7] and Vũ Trọng Bình[8] wanted to fight. They proposed that, if we fought, we should spend money to go abroad to purchase weaponry, otherwise there would be no chance of winning. But the king was not prepared to spend money for that purpose, wanting to bury it in the ground and purchase nothing. He told the military officials: "If you want to fight, you may. But if you do not win, what will happen to my mother and myself?" His irresolute attitude forced military officials such as Vũ Trọng Bình to retire from their positions and led to Nguyễn Tri Phương's arrest by the French and eventual death during a hunger strike. There were also those with broad knowledge, like Nguyễn Trường Tộ, who advised the king to travel to France to observe its culture and civilization and to

---

[5] The conflict in Korea in the late nineteenth century was complicated because of its factional politics. When Phan Châu Trinh talks about the king, he seems to imply that he is referring to King Yi Kojong (Viet. Lý Cao Tông). Historians nowadays tend not to talk too much about the king, but instead focus on the role of his father, regent Taewonkun (Viet. Đại Nguyên Quân), for his isolationist policy and persecution of Catholics.

[6] Phan purposely addressed Emperor Tự Đức as "*ông*" (Mr.) to demonstrate his lack of respect for the emperor.

[7] Nguyễn Tri Phương (1800–73) was a native of Thừa Thiên; he made important contributions to the development and defense of Nam Kỳ throughout his long career of public service. In 1860–61, Nguyễn Tri Phương directed that the Kỳ Hòa fortress in Gia Định (present-day Saigon) be built to counter the French conquest of Nam Kỳ. With the subsequent French military expansion to the north, he was dispatched to Hanoi in 1872 to be in charge of the defense of Bắc Kỳ. In November 1873, when Francis Garnier assaulted Hanoi, Nguyễn Tri Phương was severely wounded and his son Nguyễn Lâm was killed during a fierce counter-attack. When the French offered to treat Nguyễn Tri Phương's wounds, he declined, saying, "I would prefer to die for a righteous cause." He refused to eat and died on December 20, 1873.

[8] Vũ Trọng Bình (1808–98) was a native of Quảng Bình. He is well-known for his literary and political talents. During the French conquest of Bắc Kỳ, Vũ Trọng Bình was the governor of Ninh Thái (Ninh Bình and Thái Bình) provinces, in the north.

dispatch students there for study; many civilian officials also proposed as much, but the king replied: "The Japanese are barbarians, the Siamese are barbarians; barbarians can learn from barbarians, but we are descendants of the gods and the saints, how could we possibly go to learn from the barbarians?"

Well, I am not going to pass judgment on that king; you have heard the story, and you will decide on your own what kind of king he was. If he and his mother died, they would have a place to be buried, but what about the twenty millions of mothers and children who had no one to rely on? The peoples whom the king considered barbarians have all made great progress. Our twenty millions at present have become not only barbarians, but lowly slaves!

MONARCHY OR GOVERNMENT OF MEN?

To make a long story short, "*quân trị*" (monarchy, autocracy) is "*nhân trị*" (government by men). In a country that adopts autocracy, there are laws, but these laws are deliberately made by the king, and the people are completely unaware of anything. If a country were fortunate enough to have a wise and heroic king, one who would understand the relationship between the people and their country and would be able to punish corrupt officials so that people could live in peace and be content with their lives (Viet. *an cư lạc nghiệp*), that country would enjoy prosperity and peace as long as that king was on the throne.

But if the king were a despot, who lived with concubines and eunuchs, knew nothing of national affairs, and left his country's governance to his deceitful ministers (Viet. *nịnh thần*), his country would certainly collapse because of the king, its ruler, being so negligent. Confucius thus said: "The government of King Wen and King Wu is displayed in the records ... Let there be the men, and the government will flourish; but without the men, the government decays and ceases." Xunzi (Viet. Tuân Tử), on the other hand, said: "*You zhi ren, wu zhi fa*" (Viet. *hữu trị nhân, vô trị pháp*), literally, "there are men who are able, but there are no laws which are able"[9] [implying that "there are men who are capable of governing their country, but there are no laws that, by themselves, could govern the country"]. Mencius, encompassing the views of Confucius and Xunzi, said: "Virtue alone is not sufficient for the exercise of government, laws alone cannot carry themselves into practice" (Viet. *Đồ thiện bất túc dĩ vi chính, đồ pháp bất năng dĩ tự hành*).[10]

For thousands of years, able kings and generals have done their best to prevent monarchy from being *nhân trị*, but without any success. This is because the laws were made by kings, and the laws were also abolished by them. These kings were those who concerned themselves with modifying *nhân trị* prior to the Song and the Tang dynasties, as after that monarchies became extremely autocratic. Emperor Hongwu (Viet. Hồng Vũ) [1368–98],[11] of the Ming dynasty, created a law against "having talents but not allowing the king to use them" (Viet. *hữu tài bất vi quân dụng*)

---

[9] The source for this quotation can be found in Xunzi, "Jundao" (The Way of the Sovereign). See *Kadokawa Daijiten* [Kadokawa Great Dictionary of Etymology], ed. Ozaki Yujirô et al. (Tokyo: Kadokawa Shoten, 1992), p. 1003.

[10] The source for this quotation can be found in *Mencius*, Book 7 (Li Lou, Part I). See *Han-Ying Sishu* [The Four Books in Chinese and in English], trans. James Legge, annot. Luo Zhiye (Hunan: Hunan Chubanshe, 1992), pp. 388–89.

[11] Also known as Minh Thái Tổ.

to put everyone under tyrannical rule by not allowing anyone to retire out of frustration. Emperor Qianlong (Viet. Càn Long) [1736–95] added a law against "wheedling the king," to punish those who had talents but forced the king to beg for their services. The kings in ancient times were looking for talented people, but those in later times just lay back—making no attempt at searching. Nonetheless, they would arrest those who had talents yet did not come forth.

• • •

I have spoken about the history and philosophy of monarchy as *nhân trị*. I would like to add a few concrete and easily recognizable illustrations. *Nhân trị* is a form of government that may be liberal or harsh, depending entirely on the joyful or sorrowful, loving or unloving, mood of the king, and it is a form of government in which the laws exist for nothing.

For example, Mr. Gia Long [r. 1802–20] adopted the law enacted during the time of Qianlong, of the Qing dynasty, to govern the Vietnamese. This law stipulated that "without acquiring military merits, one cannot be given the rank of marquis" (Viet. *phi quân công bất hầu*). Nguyễn Văn Thành [1757–1817] was appointed to the rank of marquis and was even promoted to military secretary (Viet. *trung quân*) because Mr. Gia Long was fair in his assessment of the military achievements that Nguyễn Văn Thành had accumulated since his youth. Afterwards, however, when Mr. Thành's son composed a poem for pleasure, quite an innocent one, Mr. Gia Long ordered the execution of his three generations [Nguyễn Văn Thành, his sons, and his father]. In other words, because he was so infuriated he ordered the execution, and this had nothing to do with the law!

I would like to tell you another story about Mr. Tự Đức, whose name I mentioned previously. In the twenty-fifth year of the Tự Đức era [1873], people in the Trung Kỳ region suffered from near starvation. After the government had provided a small measure of relief, officials requested that a portion of the tax collected in the provinces, prefectures, and districts be kept in village granaries, in anticipation of future food shortages. At that time, Mr. Tự Đức told the people that they could bring forth money or rice; in return, they would receive the titles of *bá hộ*,[12] eighth rank, or ninth rank. But the people were starving, how could they have money or rice to be collected? Mr. Tự Đức then issued a decree ordering his officials to allow submission payment on credit: with an initial installment of 300 piastres (of the 1,000 piastres that one was supposed to pay), one would receive a certificate; and upon payment of the balance, the official title would be granted. The decree mentioned specifically that the money collected in each village was to be kept there. The following year another decree appeared ordering that all the money that had been paid or was still on credit should be transferred to the provinces to be used as funds to stave off rebellions. Orders flowed down from provinces to prefectures and districts, then from prefectures and districts to villages. The people responded, saying that the king had allowed them to pay on credit, rather than requiring immediate payment; and since that year the people had experienced a bad harvest, they simply did not have the money to pay—whatever disciplinary measures might

---

[12] Literally, "one hundred households." Originally, this was the title of a low-ranking military officer during the Yuan and Ming dynasties in China; such an officer would have had one hundred soldiers under his command. The term was used in Vietnam either in the above context or to refer to persons of great wealth.

be taken. Provincial officials reported to the ministry, the ministry then reported to the king. The king decided that all the people were to be punished. In Vietnamese law, however, there was no clause dealing with transactions of money between the people and the government. The government officials thus could not find a legal basis on which to charge the people. They reported to the king. The king said that the law to be applied was *"thượng thư bất dĩ thật,"* i.e., the clause concerning "an official who makes a political report to the king untruthfully." The officials at the ministry level then brought charges against the officials at the provincial level [the very people who had received the titles for paying their taxes in full]. Some punishments were six years, some were eight years, and some were twelve years of imprisonment. In the midst of famine, and with their family members scattered, these people had thought it would cheer them up if they could make the payment and collect a low-ranking title (eighth or ninth rank), but to their unforeseen dismay they were put into prison instead. Their families and their clans were heart-broken. Fortunately, when this case reached Quảng Ngãi province, the provincial judge (Viet. *án sát*) was well-versed in legal matters and took seriously the concerns of the people and those regarding national affairs. His name was Nguyễn Thông, pen name Kỳ Xuyên (a native of Bến Tre, province of Vĩnh Long, he had escaped to Phan Thiết following the loss of the six provinces [Nam Kỳ]).[13] This man methodically demolished the charges against the low-ranking officials, sentence by sentence. He wrote to the ministry, saying: "In this case, it was the king and officials who lied to the people—the people did not lie to anyone. It is completely out of place to apply the law *'thượng thư bất dĩ thật.'"* Mr. Tự Đức realized that it was his fault, but he was ashamed of himself, so he set somebody to sue Mr. Nguyễn Thông by bringing a grave charge against him and had him deposed. But the people in Quảng Ngãi and elsewhere did all they could to support Mr. Nguyễn Thông, so damage was limited to his deposition.

The above are only a few examples; if I were to talk about Chinese and Vietnamese histories, I could go on and on for days.

A Brief Account of Democracy

In the present world, in the countries which have, more or less, adopted European civilization or are exposed to liberalism and freedom of expression, everyone understands the meaning of democracy (Viet. *dân chủ*, or *dân trị*). There are several countries in Europe that practice monarchy, but in every country the upper and lower houses have a democratic party. In Vietnam, however, the French have dominated the six provinces [Nam Kỳ] for sixty years and the term *"République"* is continually bandied about, yet no one investigates its meaning and compares it with the meaning of monarchy. This is the situation within the learned circle, and it appears to me that, within this group, monarchy is preferred. So far as people in rural areas are concerned, they know nothing about democracy; they worship the king in their heads as if he were a deity or a sage. Not only do they dare not think about the question of "whether or not we should have a king," but they act as if a

---

[13] Nguyễn Thông (1827–84) was a native of Gia Định (what is now Long An). Following the outbreak of the French military campaign against Vietnam in 1859, Nguyễn Thông participated in the defense of Nam Kỳ, led by Military Governor Tôn Thất Hiệp. Nguyễn Thông "took refuge" (Viet. *tị*) in the southern provinces of Trung Kỳ after the loss of the three eastern provinces in Nam Kỳ. The episode to which Phan refers must have taken place when Nguyễn Thông served as provincial governor (Viet. *bố chính*) of Quảng Ngãi, during 1868–71.

person raising this question would be struck by a thunderbolt, buried under rocks, trampled by elephants, and torn apart by horses.

Upon hearing the name of a king, whoever he is, people are jubilant and ecstatic, placing their hope and expectation on him. So silly was the recent case of Phan Xích Long.[14] The poison of autocracy has therefore entered deeply into the minds of our people, and their intellectual level is so low. The people understand if someone tells them, "You must be loyal to this person, or respect that person," but if anyone mentions the name of Vietnam and tells them, "That is your motherland, you must love it," they do not understand because they cannot touch it with their hands or see it with their eyes. How is it possible for them to love it? They can love only a house, a garden, and some acres of land—things they can see with their eyes.

I noticed in the last few years that, whenever journalists and public speakers open their mouths, they mention the twenty million people of our country. The tone is a mixture of pride, boastfulness, and expectation. In my opinion, these twenty million people know only their family and do not know their country. For example, if a family's sons have died and there is no heir, or a family has a lot of land and rice fields but is being sued, or a family has children who are addicted to gambling, etc.— people consider these things most important and gather to gossip. But if one talks about "the loss of national independence" (Viet. *mất nước*), not a single soul cares. How deplorable if the attitude of a people to their country is so indifferent and disinterested! Considering the state of the people, among you there are those who might be surprised at the suggestion to abolish monarchy and create a republic (Viet. *dân quốc*). In my view, since the poison of autocracy has fatally injured the patriotism of our people, there is no better way to make them aware of the fact that Vietnam is indeed their country than to throw away those lackeys, and only after that is done may they be able to find out to whom this country belongs. One day our intelligent people will find that, in this land, handed down to them over thousands of years, much still remains of their interests, much is still to be found of their rights. They will realize that those who have been called kings and officials since the olden days are, after all, just their representatives acting on their behalf, and if they cannot do a good job, there is nothing wrong with chasing them away.

When the people begin to see things in that light, they will know how to love their country. Only when they know how to love their country might one hope for their freedom and independence; otherwise, they will remain slaves from generation to generation.

Why It Is Called Democracy

To the people in Europe, there is no need to explain "why it is called democracy"; but in our country, this is not so. I will therefore provide a brief explanation so that you will follow the general line.

---

[14] Phan Xích Long's real name was Phan Phát Sanh. Son of a policeman in Chợ Lớn, Phan Phát Sanh made his living by working as an assistant for a French store in Saigon. In 1913, he declared that he was the "crown prince" of Emperor Hàm Nghi (under whose name the Loyalist Movement was launched in the late 1880s) and changed his name to Phan Xích Long ("Xích Long" means Red Dragon, the dragon being the symbol of the throne). Claiming himself to be emperor, in 1913 Phan Xích Long created a secret society and led an uprising in Saigon against the colonial government. He was soon arrested and imprisoned. See Vương Hồng Sển, *Saigon năm xưa* [Saigon of the Old Days] (Saigon: Nxb Khai Trí, 1968), pp. 252–53.

History. In any country, the intellectuals represent only a small part of its entire population. They rely on the lead of the upper class and the middle class. Peoples in European countries were different from our people, although at the beginning of their history they also revered monarchy. In ancient Greek states, a citizen body called the legislature, consisting of aristocrats, was convened by the king to decide on judicial matters. There was also a popular assembly that ratified the laws created by the king and the aristocrats. In the age of Pericles [461–429 BCE], the Board of Ten Generals dealt with national matters. Following the end of the Roman kings, the senate, or the council of elders, and a plebeian assembly were established. Consequently, even after Rome became an autocratic empire, Roman law was further developed and would eventually form a basis for the legal codes for Western countries. With the invasions of the Germanic tribes, the Roman Empire was brought to an end, the European countries became independent, and the assembly-based political system also disappeared from most countries for hundreds of years. Amazingly, the British still retained these assemblies in the House of Lords and the House of Commons, which were called by the king and assigned legislative power. Later on in the eighteenth century, the English House of Commons became a model for continental Europe. That is a brief outline of the history of popular rights in Europe.

A BRIEF DESCRIPTION OF DEMOCRACY

At present, in Europe, all nations practice democracy, with the exception of the countries whose peoples are still ignorant.

Let me describe for you the political structure of France. The Lower House, i.e., the Chamber of Deputies or the National Assembly, is the most important house. The number of seats is approximately six hundred. Citizens twenty-one years old and older have the right to vote. Those above age twenty-five have the right to become candidates in the election. If elected, one becomes a deputy in the Lower House. France's fortune is decided by this house, which has legislative power. In addition, there is also a Senate. The senators are not elected by the people, but indirectly by a *collège électoral* consisting of municipal councilors in each *département*, the administrative units into which France is divided. The Senate looks after fiscal matters. The president is elected by the two houses. The candidates for the presidency are members from these two houses, and the candidate who receives the most votes is elected. Once the president has been elected, he has to take an oath in front of the two houses, saying: "On the basis of our democratic constitution, I vow not to betray our people and not to be partisan; if I am guilty of breaking these promises, I am subject to impeachment."[15] Because of their violations against the constitution, French presidents MacMahon and, more recently, Mitterand, were removed from office.

The government is also formed from members sitting in the two houses. The party that occupies the largest number of seats is allowed to form a cabinet. The present cabinet has a few dozen ministries, but their ministers are not nonfunctional and haughty like the ministers in our country. Each of them has specific responsibilities. If they do not meet the expectations of the people, they will be criticized. Because there are two political parties in the National Assembly, one

---

[15] It is not known from what source Phan quoted that presidential pledge.

leftwing and one rightwing, if the leftwing party holds the majority of the seats, the rightwing party will be the watchdog and be ready to level criticisms; therefore, it is difficult to do anything outrageous.

Everyone in the country must observe the constitution. The power of the government is also stipulated in the constitution, and therefore there is little room for negligence and autocracy. In addition, if there is a violation of the constitution, everyone will be treated according to the same law—from the president to a common person in the countryside.

The government officers possess only administrative power; judicial power is entrusted to judges who have the required training and qualifications. The judges specialize in making judgments in the courts. They have independent power and rely on the letter of the law, fairness, and their conscience in making their decisions. They deal with government officials and private citizens in exactly the same manner. The judges belong to a separate department, the Department of Justice. The judicial power, the administrative power of the government, and the legislative power of the parliament are separate, not controlled by a single person.

The above is just a brief outline; in order to have a thorough understanding of democracy, one has to be more specific.

Seen in this light, democracy is a government of laws (Viet. *pháp trị*). The rights and duties of everyone in the country are well described by the laws—like a road on which lines have been drawn clearly, so that you can walk freely, there is nothing to stop you, and you may go on as far as you like, as long as you do not violate the rights of others. This is because before the laws, everyone is equal, regardless of whether they are officials or common people.

Comparing the two concepts of monarchy and democracy, we see that democracy is far better than monarchy. To govern a country solely on the basis of the personal opinions of one individual or of an imperial court is to treat the people of that country as if they were a herd of goats—their prosperity and joy, or their poverty and misery, are entirely in the hands of the herder. In contrast, in a democracy the people create their own constitution and select officials, who will act according to the will of the people to look after their nation's business. Even in the case where there are no excellent talents among the government officials, the people do not have to submit themselves to becoming servants for a family or a clan [as has happened under monarchies].

History has proven that the wise peoples who followed the path of self-strengthening and self-reliance to search for their common interests have, day-by-day, become happier. In contrast, the ignorant peoples who stayed idle without doing anything—only waiting for help from Heaven or favors from government officials, and entrusting their rights to the hands of a single person or government—have suffered from all sorts of hardships.

My compatriots! Now that you have seen the reasons, you should take part in tackling our national affairs; without doing so, we will not be able to raise our heads.

About the Editor, Translator

Vinh Sinh is a professor in the Department of History and Classics, University of Alberta. His major publications include: *Overturned Chariot: The Autobiography of Phan Bội Châu*, co-editor and co-translator (Honolulu, HI: University of Hawai'i Press, 1999); *Phan Bội Châu and the Đông Du Movement*, editor (New Haven, CT: Yale Center for International and Area Studies, 1987); *Tokutomi Sohô: A Critical Biography* (Tokyo: Iwanami Shoten, 1994); *The Future Japan*, editor and co-translator of Tokutomi Sohô's book *Shôrai no Nihon* (Edmonton: University of Alberta Press, 1989), which won the Canada Council's 1990 Canada-Japan Book Prize; and *Tokutomi Sohô: The Later Career* (Toronto: University of Toronto–York University Joint Centre on Modern East Asia, 1986).

SOUTHEAST ASIA PROGRAM PUBLICATIONS
Cornell University

Studies on Southeast Asia

Number 49 *Phan Châu Trinh and His Political Writings*, Phan Châu Trinh, ed. and trans. Vinh Sinh. 2009. ISBN 978-0-87727-749-1 (pb.)

Number 48 *Dependent Communities: Aid and Politics in Cambodia and East Timor*, Caroline Hughes. 2009. ISBN 978-0-87727-748-4 (pb.)

Number 47 *A Man Like Him: Portrait of the Burmese Journalist, Journal Kyaw U Chit Maung*, Journal Kyaw Ma Ma Lay, trans. Ma Thanegi, 2008. ISBN 978-0-87727-747-7 (pb.)

Number 46 *At the Edge of the Forest: Essays on Cambodia, History, and Narrative in Honor of David Chandler*, ed. Anne Ruth Hansen and Judy Ledgerwood. 2008. ISBN 978-0-87727-746-0 (pb).

Number 45 *Conflict, Violence, and Displacement in Indonesia*, ed. Eva-Lotta E. Hedman. 2008. ISBN 978-0-87727-745-3 (pb).

Number 44 *Friends and Exiles: A Memoir of the Nutmeg Isles and the Indonesian Nationalist Movement*, Des Alwi, ed. Barbara S. Harvey. 2008. ISBN 978-0-877277-44-6 (pb).

Number 43 *Early Southeast Asia: Selected Essays*, O. W. Wolters, ed. Craig J. Reynolds. 2008. 255 pp. ISBN 978-0-877277-43-9 (pb).

Number 42 *Thailand: The Politics of Despotic Paternalism* (revised edition), Thak Chaloemtiarana. 2007. 284 pp. ISBN 0-8772-7742-7 (pb).

Number 41 *Views of Seventeenth-Century Vietnam: Christoforo Borri on Cochinchina and Samuel Baron on Tonkin*, ed. Olga Dror and K. W. Taylor. 2006. 290 pp. ISBN 0-8772-7741-9 (pb).

Number 40 *Laskar Jihad: Islam, Militancy, and the Quest for Identity in Post-New Order Indonesia*, Noorhaidi Hasan. 2006. 266 pp. ISBN 0-877277-40-0 (pb).

Number 39 *The Indonesian Supreme Court: A Study of Institutional Collapse*, Sebastiaan Pompe. 2005. 494 pp. ISBN 0-877277-38-9 (pb).

Number 38 *Spirited Politics: Religion and Public Life in Contemporary Southeast Asia*, ed. Andrew C. Willford and Kenneth M. George. 2005. 210 pp. ISBN 0-87727-737-0.

Number 37 *Sumatran Sultanate and Colonial State: Jambi and the Rise of Dutch Imperialism, 1830-1907*, Elsbeth Locher-Scholten, trans. Beverley Jackson. 2004. 332 pp. ISBN 0-87727-736-2.

Number 36 *Southeast Asia over Three Generations: Essays Presented to Benedict R. O'G. Anderson*, ed. James T. Siegel and Audrey R. Kahin. 2003. 398 pp. ISBN 0-87727-735-4.

Number 35 *Nationalism and Revolution in Indonesia*, George McTurnan Kahin, intro. Benedict R. O'G. Anderson (reprinted from 1952 edition, Cornell University Press, with permission). 2003. 530 pp. ISBN 0-87727-734-6.

Number 34 *Golddiggers, Farmers, and Traders in the "Chinese Districts" of West Kalimantan, Indonesia*, Mary Somers Heidhues. 2003. 316 pp. ISBN 0-87727-733-8.

Number 33   *Opusculum de Sectis apud Sinenses et Tunkinenses (A Small Treatise on the Sects among the Chinese and Tonkinese): A Study of Religion in China and North Vietnam in the Eighteenth Century*, Father Adriano de St. Thecla, trans. Olga Dror, with Mariya Berezovska. 2002. 363 pp. ISBN 0-87727-732-X.

Number 32   *Fear and Sanctuary: Burmese Refugees in Thailand*, Hazel J. Lang. 2002. 204 pp. ISBN 0-87727-731-1.

Number 31   *Modern Dreams: An Inquiry into Power, Cultural Production, and the Cityscape in Contemporary Urban Penang, Malaysia*, Beng-Lan Goh. 2002. 225 pp. ISBN 0-87727-730-3.

Number 30   *Violence and the State in Suharto's Indonesia*, ed. Benedict R. O'G. Anderson. 2001. Second printing, 2002. 247 pp. ISBN 0-87727-729-X.

Number 29   *Studies in Southeast Asian Art: Essays in Honor of Stanley J. O'Connor*, ed. Nora A. Taylor. 2000. 243 pp. Illustrations. ISBN 0-87727-728-1.

Number 28   *The Hadrami Awakening: Community and Identity in the Netherlands East Indies, 1900-1942*, Natalie Mobini-Kesheh. 1999. 174 pp. ISBN 0-87727-727-3.

Number 27   *Tales from Djakarta: Caricatures of Circumstances and their Human Beings*, Pramoedya Ananta Toer. 1999. 145 pp. ISBN 0-87727-726-5.

Number 26   *History, Culture, and Region in Southeast Asian Perspectives*, rev. ed., O. W. Wolters. 1999. Second printing, 2004. 275 pp. ISBN 0-87727-725-7.

Number 25   *Figures of Criminality in Indonesia, the Philippines, and Colonial Vietnam*, ed. Vicente L. Rafael. 1999. 259 pp. ISBN 0-87727-724-9.

Number 24   *Paths to Conflagration: Fifty Years of Diplomacy and Warfare in Laos, Thailand, and Vietnam, 1778-1828*, Mayoury Ngaosyvathn and Pheuiphanh Ngaosyvathn. 1998. 268 pp. ISBN 0-87727-723-0.

Number 23   *Nguyễn Cochinchina: Southern Vietnam in the Seventeenth and Eighteenth Centuries*, Li Tana. 1998. Second printing, 2002. 194 pp. ISBN 0-87727-722-2.

Number 22   *Young Heroes: The Indonesian Family in Politics*, Saya S. Shiraishi. 1997. 183 pp. ISBN 0-87727-721-4.

Number 21   *Interpreting Development: Capitalism, Democracy, and the Middle Class in Thailand*, John Girling. 1996. 95 pp. ISBN 0-87727-720-6.

Number 20   *Making Indonesia*, ed. Daniel S. Lev, Ruth McVey. 1996. 201 pp. ISBN 0-87727-719-2.

Number 19   *Essays into Vietnamese Pasts*, ed. K. W. Taylor, John K. Whitmore. 1995. 288 pp. ISBN 0-87727-718-4.

Number 18   *In the Land of Lady White Blood: Southern Thailand and the Meaning of History*, Lorraine M. Gesick. 1995. 106 pp. ISBN 0-87727-717-6.

Number 17   *The Vernacular Press and the Emergence of Modern Indonesian Consciousness*, Ahmat Adam. 1995. 220 pp. ISBN 0-87727-716-8.

Number 16   *The Nan Chronicle*, trans., ed. David K. Wyatt. 1994. 158 pp. ISBN 0-87727-715-X.

Number 15   *Selective Judicial Competence: The Cirebon-Priangan Legal Administration, 1680–1792*, Mason C. Hoadley. 1994. 185 pp. ISBN 0-87727-714-1.

Number 14   *Sjahrir: Politics and Exile in Indonesia*, Rudolf Mrázek. 1994. 536 pp. ISBN 0-87727-713-3.

Number 13   *Fair Land Sarawak: Some Recollections of an Expatriate Officer*, Alastair Morrison. 1993. 196 pp. ISBN 0-87727-712-5.

Number 12   *Fields from the Sea: Chinese Junk Trade with Siam during the Late Eighteenth and Early Nineteenth Centuries*, Jennifer Cushman. 1993. 206 pp. ISBN 0-87727-711-7.

Number 11   *Money, Markets, and Trade in Early Southeast Asia: The Development of Indigenous Monetary Systems to AD 1400*, Robert S. Wicks. 1992. 2nd printing 1996. 354 pp., 78 tables, illus., maps. ISBN 0-87727-710-9.

Number 10   *Tai Ahoms and the Stars: Three Ritual Texts to Ward Off Danger*, trans., ed. B. J. Terwiel, Ranoo Wichasin. 1992. 170 pp. ISBN 0-87727-709-5.

Number 9   *Southeast Asian Capitalists*, ed. Ruth McVey. 1992. 2nd printing 1993. 220 pp. ISBN 0-87727-708-7.

Number 8   *The Politics of Colonial Exploitation: Java, the Dutch, and the Cultivation System*, Cornelis Fasseur, ed. R. E. Elson, trans. R. E. Elson, Ary Kraal. 1992. 2nd printing 1994. 266 pp. ISBN 0-87727-707-9.

Number 7   *A Malay Frontier: Unity and Duality in a Sumatran Kingdom*, Jane Drakard. 1990. 2nd printing 2003. 215 pp. ISBN 0-87727-706-0.

Number 6   *Trends in Khmer Art*, Jean Boisselier, ed. Natasha Eilenberg, trans. Natasha Eilenberg, Melvin Elliott. 1989. 124 pp., 24 plates. ISBN 0-87727-705-2.

Number 5   *Southeast Asian Ephemeris: Solar and Planetary Positions, A.D. 638–2000*, J. C. Eade. 1989. 175 pp. ISBN 0-87727-704-4.

Number 3   *Thai Radical Discourse: The Real Face of Thai Feudalism Today*, Craig J. Reynolds. 1987. 2nd printing 1994. 186 pp. ISBN 0-87727-702-8.

Number 1   *The Symbolism of the Stupa*, Adrian Snodgrass. 1985. Revised with index, 1988. 3rd printing 1998. 469 pp. ISBN 0-87727-700-1.

SEAP Series

Number 23   *Possessed by the Spirits: Mediumship in Contemporary Vietnamese Communities*. 2006. 186 pp. ISBN 0-877271-41-0 (pb).

Number 22   *The Industry of Marrying Europeans*, Vũ Trọng Phụng, trans. Thúy Tranviet. 2006. 66 pp. ISBN 0-877271-40-2 (pb).

Number 21   *Securing a Place: Small-Scale Artisans in Modern Indonesia*, Elizabeth Morrell. 2005. 220 pp. ISBN 0-877271-39-9.

Number 20   *Southern Vietnam under the Reign of Minh Mạng (1820-1841): Central Policies and Local Response*, Choi Byung Wook. 2004. 226pp. ISBN 0-0-877271-40-2.

Number 19   *Gender, Household, State: Đổi Mới in Việt Nam*, ed. Jayne Werner and Danièle Bélanger. 2002. 151 pp. ISBN 0-87727-137-2.

Number 18   *Culture and Power in Traditional Siamese Government*, Neil A. Englehart. 2001. 130 pp. ISBN 0-87727-135-6.

Number 17   *Gangsters, Democracy, and the State*, ed. Carl A. Trocki. 1998. Second printing, 2002. 94 pp. ISBN 0-87727-134-8.

Number 16   *Cutting across the Lands: An Annotated Bibliography on Natural Resource Management and Community Development in Indonesia, the Philippines, and Malaysia*, ed. Eveline Ferretti. 1997. 329 pp. ISBN 0-87727-133-X.

Number 15 *The Revolution Falters: The Left in Philippine Politics after 1986*, ed. Patricio N. Abinales. 1996. Second printing, 2002. 182 pp. ISBN 0-87727-132-1.

Number 14 *Being Kammu: My Village, My Life*, Damrong Tayanin. 1994. 138 pp., 22 tables, illus., maps. ISBN 0-87727-130-5.

Number 13 *The American War in Vietnam*, ed. Jayne Werner, David Hunt. 1993. 132 pp. ISBN 0-87727-131-3.

Number 12 *The Voice of Young Burma*, Aye Kyaw. 1993. 92 pp. ISBN 0-87727-129-1.

Number 11 *The Political Legacy of Aung San*, ed. Josef Silverstein. Revised edition 1993. 169 pp. ISBN 0-87727-128-3.

Number 10 *Studies on Vietnamese Language and Literature: A Preliminary Bibliography*, Nguyen Dinh Tham. 1992. 227 pp. ISBN 0-87727-127-5.

Number 8 *From PKI to the Comintern, 1924–1941: The Apprenticeship of the Malayan Communist Party*, Cheah Boon Kheng. 1992. 147 pp. ISBN 0-87727-125-9.

Number 7 *Intellectual Property and US Relations with Indonesia, Malaysia, Singapore, and Thailand*, Elisabeth Uphoff. 1991. 67 pp. ISBN 0-87727-124-0.

Number 6 *The Rise and Fall of the Communist Party of Burma (CPB)*, Bertil Lintner. 1990. 124 pp. 26 illus., 14 maps. ISBN 0-87727-123-2.

Number 5 *Japanese Relations with Vietnam: 1951–1987*, Masaya Shiraishi. 1990. 174 pp. ISBN 0-87727-122-4.

Number 3 *Postwar Vietnam: Dilemmas in Socialist Development*, ed. Christine White, David Marr. 1988. 2nd printing 1993. 260 pp. ISBN 0-87727-120-8.

Number 2 *The Dobama Movement in Burma (1930–1938)*, Khin Yi. 1988. 160 pp. ISBN 0-87727-118-6.

Cornell Modern Indonesia Project Publications
available at http://cmip.library.cornell.edu/

Number 75 *A Tour of Duty: Changing Patterns of Military Politics in Indonesia in the 1990s.* Douglas Kammen and Siddharth Chandra. 1999. 99 pp. ISBN 0-87763-049-6.

Number 74 *The Roots of Acehnese Rebellion 1989–1992*, Tim Kell. 1995. 103 pp. ISBN 0-87763-040-2.

Number 73 *"White Book" on the 1992 General Election in Indonesia*, trans. Dwight King. 1994. 72 pp. ISBN 0-87763-039-9.

Number 72 *Popular Indonesian Literature of the Qur'an*, Howard M. Federspiel. 1994. 170 pp. ISBN 0-87763-038-0.

Number 71 *A Javanese Memoir of Sumatra, 1945–1946: Love and Hatred in the Liberation War*, Takao Fusayama. 1993. 150 pp. ISBN 0-87763-037-2.

Number 70 *East Kalimantan: The Decline of a Commercial Aristocracy*, Burhan Magenda. 1991. 120 pp. ISBN 0-87763-036-4.

Number 69 *The Road to Madiun: The Indonesian Communist Uprising of 1948*, Elizabeth Ann Swift. 1989. 120 pp. ISBN 0-87763-035-6.

Number 68   *Intellectuals and Nationalism in Indonesia: A Study of the Following Recruited by Sutan Sjahrir in Occupation Jakarta*, J. D. Legge. 1988. 159 pp. ISBN 0-87763-034-8.

Number 67   *Indonesia Free: A Biography of Mohammad Hatta*, Mavis Rose. 1987. 252 pp. ISBN 0-87763-033-X.

Number 66   *Prisoners at Kota Cane*, Leon Salim, trans. Audrey Kahin. 1986. 112 pp. ISBN 0-87763-032-1.

Number 65   *The Kenpeitai in Java and Sumatra*, trans. Barbara G. Shimer, Guy Hobbs, intro. Theodore Friend. 1986. 80 pp. ISBN 0-87763-031-3.

Number 64   *Suharto and His Generals: Indonesia's Military Politics, 1975–1983*, David Jenkins. 1984. 4th printing 1997. 300 pp. ISBN 0-87763-030-5.

Number 62   *Interpreting Indonesian Politics: Thirteen Contributions to the Debate, 1964–1981*, ed. Benedict Anderson, Audrey Kahin, intro. Daniel S. Lev. 1982. 3rd printing 1991. 172 pp. ISBN 0-87763-028-3.

Number 60   *The Minangkabau Response to Dutch Colonial Rule in the Nineteenth Century*, Elizabeth E. Graves. 1981. 157 pp. ISBN 0-87763-000-3.

Number 59   *Breaking the Chains of Oppression of the Indonesian People: Defense Statement at His Trial on Charges of Insulting the Head of State, Bandung, June 7–10, 1979*, Heri Akhmadi. 1981. 201 pp. ISBN 0-87763-001-1.

Number 57   *Permesta: Half a Rebellion*, Barbara S. Harvey. 1977. 174 pp. ISBN 0-87763-003-8.

Number 55   *Report from Banaran: The Story of the Experiences of a Soldier during the War of Independence*, Maj. Gen. T. B. Simatupang. 1972. 186 pp. ISBN 0-87763-005-4.

Number 52   *A Preliminary Analysis of the October 1 1965, Coup in Indonesia (Prepared in January 1966)*, Benedict R. Anderson, Ruth T. McVey, assist. Frederick P. Bunnell. 1971. 3rd printing 1990. 174 pp. ISBN 0-87763-008-9.

Number 51   *The Putera Reports: Problems in Indonesian-Japanese War-Time Cooperation*, Mohammad Hatta, trans., intro. William H. Frederick. 1971. 114 pp. ISBN 0-87763-009-7.

Number 50   *Schools and Politics: The Kaum Muda Movement in West Sumatra (1927–1933)*, Taufik Abdullah. 1971. 257 pp. ISBN 0-87763-010-0.

Number 49   *The Foundation of the Partai Muslimin Indonesia*, K. E. Ward. 1970. 75 pp. ISBN 0-87763-011-9.

Number 48   *Nationalism, Islam and Marxism*, Soekarno, intro. Ruth T. McVey. 1970. 2nd printing 1984. 62 pp. ISBN 0-87763-012-7.

Number 43   *State and Statecraft in Old Java: A Study of the Later Mataram Period, 16th to 19th Century*, Soemarsaid Moertono. Revised edition 1981. 180 pp. ISBN 0-87763-017-8.

Number 39   Preliminary Checklist of Indonesian Imprints (1945-1949), John M. Echols. 186 pp. ISBN 0-87763-025-9.

Number 37   *Mythology and the Tolerance of the Javanese*, Benedict R. O'G. Anderson. 2nd edition, 1996. Reprinted 2004. 104 pp., 65 illus. ISBN 0-87763-041-0.

Number 25   *The Communist Uprisings of 1926–1927 in Indonesia: Key Documents*, ed., intro. Harry J. Benda, Ruth T. McVey. 1960. 2nd printing 1969. 177 pp. ISBN 0-87763-024-0.

Translation Series

Volume 4   *Approaching Suharto's Indonesia from the Margins*, ed. Takashi Shiraishi. 1994. 153 pp. ISBN 0-87727-403-7.

Volume 3   *The Japanese in Colonial Southeast Asia*, ed. Saya Shiraishi, Takashi Shiraishi. 1993. 172 pp. ISBN 0-87727-402-9.

Volume 2   *Indochina in the 1940s and 1950s*, ed. Takashi Shiraishi, Motoo Furuta. 1992. 196 pp. ISBN 0-87727-401-0.

Volume 1   *Reading Southeast Asia*, ed. Takashi Shiraishi. 1990. 188 pp.
ISBN 0-87727-400-2.

The Many Ways of Being Muslim: Fiction by Muslim Filipinos, ed. Coeli Barry. Copublished with Anvil Publishing, Inc., the Philippines. 2008. ISBN 978-08772-760-50 (pb.)

Language Texts

INDONESIAN

Beginning Indonesian through Self-Instruction, John U. Wolff, Dédé Oetomo, Daniel Fietkiewicz. 3rd revised edition 1992. Vol. 1. 115 pp. ISBN 0-87727-529-7. Vol. 2. 434 pp. ISBN 0-87727-530-0. Vol. 3. 473 pp. ISBN 0-87727-531-9.

Indonesian Readings, John U. Wolff. 1978. 4th printing 1992. 480 pp.
ISBN 0-87727-517-3

Indonesian Conversations, John U. Wolff. 1978. 3rd printing 1991. 297 pp.
ISBN 0-87727-516-5

Formal Indonesian, John U. Wolff. 2nd revised edition 1986. 446 pp.
ISBN 0-87727-515-7

TAGALOG

Pilipino through Self-Instruction, John U. Wolff, Maria Theresa C. Centeno, Der-Hwa V. Rau. 1991. Vol. 1. 342 pp. ISBN 0-87727—525-4. Vol. 2., revised 2005, 378 pp. ISBN 0-87727-526-2. Vol 3., revised 2005, 431 pp. ISBN 0-87727-527-0. Vol. 4. 306 pp. ISBN 0-87727-528-9.

THAI

A. U. A. Language Center Thai Course, J. Marvin Brown. Originally published by the American University Alumni Association Language Center, 1974. Reissued by Cornell Southeast Asia Program, 1991, 1992. Book 1. 267 pp. ISBN 0-87727-506-8. Book 2. 288 pp. ISBN 0-87727-507-6. Book 3. 247 pp. ISBN 0-87727-508-4.

A. U. A. Language Center Thai Course, Reading and Writing Text (mostly reading), 1979. Reissued 1997. 164 pp. ISBN 0-87727-511-4.

A. U. A. Language Center Thai Course, Reading and Writing Workbook (mostly writing), 1979. Reissued 1997. 99 pp. ISBN 0-87727-512-2.

KHMER

Cambodian System of Writing and Beginning Reader, Franklin E. Huffman. Originally published by Yale University Press, 1970. Reissued by Cornell Southeast Asia Program, 4th printing 2002. 365 pp. ISBN 0-300-01314-0.

Modern Spoken Cambodian, Franklin E. Huffman, assist. Charan Promchan, Chhom-Rak Thong Lambert. Originally published by Yale University Press, 1970. Reissued by Cornell Southeast Asia Program, 3rd printing 1991. 451 pp. ISBN 0-300-01316-7.

Intermediate Cambodian Reader, ed. Franklin E. Huffman, assist. Im Proum. Originally published by Yale University Press, 1972. Reissued by Cornell Southeast Asia Program, 1988. 499 pp. ISBN 0-300-01552-6.

Cambodian Literary Reader and Glossary, Franklin E. Huffman, Im Proum. Originally published by Yale University Press, 1977. Reissued by Cornell Southeast Asia Program, 1988. 494 pp. ISBN 0-300-02069-4.

HMONG

White Hmong-English Dictionary, Ernest E. Heimbach. 1969. 8th printing, 2002. 523 pp. ISBN 0-87727-075-9.

VIETNAMESE

Intermediate Spoken Vietnamese, Franklin E. Huffman, Tran Trong Hai. 1980. 3rd printing 1994. ISBN 0-87727-500-9.

* * *

Southeast Asian Studies: Reorientations. Craig J. Reynolds and Ruth McVey. Frank H. Golay Lectures 2 & 3. 70 pp. ISBN 0-87727-301-4.

Javanese Literature in Surakarta Manuscripts, Nancy K. Florida. Vol. 1, *Introduction and Manuscripts of the Karaton Surakarta*. 1993. 410 pp. Frontispiece, illustrations. Hard cover, ISBN 0-87727-602-1, Paperback, ISBN 0-87727-603-X. Vol. 2, *Manuscripts of the Mangkunagaran Palace*. 2000. 576 pp. Frontispiece, illustrations. Paperback, ISBN 0-87727-604-8.

Sbek Thom: Khmer Shadow Theater. Pech Tum Kravel, trans. Sos Kem, ed. Thavro Phim, Sos Kem, Martin Hatch. 1996. 363 pp., 153 photographs. ISBN 0-87727-620-X.

In the Mirror: Literature and Politics in Siam in the American Era, ed. Benedict R. O'G. Anderson, trans. Benedict R. O'G. Anderson, Ruchira Mendiones. 1985. 2nd printing 1991. 303 pp. Paperback. ISBN 974-210-380-1.

To order, please contact:
Mail:
Cornell University Press Services
750 Cascadilla Street
PO Box 6525
Ithaca, NY 14851 USA

E-mail: orderbook@cupserv.org

Phone/Fax, Monday–Friday, 8 am – 5 pm (Eastern US):
Phone: 607 277 2211 or 800 666 2211 (US, Canada)
Fax: 607 277 6292 or 800 688 2877 (US, Canada)

Order through our online bookstore at:
www.einaudi.cornell.edu/southeastasia/publications/

Milton Keynes UK
Ingram Content Group UK Ltd.
UKHW020835260624
444734UK00008B/381

9 780877 277491